More Praise for *Smart Parenting for Smart Kids*

"Having had the experience of raising a smart, perfectionistic child myself, this book is a literal godsend. Packed with familiar anecdotes and valuable advice, parents will find great wisdom in its pages."
—Stephen R. Covey, author, *The 7 Habits of Highly Effective People* and *The Leader in Me*

"*Smart Parenting for Smart Kids* is a fresh parenting book filled with vignettes and strategies for raising smart kids to become healthy, happy, and contributing adults. It shines light on the mindset needed to counter the effects on our children of our high-stakes culture and education system."
—Vicki Abeles, producer and codirector, *Race to Nowhere*

"*Smart Parenting for Smart Kids* is a really important book for parents who are immersed in the wave of pressure parenting. The authors have done parents a favor by exposing the flaws in the argument that our kids must be pushed ever harder to succeed. This book helps parents see how to encourage their children to develop as whole people with feelings, ideas, and the ability to cope with the occasional disappointment too."
—Roberta Michnick Golinkoff, PhD, professor, University of Delaware; author, *Einstein Never Used Flash Cards* and *A Mandate for Playful Learning in Preschool*

"This book offers warm, sensible, and practical ways that parents can help their children build positive relationships and develop effective coping skills. The authors make parents aware of the fine line between encouragement and over-involvement. I highly recommend it."
—Nancy Samalin, MS, parent educator and best-selling author, *Loving Without Spoiling*

"If you wish to be a smart parent, get this book and absorb its messages about how to help your children learn from experience, grow despite setbacks, work well with those around them, and find their own motivation and joy."
—Maurice J. Elias, PhD, director, Clinical Training, Psychology Department, Rutgers University; coauthor, *Emotionally Intelligent Parenting*

"This book is a treat—smart guidance for parents of bright children in a stressed-out world! Kennedy-Moore and Lowenthal engage you with their comfortable writing style, psychological expertise, compelling examples of children's core challenges, and sound parenting strategies. I recommend it for parents who want to help their children achieve and thrive, without pressure."
—Carol D. Goodheart, EdD, 2010 president, American Psychological Association

"Parents will identify their children in the case studies presented by the authors and immediately find practical strategies for guiding them with their intellectual and social-emotional needs."
—Sylvia Rimm, PhD, author, *How to Parent So Children Will Learn*

"Kennedy-Moore and Lowenthal show us how to encourage healthy self-esteem and coping in our children. In a clear manner, they translate solid strategies into easy-to-understand advice for parents to help kids stay productive and happy. Wish my parents had this when I was growing up."
—Jed Baker, PhD, author, *No More Meltdowns*

"This warm and wise book shows parents how to nurture the social and emotional skills that all children need to succeed. It's filled with practical strategies parents can use to help children discover and develop their true potential."
—Michele Borba, PhD, author, *The Big Book of Parenting Solutions*

SMART PARENTING FOR Smart Kids

SMART PARENTING FOR Smart Kids

Nurturing Your Child's
True Potential

EILEEN KENNEDY-MOORE, PhD

MARK S. LOWENTHAL, PsyD

JOSSEY-BASS
A Wiley Imprint
www.josseybass.com

Published by Jossey-Bass
A Wiley Imprint
989 Market Street, San Francisco, CA 94103-1741—www.josseybass.com

Jossey-Bass books and products are available through most bookstores. To contact Jossey-Bass
directly call our Customer Care Department within the U.S. at 800-956-7739, outside the
U.S. at 317-572-3986, or fax 317-572-4002.

Jossey-Bass also publishes its books in a variety of electronic formats. Some content that
appears in print may not be available in electronic books.

Library of Congress Cataloging-in-Publication Data

Kennedy-Moore, Eileen.
    Smart parenting for smart kids : nurturing your child's true potential /
Eileen Kennedy-Moore, Mark S. Lowenthal.
        p. cm.
    Includes bibliographical references and index.
    ISBN 978-0-470-64005-0 (pbk.); ISBN 978-0-470-93999-4 (ebk);
978-0-470-94000-6 (ebk); ISBN 978-1-118-00289-6 (ebk)
    1. Gifted children. 2. Parents of gifted children. I. Lowenthal, Mark S., date. II. Title.
    HQ773.5.K467 2011
    649'.155–dc22

                                                                           2010043005

Printed in the United States of America
FIRST EDITION
PB Printing   10 9 8 7 6 5 4 3 2 1

*This book is lovingly dedicated to
our spouses and partners on our parenting journey,
Tony Moore and Sandy Voremberg*

CONTENTS

NOTE TO THE READER

The vignettes in this book are based on composites of children we have known. Names and identifying information have been changed or omitted. The dialogues are fictional. They are intended to represent typical behavior and problems, and they do not refer to specific people or real events.

This book is for general educational purposes only. It does not constitute and should not substitute for individual professional advice, psychotherapy, or the provision of psychological services.

ACKNOWLEDGMENTS

This book was both a pleasure and a challenge to write. The issues we discuss are neither simple nor quickly resolved, but we believe they are at the core of a life well lived. Writing this book caused us to examine our own values, experience, and parenting practices, and deepened our understanding in meaningful ways.

We are especially grateful to the children and parents who are or have been our psychotherapy clients. Thank you for sharing your observations, insights, struggles, and strengths with us, and for trusting us to help. You are the inspiration for this book.

We thank our wonderful agent, Betsy Amster, who understood the heart of this book from the beginning, and who has been an invaluable source of support and encouragement throughout the process of writing it. We thank our editor, Alan Rinzler, for championing this book, for using a light but very perceptive editorial hand, and for being amazingly responsive with his feedback. We also thank the dedicated staff at Jossey-Bass for turning our manuscript into a "real-live" book.

Our friends and colleagues have contributed moral support and brainstorming efforts through the ups and downs of writing this book: Sheila Kennedy Hickey (who counts as both a friend and a sister!), Julie Shadd Kennedy (who counts as both a friend and a sister-in-law!), Bob Harrell, Brian Gross, Jill

Degener Smith, Julie Abrams, David Sacks, Karen Cohen, Laura Skivone Fecko, Eliot Garson, Jeffrey Segal, Bonnie Lipeles, Kathy Newman, and Jane Simon. Your support has meant a lot to us!

Most of all, we thank our families. Eileen thanks her husband, Tony Moore, who has been a wonderful source of both practical and emotional support, listening to half-formed ideas, solving computer glitches, tackling or ignoring unfinished household chores, and making necessary late-night ice cream runs to cheer her on. She also thanks their children, Mary, Daniel, Sheila, and Brenna Kennedy-Moore, for filling her life with love, laughter, and learning. Mark thanks his wife, Sandy Voremberg, who has been there for him in every way possible over the past seventeen years and throughout the writing of this book. He also thanks their children, Ian and Haley Lowenthal. They continue to teach him about becoming a better parent as well as a more patient, sensitive, and loving person.

INTRODUCTION

Rethinking Potential

Potential is a dangerous word.

When someone tells you that your child has "real potential," you probably feel delighted. Maybe you imagine your child soaring through life, surpassing all your accomplishments, suffering none of your setbacks, while you watch with loving admiration.

But then the worries start, because potential, after all, is a possibility, not a guarantee. What if your child doesn't live up to that potential?

THE PRESSURE TO
HELP OUR KIDS ACHIEVE

Friends, neighbors, and the "child improvement" industry are quick to tell us everything we need to do to help our children reach their potential. They insist:

- Play Mozart while your baby is in the womb.
- Use the "brain boosting" baby formula.
- Sign your toddler up for gym classes to develop gross motor skills.
- Arrange for music classes to develop your child's mathematical thinking.

1

- Start soccer by three, or it will be too late.
- Language immersion must take place before the critical period ends.
- It's not enough to do one activity; you have to make sure your child is well rounded.

From all sides, the message is "Start early; go faster; do more." The earnestness and intensity of this advice makes it seem as though any parent who doesn't sign her children up for a bevy of enriching activities is neglectful.

We all know that overscheduled children (that is, kids who do more activities than ours do!) are a national problem, but the pressure and competition continue, and nothing changes. Philosophically, we might appreciate the value of downtime, but as parents, we're afraid to do anything less than everything possible to develop our children's potential.

In our zeal and anxiety to make sure our children fulfill their potential, we look to grades, test scores, and class placement as if they were crystal balls into the future—objective and infallible indicators of what lies ahead. We fret if a grade is low. We worry that our children might not be working hard enough. We fear that the curriculum offerings might not be challenging enough. Again, we are bombarded by advice: "Oh, isn't your daughter doing the computer-based tutoring that will advance her test scores one whole year?" We monitor homework, help them study for tests, critique their papers, supervise their science projects, and worry we're not doing enough. We wouldn't want our children to waste their potential.

THE BURDEN OF POTENTIAL

It's very easy for thoughts about potential to slip from "possibility" to "expectation." Conscientious efforts to support and encourage our children's achievement can drift into anxious concerns about what they *could* accomplish, if only they apply themselves diligently enough and take the right classes and get the right opportunities and score high enough . . .

Potential becomes a burden when we see it as a predestined calling to impressive accomplishments. Both parents and children can become seduced into focusing on performance rather than growth, on being The Best rather than making progress, and on accumulating external awards and accomplishments as the primary measures of worth. Worst of all, this one-dimensional perspective on potential creates a terrible fear of failure.

A DIFFERENT IDEA OF POTENTIAL

A narrow view of potential suggests that there is some lofty gold ring of success, and our children will either jump high enough to reach it or else fall short. But life doesn't work that way. In real life, there are lots of choices, lots of chances, and lots of paths. It makes no sense to talk about kids "not living up to their potential" because the miracle of children is that we just don't know how they will change or who they will become. The path of development is a journey of discovery that is clear only in retrospect, and it's rarely a straight line.

This book is for parents who understand that potential is not an end point but a capacity to grow and learn. Nurturing children's potential, in the broadest sense, means cultivating their humanity. It involves supporting their expanding abilities to reach out to others with kindness and empathy, to feel part of something bigger than themselves, to find joy and satisfaction in creating a life that is personally meaningful . . . and so much more.

THE DOWNSIDE OF BEING SMART

Concerns about "achieving potential" tend to be especially prominent when it comes to school performance. Maybe this is because kids spend so much time in school. Maybe it's because school is often a segue to future careers. Or maybe it's because nowadays children's academic performance is constantly rated and ranked.

What's surprising to us is that the greatest anxiety about achievement—in both parents and kids—often surrounds the children who have the most scholastic aptitude. These children spend a lot of time thinking and hearing about what they could or should achieve—because of their potential.

There are lots of ways to be smart, but in this book, when we refer to "smart" or "bright" kids, we're talking about children who are able to earn A's and B's, even if they aren't currently producing in school. Because they are so capable, they often face a lot of pressure to achieve. And sometimes that can lead to too much focus on what they do rather than on who they are.

WHY WE WROTE THIS BOOK

Kids today face unique challenges in developing a healthy perspective on achievement. We've observed this in our own children, in our friends' kids, and in the children we work with in our psychology practices. Too often, we've seen smart kids who

- Give up at the first sign of difficulty
- Become distraught over minor mistakes
- Seem unmotivated and put forth minimal effort
- Find working with classmates intolerable
- Get into needless power struggles with adults
- Feel lonely and disconnected from peers

As clinical psychologists, we've seen a lot of bright but unhappy children. In fact, some of the most miserable, angry, or stressed-out kids we've worked with were also the most academically capable.

We live in a narcissistic age that emphasizes being impressive and seeking admiration. Sadly, smart kids are often the ones who are hurt most by this focus on externals. Because they *can* perform, and that performance seems so important to everyone around them, they may start to believe that they *are* the performance.

A real danger facing bright children is that they will come to define themselves solely in terms of their accomplishments—to believe, "I'm smart, but that's all I am." This makes them terribly vulnerable. If they don't perform perfectly, if someone else is "smarter," if they have to struggle to learn something, or if they encounter any setback, they feel inadequate or even worthless. A minor criticism leaves them feeling wounded or enraged. Even their victories can feel empty because admiration is a cold substitute for closeness. When kids measure their worth solely in terms of achievement, their self-image becomes distorted and their ability to connect with others is crippled.

The antidote is to help children cultivate a broad self-definition that encompasses not only their abilities but also their humanity. This does *not* mean either settling for mediocrity or creating "superkids"; it means helping children develop the foundation they need to discover their passions, build relationships, sustain effort, and create a life with authentic happiness.

We wrote this book because we wanted to be a voice of clarity and comfort for parents who care about developing their children's inner strength. Compassion, perspective, grit . . . these qualities aren't necessarily impressive—your kids won't win a certificate for developing them—but they are essential to a well-lived life.

SEVEN FUNDAMENTAL CHALLENGES

All children face challenges growing up, but for bright children, concerns about achievement can eclipse and complicate "normal" developmental tasks. The chapters in this book highlight seven fundamental challenges:

1. Tempering perfectionism

2. Building connection

3. Managing sensitivity

4. Handling cooperation and competition

5. Dealing with authority

6. Developing motivation

7. Finding joy

These are the core issues that kids struggle with and parents worry about. Each of these issues involves children figuring out who they are, how they relate to others, and what achievement means to them. These are complex issues that call for deeply personal responses, but there are things you can do to help your child navigate them.

This book is solution-focused and filled with practical strategies that you can use today and continue to use as your child grows and develops. The strategies that we describe are doable in the course of everyday life. A lot of them involve conversations, explanations, or ways of responding to your child's behavior.

THE IMPORTANCE OF
THE ELEMENTARY SCHOOL YEARS

The examples and strategies described in the book focus on children approximately six to twelve years old. This age range covers the period when academic pressure starts, but the stakes aren't yet so high. Children's coping abilities can increase dramatically during these years. It's a period of intense intellectual growth, during which children gain the ability to reason logically, understand cause and effect, and solve problems.

In elementary school, children begin to develop a stable sense of identity, and they tend to be less self-centered than younger children because they can understand that other people have different thoughts, feelings, and wants. They also begin to compare themselves to peers and to make judgments about their own relative competence. All of this means that this is a time when kids are ready and able to expand their social and emotional coping skills, and they are still young enough to be open to parental guidance. Taking steps to bolster coping skills during these early school years can equip children to deal with the stresses that lie ahead in high school and beyond.

REFLECTING ON YOUR OWN THOUGHTS, FEELINGS, AND EXPERIENCES

Chances are, if you have a bright kid, you're pretty bright yourself, which means you'll probably remember grappling with some of the issues we describe. Maybe you still struggle with them. Although this book is about supporting your child, it also offers an opportunity to reflect on your own experiences. What messages did you get about achievement from parents and teachers when you were a child? What have you found to be effective in managing multiple demands on your time? How do you relate to people who are less capable than you? How about those who are more capable than you? How do you cope when you make mistakes or things don't go your way? What brings you a sense of satisfaction and contentment?

The issues that we discuss are lifelong challenges, not problems that people can deal with at age seven and be done. In each chapter, we have a section called "Show the Way" that describes how these issues play out in adulthood and what parents can do to address them in their own lives or to model effective coping for their children.

HOW TO USE THIS BOOK

There's a wrong way and a right way to use this book. The wrong way is to view it as over two hundred pages of stuff you need to "fix" or "improve" about your child or a long list of even more things you ought to be doing, on top of everything else you're doing, to be a good parent. The right way to use this book is as a resource to support your current efforts to raise a happy, healthy, productive, and kind child. Our goal is to provide you with a deeper understanding of how and why your child might struggle and to give you options for helping your child move forward. You may want to scan this book for the chapters or vignettes that are most relevant for your child. Read these sections and give yourself time to reflect on how they relate to your beliefs, values, and parenting challenges. Please view the strategies we suggest as possibilities rather than prescriptions, and use only those that make sense for you. Every child is unique, and nobody knows your child and your family better than you do.

It's also important to take a long-term view. You can't rush cognitive and emotional development. Kids grow at their own pace, and our role as parents is to support that growth, not force it. Although the book is filled with doable strategies, there are no gimmicks or quick fixes. Instead, the book focuses on ways you can communicate with, guide, and support your child. Throughout the book, we emphasize learning and growing, rather than performing.

THE COMPONENTS OF SMART PARENTING

Parenting involves a delicate balance. On the one hand, we need to cherish who our children are at this very moment. On the other hand, we need to support our children in moving forward. Achieving this balance requires four essential components of smart parenting:

1. A compassionate ability to view the world through our children's eyes

2. The confidence to set judicious limits

3. A commitment to turn toward our children more often than away

4. Faith in our children's ability to grow and learn

These four components underlie everything in this book.

Test scores and grades are good predictors of academic performance, but whether our children will be able to develop happy, productive, and fulfilling adult lives depends on much more than school smarts. All children need wise and caring guidance so they can develop the social and emotional skills that will serve as a foundation for everything they do. Our goal with this book is to support you in helping your kids develop internal tools so that they can pursue their passions, cope with difficulties, build relationships, and make what they wish of their lives. This book is about raising children rather than creating impressive products.

CHAPTER 1

TEMPERING PERFECTIONISM
What Is "Good Enough"?

 Does your child

- Fret and worry about minor mistakes?
- Focus on the one thing that's wrong rather than everything that's right?
- Act as his own worst critic?
- Make snap judgments and all-or-nothing pronouncements about whether she is "good at" some activity?
- Insist, "I'm so stupid" after making a mistake?
- Tend to make excuses and blame others for failings?
- Become teary or furious when some skill or activity doesn't come easily?
- Often forgo sleep, relaxation, and time with others because there is "too much work to do"?
- Procrastinate about big projects?
- Have trouble letting go and finishing projects?

When children are very capable, it's all too easy to fall into the trap of perfectionism. Because they *can* do extremely well, they come to believe that they *must* do everything flawlessly. Because they *have* done extremely well, they conclude that they *must always* meet or surpass the highest standards. Their self-worth depends on it.

THE FEELINGS AND BELIEFS UNDERLYING PERFECTIONISM

On the surface, perfectionism seems like a work issue, but it's really a relationship issue. Perfectionistic children (or adults) feel as though they live their lives on stage, in front of a harshly critical audience. The expectations stemming from their high abilities somehow become twisted and distorted into unyielding internal demands. When they fall short, perfectionistic children may respond with anger, tears, blame, or withdrawal, but fueling these reactions is an underlying sense of worthlessness. Perfectionists believe that their value lies not in who they are but in what they produce. In their hearts, perfectionists believe that love has to be earned and that nothing less than 100 percent will do.

Perfectionism Versus Healthy Striving

Researchers disagree about whether perfectionism is simply "too much of a good thing" or whether it's completely separate from healthy ambition and a desire to do a good job. On the one hand, having high standards is associated with better performance. On the other hand, studies show that perfectionism is linked to depression, suicidal thoughts, anxiety, substance abuse, eating disorders, and various physical symptoms. The critical factor may be whether there's a mismatch between expectations and self-evaluation: when kids believe that they *must* perform extremely well but also think they *didn't* or *can't*, they're likely to feel bad about themselves and to respond with either hopeless withdrawal or desperate efforts to measure up.

We're convinced, based on our clinical experience, that there's a blurry but important line between healthy striving for excellence and unhealthy perfectionism. This distinction is easiest to see at an emotional level. Healthy striving feels hopeful, engaged, optimistic, energetic, and enjoyable. It requires effort, but that effort feels satisfying and voluntarily chosen, and the goals feel achievable. Perfectionism, in contrast, is driven by dread of humiliation and fear of failure. The effort seems forced, painful, and imposed rather than chosen—and it never ends. The goals are moving targets, and the performance could always be better. By anyone else's standards, perfectionistic children may be performing extremely well, but it's heartbreaking to hear the self-contempt they feel, as they struggle to meet their own impossible expectations. It's this unhealthy form of perfectionism that we consider in this chapter.

The Lure and Pitfalls of Perfectionism

Rigid, unrelenting perfectionism makes people miserable, yet they cling to it. If your child has perfectionistic tendencies, it won't be easy to temper them. Letting go of unrealistically high standards may seem like a sensible thing to do, but it's terrifying for perfectionists. Despite the personal cost, striving to perform perfectly gives them a sense of control. They worry that if they let up an inch, their secret inadequacy will be exposed, they'll never achieve anything, and they'll earn the scorn or disappointment of others.

Grades, contests, rivalry with peers, and spoken or unspoken demands from teachers and parents can contribute to this all-or-nothing thinking. Smart kids get a lot of praise and recognition for performing perfectly. They don't often hear, "Wow, you did a great job of setting sensible limits and refraining from overdoing."

Sometimes the pressure to perform comes from inside. Bright children are often proud of their perfectionism, seeing it as central to who they are and what they've achieved. They would be ashamed to do a less than perfect job. Mistakes seem like personal failings and signs of a frightening loss of control. To perfectionists, the suffering that comes from striving to perform flawlessly seems necessary and unavoidable. They are convinced that perfectionism is desirable and the only path to success.

But the fact is that people generally achieve *despite* perfectionism, not because of it. Perfectionism can stifle output by leading to paralyzing procrastination that makes it hard to start, work on, or finish projects. It can waste energy when it causes children to worry, rather than take action. It often leads to excessive focus on trivial details. Perfectionism also kills creativity. When children are anxiously focused on judging the merit of their work and fretting about the possible reactions of their real or imagined audience, they are not free to invent, discover, or try new approaches.

Tempering Perfectionism

To make the most of their abilities, smart children need to embrace high standards but move beyond rigid perfectionism. They need to understand that it's possible to be capable and accomplished without being perfectionistic. They need to learn to treat themselves with compassion and open their eyes to the possibility that relationships don't have to be earned. In this chapter, we'll describe some common scenarios involving perfectionistic children and offer ideas about how you can help.

 ## MICHAEL: FOCUSING ON FLAWS

"I blew it! I totally blew it!" Michael whispered, as he sat down next to his parents in the auditorium. He crumpled the program for the piano recital, wishing he could rip it into shreds.

"I think you did a wonderful job, honey," his mother insisted.

"Are you kidding? I messed up the beginning of the second piece." Michael blinked frantically, trying not to cry.

"You're the only one who noticed. Didn't you hear the applause?"

"They clap for everyone, Mom," Michael insisted miserably. "They probably felt sorry for me. I'm just no good at piano. I've been practicing for weeks for this stupid recital, and I totally messed up. I'm never doing another piano recital as long as I live. Can we leave now?"

※

The only thing that Michael remembers about his performance is his mistake. It eclipses everything that came before or after. He's also convinced that that's all anyone else heard, so his mother's praise feels empty and unbelievable.

Michael's story is about a musical performance, but this kind of overfocusing on flaws can involve schoolwork, athletic events, or even social interactions. Perfectionistic children constantly and harshly critique their own behavior.

Magnifying Mistakes

If pressed, Michael would probably admit that he was not the only child to make a mistake during the piano recital. But somehow, although other children's errors seem excusable or understandable, his own mistake feels humiliating. He sees it as proof of his inadequacy as a pianist. He cringes as he imagines his audience's pity and disdain, and he longs to escape. In Michael's view, the only possible and appropriate response to errors is to slink away alone in shame. For perfectionists like Michael, mistakes that other people would shrug off, or perhaps not even notice, fuel their vicious internal litany: "I shouldn't have done that. I'm no good."

The Slippery Slope Theory

Matt Stone, the cocreator of *South Park*, once remarked,

> I remember being in sixth grade and I had to take the math test to get into Honors Math in the seventh grade. And they're, like, "Don't screw this up. Because if you screw this up, you won't get into Honors Math in seventh grade. And if you don't get in in seventh grade, you won't in eighth grade, then not in ninth grade. And tenth and eleventh grade and you'll just die poor and lonely."

This seems laughable, yet it's exactly what perfectionists fear—that a minor slipup now could irrevocably destroy all opportunities for future success and happiness.

Kids, by definition, lack perspective. No matter how smart they are, they just haven't been around long enough or seen enough of the world to be able to understand events in any kind of broad context. The narrowness of their experience contributes to perfectionistic children's "step off the path and it's all over" fears.

Yes, it's important to do well in school, but "do well" doesn't have to mean performing flawlessly at all times. Research consistently shows that grades and test scores are not the whole story when it comes to predicting adult accomplishment. This is probably because adult job performance has nothing to do with taking multiple-choice tests and everything to do with being able to solve problems, adjust to changing circumstances, think critically, communicate effectively, work dependably, and get along with clients, colleagues, and bosses. These are the real lessons that your child needs to learn from school and from life.

The fact that your son got a bad grade on a fourth-grade math test doesn't mean that he's destined for a life of failure any more than the fact that your daughter liked to run around naked when she was two means that she's destined for a career as an exotic dancer. Children are constantly growing, learning, and developing.

One of the most precious gifts that we can give our children is to share our confidence in their growth and their ability to surmount difficulties and move beyond disappointments. Believe in your child's future. Convey your faith that even if there are some stumbles along the way, your child will find a path that's right for him or her.

STRATEGIES TO HELP YOUR CHILD TEMPER SELF-CRITICISM

Children like Michael need to learn to temper their internal critic, so that their inner voice is inspiring rather than self-defeating. They need help managing their feelings of anxiety or disappointment, and they need to develop a more compassionate, multifaceted view of their work. Here are some ideas about how you can help.

Reflect but Downshift

When smart kids are convinced that they "totally messed up," loving parents instinctively want to respond with reassurance. The problem is that the more we insist, "Oh, sweetie, of course you're not stupid! How can you say such a thing? You know that's not true!" the harder they argue the contrary.

A basic principle for working with children is to start by meeting them where they are. This means that if your child is upset about a perceived failure, you need to acknowledge that upset before you can help your child move on. Obviously you don't want to agree with outrageous statements ("Yes, your life truly is over"), but you can help wrap feelings in words. Name feelings. Summarize facts. Describe wishes or fears. Offer affection. Your goal is to stay true to your child's emotional reality while gently shifting the reaction in a less extreme direction. Here are some examples of how you might respond:

Child's Comment	Parent's Reflection
"I totally blew it!"	"You didn't do as well as you'd hoped."
"I'm such an idiot!"	"You're feeling frustrated about your mistake."
"I'm no good!"	"You're disappointed."
"My life is over!"	"You sure had a rough day."
"I'll never be able to show my face in public!"	"You're worried about how they'll react."
"I messed up!"	"Do you need a hug?"

This strategy of reflecting but downshifting can help children see their feelings as more manageable. While children are emotionally wound up, they simply can't hear reason, so hold off on any reassurances or suggestions. Just keep listening and reflecting until your child is in a calmer frame of mind.

Resist the Temptation to Offer Pointers

It's natural for parents to want to share their wisdom with their children. Unfortunately, children under the age of thirty usually don't respond well to this. Although our intent is to offer the benefit of our learning and experience, kids tend to hear our helpful tips as personal criticism and rejection. This is especially true when children are feeling vulnerable because they're disappointed in their performance.

In general, it's best to leave the teaching and coaching to your child's teachers and coaches. It's just less complicated, psychologically, for children to accept criticism from nonparents. Research suggests that children do better in school and feel happier when they perceive that their parents have high expectations for them in the sense of generally wanting them to do well, but chronic parental criticism is linked to anxiety, depression, and poor school outcomes. It's painful for children to feel as though they can't live up to their parents' standards.

What if your child specifically asks you for feedback on a performance? Resist answering. This is a no-win situation for parents. If you say something good, your perfectionistic child will discount it; if you say something bad, your child will feel wounded. So give a hug and toss the question back. "You tell me. What were your favorite parts?" Be careful not to get sucked into arguing about your child's evaluations. Either reflect (as described earlier) or respond with an interested but noncommittal "Hmm."

If you must say something, stick to encouraging comments about process: "It looked like you were having fun." "I could tell you were really concentrating." "You were really trying hard." You can also offer an affectionate comment like, "I always enjoy hearing [watching] you play."

The temptation to offer pointers is especially great when children are working in fields where their parents excelled. Whether or not anyone acknowledges it, there is an underlying current of comparison and even competition when kids work in their parents' talent areas. Kids wonder if they can measure up to their parents' accomplishments. They may feel worthless if they fall short of their parents' high levels of achievement, even if, objectively, their performance is excellent. Parents hope that their children will surpass what they have done. When parents are disappointed in their own accomplishments, there is a danger that they will consciously or unconsciously push their children to fulfill the parents' own frustrated dreams.

A shared interest can be the basis of a wonderful bond between kids and parents, but only if parents can resist entering the role of chief judge and critic. Never offer pointers immediately after a performance or test—children are just too vulnerable at that point. Concentrate on sharing your enjoyment and interest rather than your performance standards. If you do offer tips, make sure you do so in a casual way, in a relaxed setting. "I've found it helpful to . . ." "You might want to try . . ."

Keep a close eye on your child's emotional reaction. If your child seems interested and encouraged, you're doing fine. If you sense your child becoming upset, say "Let's take a break" or even "Why don't you talk to your teacher [coach] about that?"

Identify What Went Right

Perfectionistic children tend to be black-and-white thinkers: either something is perfect or it's worthless. Helping your child recognize partial success can ease some of the sting that comes when they fall short of perfection.

Talk with your child to come up with a list of qualities that make up a good performance. For instance, a fine musical performance could involve

- Having the courage to get up on stage
- Playing the notes without error
- Getting all the way to the end of the piece without stopping
- Phrasing the melodies correctly
- Using changes in volume or tone to highlight melodies
- Coordinating with other musicians
- Conveying the emotional feel of a piece

A fine work of nonfiction writing could involve

- Accurate spelling
- Correct grammar
- Clear organization
- Use of transitions
- Precise or intriguing word choice
- Compelling arguments
- Natural, readable phrasing

Your goal is to come up with a bunch of criteria so that your child can gain a multifaceted view of the performance. Be sure to "stack the deck" so that most of the criteria are things that your child does well and only one or two pertain to areas of difficulty.

Tell your child, "It's true that recognizing and correcting mistakes are important parts of improving performance, but so is recognizing what went right. You need to acknowledge the things you did well, so that you can continue to do them."

KIRSTEN: DEFLECTING BLAME

"My math teacher is a complete idiot!" Kirsten snarled as she flung her backpack down. "I don't know why they even let her teach! I mean, could they find anyone stupider? I hate her stupid voice. She talks to us like we're kindergartners. And she's so boring. Plus, she dresses like a flight attendant, and she has a really big butt."

"Did something happen in math class today?" Kirsten's mom asked cautiously.

"She's such an idiot! Mrs. Warner gave us a test, and it was all on stuff that she didn't even cover in class. She's so unfair!"

"Well, how badly did you do?"

"I did terribly. It's the worst grade I've gotten this whole year. I don't want to talk about it."

"Did you fail the test?"

"Just about!"

"What did you get?"

"I said I don't want to talk about it."

"Kirsten, show me the test."

"Fine, but then I'm going to burn it."

"It's a B! That's not so bad!"

"Yes it is. Only stupid people get B's. It's not fair!" Kirsten burst into tears and ran up to her room.

Kirsten rants about the teacher. She bemoans the unfairness of the test. This is all just noise to cover up the fact that, for her, a B feels like a personal failure.

Lashing Out in Response to Failure

Like Michael in the first story, Kirsten is intolerant of her own mistakes, but instead of responding with self-criticism and withdrawal, her first impulse is to lash out. Her angry, defensive accusations are a short-lived attempt to cover up the fact that she feels very, very bad about herself.

The challenge for Kirsten's mom is to avoid being diverted by her daughter's anger. Kirsten is looking for a fight. There's a natural temptation to meet anger with anger, but for now, Kirsten's mom needs to bite her tongue. This is not the time to confront Kirsten about her outrageously rude comments or her annoying tendency to blame others for her mistakes. Kirsten is spewing venom, looking for a target for her frustration and disappointment. If Kirsten's mom tries to address the rudeness now, Kirsten is likely to respond by blaming her mother for her difficulties. Until she calms down, Kirsten just isn't capable of thinking clearly about the situation or responding in any kind of productive way.

Avoiding Getting Pulled into the Fight

It would be counterproductive for Kirsten's mom to join her daughter in raging at the teacher and the unfairness of the situation. Although this might seem like a supportive response, it actually hurts Kirsten because it validates her excuses and prevents her from taking responsibility for her actions.

Even if Kirsten's complaints about the test have some validity, it would be a mistake for Kirsten's mother to call and angrily demand that the teacher change Kirsten's grade. Complaining about a grade comes across as disrespectful and intrusive, and it's sure to antagonize the teacher. It also shifts responsibility for the unsatisfactory performance away from where it belongs—with the child. What's more, it completely misses the point. In the long run, the fact that Kirsten got a B on a test when she was a kid has absolutely no significance, but her ability to cope effectively with disappointment will be relevant throughout her life. Save your advocacy efforts for the more serious or ongoing issues that are beyond your child's ability to handle.

Kirsten's mom should also think carefully about how she usually responds to her daughter's mistakes. Harsh responses to children's errors can fuel perfectionism. Sometimes bright children have emotional outbursts in an effort to head off their parents' intense displeasure. At some level, these children think that if they are already upset, then their parents won't scold or punish them, or their parents' disappointment will be diverted away from them and toward the teacher.

STRATEGIES TO HELP YOUR CHILD RESPOND TO MISTAKES PRODUCTIVELY

Children like Kirsten need help learning to tolerate the hurt and disappointment behind their anger. They also need to develop more adaptive ways of responding to setbacks. Here are some ways you can help your child see mistakes as manageable.

Highlight the Learning Zone

Bright children often hear, "Mistakes are part of learning," but, in general, they don't believe this. Perfectionistic kids are convinced that mistakes should be avoided at all costs. Helping them understand more about the learning process can alleviate some of their anxiety and dread about mistakes.

Show your child the diagram here, and explain, "This is a picture of how you learn." The vertical arrows show difficulty—

higher up means harder problems. The left column shows the starting point. The lower rectangle, filled with check marks, is the mastery zone. That's the easy stuff that your child knows well and gets right every time. The upper rectangle, filled with X's, is the undeveloped zone. That's the stuff that's too hard. Your child just hasn't developed the ability to do these tasks yet. The most important part of the graph is the center rectangle, the learning zone. This rectangle is filled with both checks and X's, to reflect both right and wrong answers, because your child can do some, but not all, of the tasks at this level.

Work in the learning zone to expand the mastery zone.

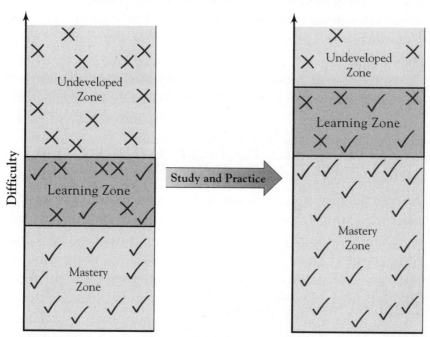

Explain to your child that kids who stick to the mastery zone are playing it safe. They never make mistakes, but they also never learn.

Kids who are brave enough to work in the learning zone are going to make mistakes. But that's okay, because through study and practice, they're going to learn from those mistakes.

They'll figure out how to turn all those X's into checks. They'll move over to the column on the right, which shows an expanded mastery zone and a new, higher-level learning zone.

Tell your child, "To learn, you have to be brave enough to make mistakes." When your child comes home with red marks on a school paper, say, "It looks like you're in the learning zone. Have you figured out yet how to fix the mistakes?"

Don't Correct Your Child's Work

Parents of bright children tend to be very conscientious. They are strongly invested in doing a good job as parents. They want to do everything they can to help their children succeed. But sometimes the best thing a parent can do is to take a giant step back.

Don't correct your child's work. This advice runs counter to what you might expect and to what you probably see most parents doing. But we believe it's one of the most important things you can do to benefit your child in the long run.

Parents who are actively involved with their children's homework every night, or who check over their children's work before they turn it in, are establishing a dangerous pattern. First, they're creating confusion about whose responsibility the homework really is. Second, they're cutting off essential feedback that teachers need about what children do or don't understand on their own. Third, they're unwittingly criticizing their children's abilities, implying that what their kids can do alone isn't good enough to be seen in public. Parents who correct their children's homework are trying to be helpful, but they're unintentionally communicating to their children that mistakes are intolerable and must be hidden. This can be particularly harmful for perfectionistic children.

If you're in the habit of correcting your child's work, it may be hard to refrain from doing so. You may feel (and your child may argue!) that you're abandoning your child. You may worry that the teacher will think you're a bad parent for letting your child turn in less-than-perfect work. You may feel embarrassed at back-to-school night, when your child's sugar cube sculpture looks like (and was!) the work of a third grader, whereas many classmates' projects look like (and were!) the work of professional engineers. These feelings are understandable, but try to take a long-term perspective. Whatever short-term pain might be involved now in changing this pattern of schoolwork overinvolvement is worthwhile in the long run. It's an investment in your child's future coping abilities.

Children need to take responsibility for their own learning. They need to experience that the world won't end if they make a mistake. Allowing children to experience and overcome many small failures leads to real learning and resilience. And when they do well, the victory will be sweeter and more satisfying if they know they did it all by themselves.

The phenomenon of parental involvement with homework is fairly recent. Most of us grew up with parents who expected us to do our homework by ourselves. Yet parents today have somehow gotten the idea that to be a good, supportive parent, they need to actually sit down and do homework with their children. Often this doesn't go well. One of the most frequent complaints that we hear from the families we work with is frustration about the tension surrounding homework time. In general, our recommendation is that parents do less so that more of the onus falls on their children.

Does this mean you should never do anything to help your child with homework? Not necessarily, although most of the time having no parental involvement with homework is perfectly fine and even desirable. If you do help, the key is to make sure that your child retains ownership of the work. Providing structure and limits for children, such as a rule that there's no TV until homework is done, is often helpful and sometimes essential. Kids with attentional issues may do better doing their homework in the dining room or kitchen, where an adult is nearby, rather than disappearing into their room, where the temptation to do other things is too high. But even with these kids, hovering or sitting next to them is likely to create unnecessary and unproductive tension. An occasional one-word reminder, "Focus!" is likely to work better.

When your child is about to start a big project, you can offer various ideas ("How about writing about the Japanese internment or the Tuskegee airmen?") or suggest possible approaches ("Do you want to use Model Magic or papier-mâché for the diorama?"), but avoid physically touching the work. If your child doesn't understand the instructions on a worksheet or doesn't know how to do a math problem, you can explain, but let your child come to you asking for help; don't offer help before it's needed.

If your child likes to review spelling words aloud with you, that's fine, but again, let your child come to you. What if your child doesn't remember to study and does poorly on a test? Well, that's an important life lesson for your child about responsibility. Next time your child can make a better choice. You can also help your child come up with a more effective study plan.

Written assignments can easily lead to overdoing parental help. Ask your child's teacher whether you should even read your child's papers before they are handed in. The teacher may prefer that you do nothing, or the teacher may appreciate your helping your child with spelling or organization. If you do get involved, stick to consulting and let your child do any revising. Point out the misspelled words, but let your child fix them. Ask questions ("What are your three main points?" "What is your topic sentence?") rather than give answers. Make general comments ("I'm having trouble following you here"; "This seems like it fits better with your earlier point"), but don't rewrite anything. Also, don't read the books or articles that your child is using as a basis for the paper. This ensures that your child is the expert on the topic, rather than you.

Although it may make you uncomfortable to let your child turn in less-than-perfect work, when you refrain from fixing the mistakes, you send your child a powerful message about acceptance and bravery and love.

Don't Protect Your Child from Disappointment

When our children suffer, our protective parental instincts automatically kick in. Our first impulse is to do whatever we can to make things all better, just as we did when they were babies. But allowing children to cope with ordinary disappointments can help them become more resilient. It lets them discover that setbacks are unpleasant but tolerable and often temporary.

If your child is upset about a grade or the results of a contest or audition, don't make it your job to fix it. Acknowledge your child's frustration or sadness, but also communicate that setbacks happen to everyone. That's just the way the world works. All we can do is lick our wounds and get up, determined to face another day.

Insist on No Excuses, Only Plans

When kids are convinced that mistakes are unacceptable, they often respond defensively by blaming everyone in sight for their failings. This behavior is counterproductive, and it can also come across as obnoxious.

If your child is very upset, wait for a calmer moment to discuss this, but if your child is just whining, put a stop to it. Say, matter-of-factly, "Excuses don't help. If you're not happy with how you did, then you need to come up with some plans about how you can do better. What could you do that might help?" If your child continues to whine, remain unimpressed. Say, "You can't change the situation; you can only change how you respond. Let me know when you're ready to talk about plans." Then walk away.

For some children, making excuses has become a habit. They do it automatically to explain away disappointment. If your child has this tendency, you may want to agree on a nonverbal signal, such as crossing two fingers to make an X, as a gentle reminder to avoid excuses. You could also discuss with your child how *excuses take away our power to make things better*. Have your child explain what this means. You may even want to post this as a motto on your refrigerator.

Coach Coping Efforts

Because they haven't had much experience "messing up," smart kids may not know how to cope when they do badly. We've been surprised to hear how many bright children secretly fear that they are not really as smart as other people think they are. They see poor performance as a threat to their whole identity. With their self-worth hanging in the balance, they may resort to casting blame or giving up simply because they don't know any other options for coping with setbacks. They just want to erase their error.

You may need to coach your child about possible coping strategies. Take a problem-solving approach. Help your child brainstorm possible responses, then choose the best ones. Be sure to generate a list of alternatives before evaluating them. Otherwise your child is likely to dismiss each option as it comes up ("That won't work because . . ."). Try to ask questions more than you give suggestions, because coming up with alternatives is a good learning experience for your child. Also, your child will be more invested in trying ideas that he or she generates. Stay focused on ideas about what *your child* (rather than you or the teacher) can do to improve the situation, and let your child make the final decision regarding which plans to implement.

Here are three general coping options that you'll want your child to consider:

1. *Clarify expectations*. Sometimes children fail to do well because they don't know what the teacher wants. They ignore or misinterpret directions, which hurts their performance.

Reading the instructions and grading criteria before starting and talking with the teacher are ways that your child can clarify expectations. Understanding expectations ensures that your child's efforts are focused in the most important direction.

2. *Change strategy.* Sometimes children need to learn a different approach to tasks. For instance, many smart kids eventually reach a point in school where their usual study strategy of casually flipping through notes right before a test or relying on their memory of what a teacher said in class just isn't enough anymore. They need to learn more effective study skills involving active learning, deliberate memorization, and thoughtful synthesis of material. Similarly, many smart kids are convinced that they can count on their "muse" to strike if they put off starting a written assignment until the last minute. With larger or more complicated writing assignments, this strategy won't work. Children need to plan out their efforts, setting mini-deadlines to keep themselves on the path toward completion.

If your child protests, "That's not the way I like to do things!" point out that the old strategy isn't working. Tell your child that there's a mountain of research showing that several shorter learning sessions work better than one long memorization marathon. There's also ample evidence that a steady approach to writing yields more output and higher-quality work than do frantic writing binges.

Your child might find it helpful to read a book about strategies for studying, taking tests, or writing papers. We like *How to Do Homework Without Throwing Up*, by Trevor Romain and Elizabeth Verdick, for younger children or *Super Study Skills*, by Laurie Rozakis, for older students. Don't assume that your child knows these strategies just because he or she is intelligent. In fact, other children might be ahead of your child in learning study skills because they had to learn them earlier, so they've been using them longer.

3. *Get help.* It's not easy for smart kids to ask for help. They believe that needing assistance implies failure because

they couldn't do it by themselves. Explain to your child that in the adult world, very few people work completely on their own, so knowing when to ask for help is an important life skill. Encourage your child to think about who might be able to help and how. Don't forget peers—having a study buddy can be both productive and fun.

SAM: AVOIDING ACTIVITIES AT WHICH HE DOESN'T EXCEL

"Swimming lessons are stupid." Sam grumbled from the backseat of the car. His father ignored him. "I mean, who even cares about different strokes? As long as I can save myself, why do I have to do that breathing? If I get thrown off a boat, which is not likely to happen, since we live three hundred miles away from any body of water, I'll do backstroke."

"Swimming is a basic life skill. Everybody needs to know how to swim. Besides, it's a good way to make friends."

"No, it isn't. How can I make friends if they make me put my face in the water? Am I supposed to talk to people underwater? Besides, I'm the only one in the class who can't do stupid freestyle."

"That's why you're taking lessons. I'm sure you'll figure it out."

"No, I won't. Some people are born to be swimmers. Others are not. I'm not."

"Sam, it just takes practice. We don't expect you to be an Olympic swimmer, but if you keep at it, you'll definitely improve. Besides, once you can swim, you won't feel shy about going to the town pool this summer."

"I don't want to go to the town pool. It's hot. The chlorine smells. The sunblock gets in my eyes. And anyway, it's boring."

Sam offers a laundry list of elaborate excuses about why he doesn't want to go to swimming lessons, but the real reason is that he's uncomfortable doing an activity in which he doesn't immediately excel.

Expecting Instant Success

Because they are used to doing well with minimal effort, bright children are often quick to conclude, "I'm no good at this" when they aren't instantly accomplished at some task. Their impulse is to give up rather than to try harder. These children have little tolerance for the process of developing skills. Because they've rarely experienced it, they don't grasp and may even actively resist the idea of step-by-step improvement.

Fearing Exposure

When perfectionists balk at doing something new or difficult, it may be because they fear exposing what they consider their inalterable weaknesses. This kind of perfectionistic thinking fits with what Stanford University psychology professor Carol Dweck calls a *fixed mindset*. Children with a fixed mindset believe that abilities are innate. They think that people are born with a certain amount of talent or intelligence, and their performance "proves" how capable they are. In contrast, children with a *growth mindset* believe that innate abilities can be expanded through learning. For them, performance is a measure of a temporary state rather than a permanent trait. Whereas fixed-mindset children feel compelled to guard against looking stupid, growth-mindset children are more willing to take chances, ask questions, and try harder in order to expand their abilities.

STRATEGIES TO HELP YOUR CHILD BECOME LESS AFRAID OF TRYING

Ability is not something that's either present or absent, like the answer to a true-false test. Children like Sam need to understand that knowledge and skills develop with effort over time. The following strategies can help your child become less afraid of trying.

Read About Famous People's Path to Success

Bright children tend to assume that high ability should translate into instant and consistent success. They're quick to conclude that a lack of success means a lack of innate talent. A look at the lives of eminent people shows that none was successful 100 percent of the time, many did not show promise initially, and all of them had to overcome setbacks, difficulties, or challenges of some sort. Thomas Edison tried over ten thousand experiments before inventing the incandescent light bulb. Albert Einstein failed the entrance exams for the Swiss Polytechnic Institute. J. K. Rowling was on welfare. Oprah Winfrey was fired from a job as a television reporter. The book *Famous Failures: Hundreds of Hot Shots Who Got Rejected, Flunked Out, Worked Lousy Jobs, Goofed Up, or Did Time in Jail Before Achieving Phenomenal Success* is filled with interesting facts like these. For a more in-depth look at famous lives, have your child read *Great Failures of the Extremely Successful: Mistakes, Adversity, Failure and Other Stepping Stones to Success*, by Steve Young. Biographies of people your child admires can also be inspiring and help temper the naïve view that there's a short, straight line to success.

Emphasize Deliberate Practice

Smart kids often fantasize about success and recognition, but they have no idea what it really takes to make their fantasies reality. Research by Anders Ericsson at Florida State University shows that there are no shortcuts to expertise. He and his colleagues have studied experts in a wide range of fields, including musicians, writers, athletes, doctors, and chess players. They've concluded that it takes a *minimum* of ten years or ten thousand hours of deliberate practice to become an expert.

Usually we think of practice as dull repetition, but that's not what Ericsson and his colleagues are talking about. Deliberate practice involves focused and sustained efforts to learn something that's beyond current competence and comfort. It means concentrating, analyzing, using feedback, and actively working to eliminate weaknesses. Deliberate practice is hard work. It's much easier and often more fun to practice what we already know, but deliberate practice of what doesn't come easily is the only path toward improvement and the deep satisfaction that comes from having worked hard to reach a goal.

Do Something Ridiculous Together

Perfectionistic children fear making fools of themselves. You can help your child reduce this fear by doing something ridiculous together. Try learning to juggle, especially if you think you'll be bad at it. Make up your own silly words to a song. Check out the book *Kids Shenanigans*, by the editors of Klutz Press, for instructions on a variety of silly handshakes, classic tricks like hanging a spoon from your nose, speaking pig latin, and many other fun but pointless activities. Laughing together is one of the best ways to defuse perfectionists' rigid standards.

ANGELA: FEELING INADEQUATE

"I can't do it," Angela thought, as she swallowed nervously. The paper was due tomorrow, and it was already 11:48 P.M. Piles of notes and books lay spread across her desk, but the computer showed only two sentences and a lot of empty space. She'd written and rewritten those two sentences a bunch of times, but they still sounded stupid. All week, she'd been working on the paper, reading and gathering information, but she just couldn't seem to pull it together.

"You're an idiot!" she said aloud. "Just get it done!" But nothing came to mind. Her stomach churned. Maybe she was getting sick.

She imagined her teacher's disappointment if she said she didn't finish the paper. Mrs. McKinley was constantly telling Angela what a good writer she was, but she had no idea what Angela went through every time she had a paper to write. How would she react if Angela turned in a page with only two sentences? She'd probably kick Angela out of the advanced language arts program.

"Write something!" Angela ordered herself, but the thought echoed in her mind, "I can't. I just can't."

Somehow, Angela will manage to finish this paper. She has always done it in the past, so she'll do it this time, too. But she's suffering.

Freezing Up

High personal standards are laudable, but for Angela, those standards have slipped into paralyzing perfectionism. She judges herself with brutal harshness, and expects others to do so too. She believes her teacher will kick her out of the advanced program if she messes up just once. The idea of turning in a so-so paper and figuring out a better strategy for next time is inconceivable to Angela. She demands nothing less than 100 percent excellence from herself. For Angela, struggles are a shameful sign of personal inadequacy rather than an indication that she needs help, guidance, extra time, or just a good night's sleep.

Driving Too Hard

Angela is exhausted and not thinking clearly. The most helpful thing her parents could do at this point is to say, "That's enough.

Go to bed." If she wants to, she can get up early in the morning to work. Otherwise, she needs to talk with the teacher about her struggles and work out a plan for finishing the paper and preventing these problems in the future. Angela needs to get the message that nobody expects her to drive herself into the ground. That kind of pushing isn't appropriate for a child (and it's not particularly healthy for adults, either).

Perfectionism like Angela's is common in certain cultures in which a child's performance is thought to reflect on the honor of the extended family. For these children, anything less than extraordinary performance feels unbearable because they believe they are bringing shame on their family and letting down the people they love. Although a sense of responsibility toward family is desirable and admirable, sometimes these children magnify their parents' expectations to an extreme degree. If you have a child who seems to be pushing too hard to succeed, you may need to offer a reminder that doing well is important, but not at any cost.

STRATEGIES TO HELP YOUR CHILD ACCEPT "GOOD ENOUGH"

Children like Angela need to develop more compassionate standards for themselves. They need to find a way to embrace effort without pushing themselves to desperate lengths. They also need to learn practical strategies for breaking through procrastination.

Focus on "Reasonable Effort"

Never tell a perfectionistic child, "Just do your best." Other children hear this as sensible or even reassuring advice, but perfectionists interpret it as "Do the best job you can possibly imagine, even if it kills you."

A healthier message for perfectionists is, "Make a reasonable effort." What constitutes a reasonable effort? Well, that's a judgment call. It depends on the importance of the task and how much time is available. Just getting your child to think about this before starting a project is an important step in helping your child understand that effort levels can and should vary. Working a certain amount each day on a large project is reasonable. Frequently getting too little sleep or never having time off is not reasonable.

You may also want to help your child identify the vital elements of a task. If it's a school assignment, what parts does the teacher care about most? If the basis for the grade will be 70 percent clarity and organization of writing, 20 percent thoroughness of research, and 10 percent attractiveness of illustrations, those percentages should guide your child's efforts. Obsessing about reading every possible reference or making the illustrations perfectly beautiful would be a mistake, especially if these efforts take away from working on the writing.

Teach Anti-Procrastination Tips

Many perfectionists struggle with procrastination. Their extremely high standards, and their fears about falling short of those standards, interfere with both starting and finishing projects. Here are some strategies that you might want to share with your child for cutting through procrastination:

- *Break down big jobs into small steps.* Help your child make a list of what needs to be done. Having a step-by-step game plan will seem less daunting than a giant leap from nothing to a fully finished project. Crossing off steps on the way to the final goal can also provide a sense of progress.

- *Set mini-deadlines.* Deciding on deadlines for intermediate steps can help your child pace efforts to avoid a frantic rush at the end. Remind your child to allow some leeway for unexpected delays. Mini-deadlines can also be useful for preventing overdoing. Help your child decide how much time a certain task is worth and then do no more than that.

- *Do the most important and most difficult things first.* Once these are out of the way, your child can relax.

- *Set up routines.* Establishing regular times for certain activities avoids wasting time wondering when to do something or what to do next.

- *Take short planned breaks to stay fresh.* Ten minutes of exercise or relaxation at regular intervals or after finishing certain tasks can help your child stay focused and reduce fatigue.

- *Plan the next work session.* Before stopping work on a large project, have your child make some notes about what to do next, so that there's no delay in getting productive at the start of the following work session.

- *Use quick tasks to build momentum.* Doing some small jobs that can be accomplished quickly and easily can help your child get moving on a project.

- *Work on one task at a time and fully finish.* Your child will feel more relaxed with three tasks completely done than six tasks half finished.

- *Get all the way through before polishing.* It's usually more important to finish a task than to do it perfectly. Tell your child to do a full draft or complete rough project, so that there's something to turn in, then revise or improve as time allows.

- *Celebrate accomplishments.* Encourage your child to plan self-rewards for completing intermediate goals and the whole project.

Share a Fable

Throughout history, people have used stories to convey important messages. Try reading this fable to your child:

THE LAST HANDFUL OF GRAIN

Once there was a farmer who had two sons. Early one morning, in late summer, when the grain in the fields was golden and ripe, the farmer said to his sons, "You're old enough now to be trusted with the important work of harvesting. One of you take the east side and the other the west. Go into the fields and gather the grain, and tonight at dinner we'll celebrate your new responsibility."

The sons eagerly gathered their tools and climbed into their wagons. The first son drove to the east fields. He worked for hours, cutting the tall grass and gathering the grain in his wagon. When the whole field was cut, he went over it again, checking for grain that had fallen on his first pass. Then, because he knew the harvest was important to his family, he passed through the field a third time, gathering the gleanings. By then it was late, and the sun was going down. The first son sighed and stretched as he eyed his loaded wagon with satisfaction. He climbed onto the wagon and headed for home.

The second son drove to the west fields. He also worked for hours, cutting the tall grass and gathering the grain. And he too went over the field a second and a third time to gather the gleanings. When the sun was going down, he looked, not at his loaded wagon, but out into the fields, fretting about the grains he might have missed. He was tired, and his body ached from his hard work, but the thought that there might still be some grain in the field gnawed at him. It was too dark now to walk through the fields, so he grabbed a lantern and began to crawl on his hands and knees, looking for fallen grains.

At home, the father waited eagerly for his sons to return. When the first son drove in, the father exclaimed happily over the loaded wagon and hugged him. As the first son went in to get ready for dinner, the father stayed outside to wait for his second son. He continued to wait, as it got darker and later, and still the second son didn't return. The father became worried. It was hours past sunset. Where was his son? Was something wrong? Was he hurt? The father was just about to send out a search party when he spotted the second son's wagon pulling in.

The second son was covered with scratches, and his shoulders drooped with exhaustion. "What happened?" the father asked, as he rushed to his son.

The son slowly and painfully climbed down from the wagon. "I wanted to do a good job," the son explained. "So I crawled through the field to make sure I didn't miss a single grain. And I did find this last handful."

The father gathered the son in his arms and hugged him tightly. "My son," he said. "You are more precious to me than a handful of grain." The son hugged his father back, and as he did, he opened his fist, and let the last handful of grain . . . go. They walked into the house together.

You can use this fable to open a discussion about perfectionism with your child. Ask questions to help your child figure out what the story means.

What was different about the two sons' approaches to gathering the grain?

Why did the second son choose to go over the field a fourth time?

Why did the first son stop after three times?

How did each son feel at the end of the day?

How did the father feel when each son returned?

Why did the second son let the last handful of grain go?

You may want to explain to your child the idea of diminishing returns: at some point, additional effort yields little improvement in results. Use examples your child can relate to, such as washing dishes versus scrubbing every plate with a toothbrush, or studying spelling words versus spending every waking moment reviewing spelling words. Ask for your child's thoughts about how to decide when efforts are good enough.

The fable can also be an opportunity to talk about unconditional love. Hard work can be satisfying and rewarding, and it often leads to achievement. But achievement is not what underlies loving relationships. Perfectionistic children need to hear explicitly that they are loved for who they are, not for what they accomplish.

SHOW THE WAY

The best way to teach children to move beyond unhealthy perfectionism is through our own example. Kids learn more from what we do than from what we say. Let your child see you actively choosing alternatives to perfectionism. The next sections offer some ideas about how you might do this.

Put It Away

With our 24/7 access to cell phones and the Internet, modern careers can be all-consuming. Even if you aren't employed outside the home, the to-do list is endless. You really could work every waking hour, but is that what you want for yourself? Is that what you want your child to think is "normal"?

Let your child see you shut down the computer, close your briefcase, or put down the chore list and say, "Well, there's always more I could do, but I've done enough for now." Then relax. Chat with your spouse. Call a friend. Take a walk. Watch a movie. Read a book with no redeeming literary value. Do something fun and completely unproductive with your child.

Try setting up some regular work-free time that you spend doing something you enjoy. Start small if you need to, but guard this time zealously. Tell your child what you are doing and why.

Make the Effort Fit the Task

Be clear about what matters to you, so that you can cut corners on the rest. Question your "shoulds" so you avoid overdoing. Sometimes, through habit or observation, we assume that things have to be done a certain way. Decide what tasks you are willing to do in a quick-and-dirty way so that you can have more time for whatever is more important to you. Share your thoughts with your child. "I have to do this. I could spend a lot of time on it, but it's not worth that much effort. I'm just going to do the minimum, to get it done." "In the past, I've always done it this way. Now, I'm thinking that I'd rather spend my time . . ." Whether you're talking about writing a report or making a Thanksgiving dinner, you're showing your child that a variety of approaches are possible and that it makes sense to match the effort to the importance of the task.

Acknowledge Mistakes and Share Plans

When you acknowledge your own mistakes, you give your child permission to make mistakes. Say you're sorry, sincerely but simply. Admit it when you didn't do something as well as you would have liked, but don't put yourself down. And don't stop there. Follow the admission by sharing your plan for doing better next time. This shows that mistakes are not an end point.

Try Something New

Young children believe that parents can do everything well and have always been able to do everything well. Let your child see you trying something new, especially something that will take time and effort to master. Talk about how you enjoy the activity even though you're not good at it yet. Explain how engrossing the process of learning can be, regardless of the level of performance.

Too many bright children suffer because their self-worth is tied to flawless performance. They believe they have to earn love and approval by being perfect. They respond with vicious self-criticism, angry blame, or painful withdrawal if they fall short of their lofty ideals. Although high standards are laudable, when they cross over to unhealthy perfectionism, they interfere with both productivity and happiness.

Parents can help by leading children toward a more compassionate view of themselves. This can involve tempering children's self-evaluations, expanding their understanding of how people learn, and guiding their efforts to cope with fears and frustrations. Parents need to be especially cautious about critiquing or being overly helpful with their children's work, because these well-intentioned efforts can inadvertently contribute to fear and shame about making mistakes. Above all, parents need to model healthy alternatives to perfectionism through their own choices and actions.

In the next chapter, we describe ways to help bright children make and keep friends.

CHAPTER 2

BUILDING CONNECTION

How Does Your Child Reach Out to Others?

 Does your child

- Struggle to find other kids who share his interests?
- Try to impress peers but end up pushing them away?
- Unintentionally annoy other kids?
- Avoid typical social situations because she feels uncomfortable around kids her age?
- Hang back rather than participate in group activities?
- Feel as though he has nothing in common with his classmates?
- Complain about how all the other kids are mean?

Do you remember playing with friends and being so absorbed in your game or adventure that you lost track of time? Do you remember the delight of discovering and creating a whole world apart from adults? Do you remember feeling disappointed when your parents told you it was time to go home?

The favorite childhood memories of many adults involve friends. In a sense, friendship is what childhood is all about. But some smart kids struggle painfully to make and keep friends. Their advanced intellectual skills don't necessarily translate into advanced social skills.

FRIENDSHIPS MATTER

Friendships are not only a source of fun; they also help children grow in meaningful ways. School-age children are discovering who they are outside the family, and an important part of their emerging identity is how their peers react to them. Having one or more friends creates a sense of belonging through shared interests: "My friends and I play soccer," "We like this kind of music," "We're always cracking jokes." Friendships can also provide a refuge of acceptance that can temper self-criticism. Knowing, for example, "Michelle is my friend, and she wants to play with me," can help a child understand that we don't have to be perfect to be liked. Having friends also means that kids have allies for facing whatever life throws at them. This makes it easier for them to tolerate stress, rebuffs, or aggravations.

Perhaps the most important benefit of friendship is that it encourages children to grow beyond self-interest. It helps them shift from thinking solely about what they want toward a more empathic perspective that considers others' concerns as well as their own. Caring about a friend, or just wanting to play with that friend, can temper selfish urges and open the way for negotiation, compromise, and even generosity.

Friendship Challenges

It's harder nowadays for kids to learn about getting along with peers. Families are busy. Parents often work long hours, and children's schedules tend to be packed with homework and after-school activities, so there's just less time available for casual get-togethers with friends. Children's activities also tend to be orchestrated by adults. Parents feel responsible for providing their children with as much enrichment as possible, rather than just telling them, "Go outside and play." Families also tend to be smaller and more dispersed, which means fewer day-to-day, unstructured interactions with other kids.

Over the past decade, a big change in children's social lives, especially for boys, involves the increase in technology-related play. Most boys enjoy video games and computer games. They talk about them and play them frequently. But for some kids, virtual friendships are their main way of relating. We often hear socially isolated boys tell us, "I get together with my friends all the time on Xbox LIVE!" They don't understand that this is a very diluted form of social contact. Handheld video game units, which can be brought everywhere, can also be an easy way for kids to tune out the social world.

There's no point bemoaning the passing of a "simpler" era. The times are what they are. However, all of this means that children may need additional support to learn how to make and keep friends.

Supporting the Development of Friendship Skills

In many ways, learning friendship skills is not unlike learning how to do math word problems. Both involve three processes: seeing, thinking, and doing.

To solve a math word problem, children need to be able to read the problem and *see*, for example, "Ah, this is a subtraction problem!" They then need to *think* of a strategy for setting up an appropriate equation so they can solve the problem. Finally, they need to implement that strategy and get lots and lots of practice, so that they can *do* these types of problems accurately and confidently.

As shown in the figure, these same three processes are involved in navigating social situations. First, children need to be able to *see* what's going on. This means picking up on social cues. Children need to be aware of the setting, because different situations call for different behaviors. They need to distinguish, for example, whether they're in a casual setting, like a playground, or a more formal setting, like a classroom, or whether they're with close friends or acquaintances. Noticing what other kids are doing provides an important clue about how to fit in. Children also need to be able to recognize what they are doing that might contribute to problems. They need to be able to monitor other people's reactions, moment by moment, so they can change course if things aren't going well. Children who have trouble "seeing" in social situations tend to be oblivious to social cues. They often unwittingly offend others or persist in doing things that others find strange or irritating.

Three processes involved in learning friendship skills:

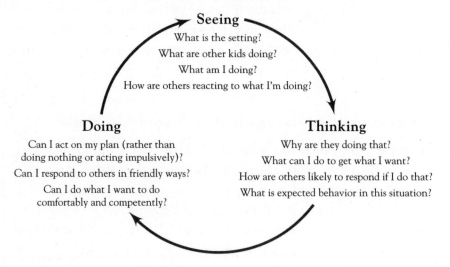

Seeing

What is the setting?
What are other kids doing?
What am I doing?
How are others reacting to what I'm doing?

Doing

Can I act on my plan (rather than
doing nothing or acting impulsively)?
Can I respond to others in friendly ways?
Can I do what I want to do
comfortably and competently?

Thinking

Why are they doing that?
What can I do to get what I want?
How are others likely to respond if I do that?
What is expected behavior in this situation?

Kids also need to be able to *think* about social situations. This involves interpreting other children's behavior, to understand what it means or why they're doing it. For example, children need to be able to discern whether their peers are feeling bored, angry, or friendly, and whether their actions are deliberate or accidental. Social thinking also involves coming up with effective strategies for influencing peers in desired ways. To do this, children need to understand what is expected behavior in a particular situation, and they also need to be able to predict others' likely responses to their actions. Research shows that children who struggle socially often misinterpret others' intentions, and they are less able to come up with a variety of possible solutions to social dilemmas.

Finally, kids need lots and lots of practice having positive interactions with their peers, so that they can feel genuinely comfortable and confident in social situations. Some children know what they ought to do but have trouble actually doing it. They may feel anxious and freeze up, so they're unable to respond to friendly overtures. They may tend to act impulsively, blurting out inappropriate comments. They may be socially clumsy and end up acting in ways that unintentionally offend or annoy others.

Continually experiencing social failure doesn't help children learn. They need guidance and support so they can "get it right" socially by behaving in ways that help them connect with their peers.

Responding to Friendship Problems

When children are feeling rejected, they need some extra love and understanding from their parents. Just listening and empathizing can help a lot. You could say, "Sounds like you had a rough day," "That must have really hurt your feelings," "How embarrassing!" or "How frustrating!"

Although empathizing with your child's feelings is important, be careful not to overreact. This can be a hard thing to do. Hearing that your child is unhappy may make you feel helpless or ferociously protective. Your child's friendship problems may even remind you of painful incidents from your own childhood. ("This is exactly like what Erin Donohue did to me in second grade!") However, it's not helpful to burden your child with your strong feelings about the problem.

Resist the urge to rush in with advice or suggestions, because your child may be able to solve the problem without your intervention. Most friendship problems just blow over. Kids often forgive, forget, and move on faster than their parents. Today your son may insist he hates Stuart's guts; next week he might claim Stuart is his best friend. You may stay up late worrying about the crisis that had your daughter in tears, but the next day she might dismiss the whole situation, saying "It's fine." So while you want to acknowledge your child's feelings, try not to dwell on misery. Psychologist Michael Thompson and his colleagues, authors of *Best Friends, Worst Enemies*, caution against "interviewing for pain." Asking your child, "Was anyone mean to you today?" encourages your child to focus on slights and feel like a victim.

If friendship problems persist, it's critical to talk to your child's teacher to get the facts. The teacher sees your child interacting with peers every day and may have important information about how typical, common, enduring, or pervasive the problem is, and how your child might (perhaps unwittingly) be contributing to the problem. The teacher can also be an important ally in guiding your child toward better choices or intervening with other children.

Because social interactions are complicated, friendship problems can take many forms. Some kids are quirky or different in ways that push other kids away; some hold back too much; some come on too strong. In this chapter, we describe several of the most common friendship struggles we've seen with bright children and emphasize ways to help these children learn to reach out to their peers.

ANDREW: SEEKING AN AUDIENCE RATHER THAN A FRIEND

"What kind of computer do you have?" Andrew asked.

"It's a Mac," Robert said.

"Does it have an Intel Core 2 Duo processor?"

"Um, I don't know." Robert shrugged. "I mostly just use it to play games."

"I have a Dell XPS-700 with an NVIDIA quad graphics card and a PhysX Accelerator."

"Hmmm," Robert mumbled. "Well, do you have any games?"

"I develop my own computer games using Autodesk 3ds Max 9. I use basic polygon modeling to design articulated 3-D characters. Watch. I'll show you," Andrew said, booting up the computer.

"Well, how about if we go outside and shoot some hoops?" Robert suggested, glancing out the window.

"In a minute. First, I want to show you my production workflow," Andrew insisted.

❧

This play date is not going well. Andrew's in-depth knowledge of programming might be shared by certain high school students, but it leaves Robert, his elementary school classmate, feeling bored and bewildered. Andrew's interest in computers is beyond his years, but his ability to relate to peers is underdeveloped.

Andrew wants to connect with Robert by showing him what he can do with his computer, but he comes across as arrogant, rather than just enthusiastic. He starts by asking about Robert's computer, but this question is just a perfunctory prelude to Andrew's monologue, rather than an expression of genuine interest. Andrew is talking *at* Robert, not to him, and Robert is probably thinking he can't wait to get away.

Trying to Impress Rather Than Connect

Andrew appears conceited, but underneath his bragging, he's probably feeling insecure and a little desperate. We suspect he was very excited about the play date and eager for Robert to like him. After the play date, he'll feel hurt and baffled when Robert rejects him.

What drives Andrew's bragging isn't arrogance but igno-rance. He's working very hard to make Robert like him, but he's going about it in the wrong way, because he's trying to impress rather than connect.

Bright children tend to get a lot of attention from adults for performing, so they think that's what they're supposed to do to build relationships. Unfortunately, although parents and grand-parents may be delighted to watch children demonstrate their precocious skills and advanced knowledge, other kids are not interested in playing the role of an audience.

Andrew seeks Robert's admiration. He imagines that Robert will be attracted by his superior skills in the same way sunflowers turn to bask in the light of the sun. Andrew doesn't realize that admiration involves distance rather than closeness. It's not a path that leads to a mutual friendship.

Ignoring Social Feedback

Andrew's biggest social mistake isn't his bragging; it's his failure to respond to social feedback. He ignores Robert's lack of enthu-siasm for esoteric computer details and plows on relentlessly. Robert's curt comments, his shrug, glance away, and explicit suggestions of alternative activities all shout, "I'm not enjoying this!" But Andrew either doesn't notice these cues, or he dis-counts them. Maybe, because he loves programming so much, he can't imagine that anyone would not be enthusiastic about it. Maybe he hopes that if he persists, Robert will somehow become eager to watch him demonstrate his computer expertise. Or maybe he just doesn't know any other way to try to engage a peer.

The hardest part about friendship skills is that they require constant adjustments guided by ongoing reading of social cues. Almost everyone has had the experience of telling a joke that doesn't get a laugh or making a comment or suggestion that doesn't elicit interest. This is no big deal if we stop there and adjust our behavior accordingly. But if we continue despite negative feed-back, we're likely to irritate others or even drive them away. Noticing others' responses helps us recognize whether our comments or actions are on target, which helps us decide whether to continue or change directions. Ignoring these cues is like driving with our eyes closed—a crash is extremely likely.

STRATEGIES TO HELP YOUR CHILD REACH OUT TO PEERS

Children like Andrew need to learn to be better attuned to their peers' reactions, so they can build relationships. They also need to understand that sharing the limelight with others doesn't diminish them, but instead opens the door to mutual friendships.

Plan Activity-Based Play Dates

Most children's friendships are based on doing things together. You may want to help your child plan an activity-based play date. Go bowling, ice skating, miniature golfing, to a movie, to a local farm, or to a dog park. These kinds of activities are fun, and they minimize awkwardness because the context dictates what children should do. An activity-based play date can start or build a friendship. Keep the play date short: two hours is a good length for elementary students. It's better to have the kids leave wanting more than to let things drag on to the point of irritability.

Go over Host Etiquette

Explain to your child that the host is responsible for making sure the guest has a good time. Some kids are territorial. They may believe, "My house, my rules," and act bossy. You may need to talk with your child about hospitality and brainstorm together some ways to take care of guests. Here are some possibilities:

- Offer the guest a nice snack and drink when the guest arrives.
- Offer the guest a choice of two or three activities. (Just asking, "What do you want to do?" usually elicits "I dunno.")
- Allow the guest to go first.
- Watch the guest's facial expression and body language. If the guest seems bored or unhappy, suggest an alternative activity. ("Do you want to get a snack?" or "Do you want to do something else?")
- Say, "Good game!" cheerfully, whether you win or lose.
- Before the guest comes over, put away anything you're not willing to share so that you don't have to tell the guest, "Don't touch that!"
- Say "Thanks for coming!" when the guest leaves.

Offer Sincere Compliments

Some kids believe that making friends involves being impressive in order to draw others to them. This is backwards. Making friends involves reaching out to others. An easy way to do this is by offering sincere compliments. Help your child come up with situations that provide an opportunity to offer a compliment. Keep it simple and genuine. "Great shot!" "I like your sweater." "Your project turned out really good." Genuine compliments make people feel good about themselves and have warm feelings toward the compliment giver. You may need to remind your child to offer only one compliment at a time. Too many in close succession will seem insincere.

Seek Common Ground

Friendships grow out of shared activities and interests. When Andrew emphasizes how he's different (or better) than Robert, this creates a sense of distance rather than connection.

Have your child draw two overlapping circles. One circle represents your child. The other represents a potential friend. In the overlapping area, have your child list things he or she has in common with the potential friend. Emphasizing these similarities, either in conversation or by doing the activities together, can help build a friendship. If your child doesn't know enough about the potential friend to find similarities, then listening, observing, or asking friendly questions could be ways to find out more about the other child's interests and to discover common ground.

What we have in common:

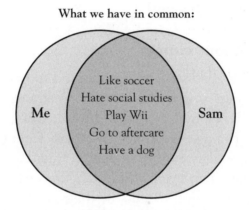

Me | Sam

Like soccer
Hate social studies
Play Wii
Go to aftercare
Have a dog

Avoid Monologues

Many smart kids are prone to monologues. Buoyed by their own interest, they go on and on in painful detail. They may feel hurt and puzzled when other kids walk away or yell "Shut up!" at them.

If your child has this tendency, you may need to explain that conversation involves taking turns. Going on too long is like hogging the ball in a game of catch—it wrecks the game.

Persisting despite signs of irritation can infuriate others. Encourage your child to watch the listener's reactions while speaking and to say no more than three or four sentences before asking a question that gives the other person a chance to speak. If the other person is looking away or appears bored, your child should stop speaking—even if it's in the middle of a story or list.

Your child could use an ending statement, such as "Well, you get the idea" or "Well, that's enough about that" to wrap things up, then ask a question and listen carefully to the other person's response.

You may want to help your child practice speaking briefly. Can your child tell you about a recent event or a book or movie in three or four sentences? You may also want to warn your child that lists are fine in written work, but they don't work well in conversation unless they are extremely brief (that is, no more than three words or phrases).

Be Careful About Humor

Children with a good sense of humor tend to be well liked, but trying to be funny is generally *not* a good strategy for kids who struggle socially. Humor can be a difficult thing to pull off. It requires good timing, sensitivity to others' feelings, and subtle understanding to defy expectations in a way that is appealingly surprising rather than aggravating. Children who have trouble reading social cues tend to miss in their attempts to be funny, and they end up annoying or offending people. They may say something inappropriately crude or hurtful. They may persist in doing something that's not funny, hoping it will become funny, which it never does. When other kids get mad, they protest, self-righteously, "I was just kidding! Can't you take a joke?" If this sounds like your child, encourage him or her to save humor for family and focus on kindness—where it's hard to go wrong—around other kids.

Practice Perspective Taking

Reading a book or watching a movie or TV show with your child can provide opportunities to practice perspective taking. You can ask your child questions about the characters' reactions and motivations, such as, "Why do you think he did that?" "How is she feeling?" "How can you tell?" "How do you think they would react if she did that?" A book or movie can provide a non-threatening context to talk about feelings, but don't ask so many questions that it ruins the fun of the story.

You may also be able to ask perspective-taking questions about events your child describes from school. Tread lightly: show only mild curiosity, ask just one or two questions, and only do this if your child is feeling calm and cooperative. You don't want your child to feel that telling you any little thing triggers an interrogation.

Don't Try to Buy Friendship

Sometimes children try to buy friendship by giving away possessions or money to their peers. The other children will usually accept the gifts, but they may also resent these attempts to manipulate them, and they often come to disrespect the overly generous giver.

Sometimes parents try to buy friendship by purchasing the most impressive toy or collection in town for their child. This strategy also tends to be ineffective. Although it may garner some initial interest, it is also likely to lead to jealousy or come across as desperate.

CLAY:
AVOIDING JOINING THE GROUP

"See, Clay, there are lots of kids from your class here," Clay's mom said, looking around and waving to friends as they walked across the field toward the school picnic.

"I hate picnics! I can't believe you made me come."

"Don't be such a stick-in-the-mud! Oh, look, there's Aidan and some of the other boys in your grade playing Frisbee. Why don't you join them?"

"I don't play Frisbee."

"Well, isn't that Pranav and William, over by the ring toss? Go say 'Hi' to them."

"No."

"Clay, you complain about not having friends, but you're not even trying!"

"I told you I didn't want to come to the picnic. Can we leave now?"

❧

Attending a large social event is pure torture for children like Clay. He actively resists his mother's cheerful encouragement to engage with his peers. Even when he sees kids he knows, he feels acutely uncomfortable and eager to escape.

Is Clay's reluctance to attend a large event a problem? Maybe or maybe not. When kids routinely pull back in social situations, it could mean that (1) they enjoy having a fair bit of time alone and prefer smaller, quieter, interactions; (2) they feel anxious and unable to reach out to peers, although they'd like to; or (3) they've been rejected by peers, so they know that if they try to reach out, they'll be rebuffed again. The first scenario is not necessarily a problem. The second and third are. It can take some detective work on parents' part to figure out which of these scenarios apply to their child.

Introversion Versus Extroversion

A classic distinction in psychology is between introverts and extroverts. Extroverts draw their energy from being around other people. They come home from a party feeling full of life. Parents of extroverts say that these children wake up in the morning making plans about who they can get together with and when. Introverts, in contrast, refuel through solitary activities. After a party, they crave silence. This doesn't mean they dislike people—introverts can be warm and caring friends. It does mean that they tend to feel exhausted and overstimulated by crowds, so they prefer get-togethers with just one or two other people, and they need a balance between together time and alone time.

American culture tends to favor extroversion, but many other cultures prefer a quieter style of interacting. Neither introversion nor extroversion is inherently better. Although there may be advantages to being outgoing, being able to feel content alone is also a crucial life skill. Introversion is not a friendship problem; it's a personality style. Introverts don't feel anxious around other people; they just prefer smaller doses of social contact.

Here are some important questions for helping determine whether or not your child's social reticence is a problem:

- Can your child interact happily with other kids under some circumstances, when he or she wants to do so?
- Does your child have at least one relationship in which he or she likes and is liked by another child?
- Does your child have someone to sit and chat with at lunch?

If the answer to all of these questions is yes, you probably don't have to worry. Some children genuinely prefer having one or two close friends, rather than a passel of acquaintances, and that's fine. Some children tend to be reserved in new situations with unfamiliar people, but open up once they feel comfortable. This is also not unusual or worrisome.

Inhibited Temperament and Social Withdrawal

Although a quieter, more reserved social style is not necessarily problematic, for some children, social withdrawal is a default rather than a choice. They feel painfully shy and awkward around other kids. These children need help.

Research tells us that one out of every five babies is born with an "inhibited" temperament. Inhibited babies are easily overwhelmed, and they tend to get very upset when they encounter new people or new toys. The theory is that these children have more sensitive nervous systems that make them emotionally reactive and hard to soothe. Many of these babies become shy toddlers who refuse to talk or even look at unfamiliar people, and they're prone to anxiety as they get older.

Often, there's a vicious cycle that keeps these children trapped as outsiders: kids who feel anxious and awkward in social situations tend to avoid them, which gives them less opportunity to figure out how to get along and practice interacting with other kids. Because they haven't learned essential friendship skills, they're more likely to be rejected or ignored by their peers. When this happens enough times, they come to expect social failure and to be hyperalert for signs of rejection. This makes them feel even more anxious and awkward, which makes them want to avoid social situations even more . . .

Another layer of complication is that parents often have strong feelings about their child's social withdrawal. When parents are naturally outgoing, like Clay's mother, they may feel frustrated, disappointed, baffled, or embarrassed by their child's tendency to pull back around other people. When parents themselves are uncomfortable in social situations, they're often anxious to ensure that their child doesn't suffer the way they have. They may be overly cautious, working too hard to protect their child from fearful situations. Or they may be overly demanding, pressuring their child to become more social. All of these parental reactions can compound children's anxiety and make them more determined to avoid contact with peers.

The most interesting finding from temperament research is that about a third of inhibited babies and toddlers somehow do *not* continue to be inhibited in later childhood. The parenting strategies linked to this improvement involve a delicate balance between accepting children's feelings and compassionately nudging them forward. Instead of focusing on what you did or what most kids do or where you think your child ought to be socially, start wherever your child is now and concentrate on moving forward, bit by bit. Encourage steps that are slightly beyond your child's current social comfort level but still manageable. Small successes can add up over time to greater social competence and confidence.

STRATEGIES TO HELP YOUR CHILD JOIN IN

Just shoving inhibited children into social situations doesn't help; neither does allowing them to avoid others. Children like Clay need extra encouragement to interact, as well as extra guidance so they can manage their anxiety and learn and practice specific strategies that will help them be successful in connecting with their peers. Here are some ideas about how you can help.

Observe, Then Blend

Observational research involving children on playgrounds shows that there is a very specific sequence involved in joining a group: observe, then blend. Kids need to watch to figure out what's going on, and then slide into the action without interrupting.

One way to explain the observe-then-blend sequence to children is by using the analogy of merging onto a highway. There are two main mistakes children can make when trying to join a group:

1. They can barge in without regard to what anyone else is doing, which disrupts the game and irritates the other children. This is like driving right onto a highway without checking the traffic. Not a good idea.
2. They can hang back and never put themselves forward enough to get in the flow of things. This is like sitting on the entrance ramp without ever trying to merge, which means they never get where they want to be.

What games has your child noticed the other kids playing at recess? Help your child plan some specific ways to blend in with these activities. For example, your child might start running around to join a tag game after noticing that a new person is It, stand in line to play four-square, stand nearby and then copy kids having a long-jump contest, or bring sticks to contribute to a building project.

It's usually not a good idea to ask, "Can I play?" because this interrupts the flow of the game, as everyone stops and considers whether they want your child to join. This question also makes it too tempting for mischievous kids to answer, "No, you can't play. Hah, hah, hah!"

Look for Individuals or Groups of Four or More

Playground research shows that children are most likely to be successful when they attempt to join another individual child or a group of four or more kids. Groups of two or three tend to be more close-knit, and if your child doesn't know them well, they may be less open to a new member. Knowing this can help your child figure out whom to approach.

If the person your child approaches says your child can't play, it's usually best to just walk away and try someone else. Tell your child it's kind of like baseball. Everyone swings and misses sometimes, but there's always a chance to try again with a new pitch. One study of preschool children showed that even the most well-liked kids were unsuccessful in their attempts to join a group one-fourth of the time.

Use Friendly Body Language

Most emotional communication is nonverbal. Ask your child, "How can you show that you are feeling friendly without saying a word?" A smiling face, a relaxed and open body posture, interested eye contact, and an upbeat tone of voice all signal openness to friendship.

Body language can also communicate negative messages. If your child is hunched in a corner, reading a book and refusing to look at or interact with any other kids, this sends a very loud message saying, "I want nothing to do with you!" An adult might make the effort to draw your child out. Other kids won't. They'll just play with someone else.

What if your child protests, "But I like reading, and I hate all the other recess activities!"? Tell your child this is a manners issue. Your child is part of the school community, and it's not polite to snub other community members by refusing to interact with them. Moreover, this behavior is self-defeating. If your child already feels like an outsider, reading while the other kids are playing or talking widens the gulf and makes the other kids think your child doesn't like them.

Your child can read at home or during reading time at school, but not during lunch or recess. Help your child figure out some alternatives. Playing on swings or slides are easy activities. At a minimum, your child can walk around the playground with a pleasant, interested facial expression and open body language. Your child can try to notice how many different activities the other kids are doing and decide which might be fun (or at least not horrible) to join.

Practice Simple Conversation Formulas

Most conversation *doesn't* involve witty repartee. In fact, a lot of casual conversation is quite formulaic. The comments simply acknowledge and express interest in others. However, we've known many children who freeze up when someone says something to them because they don't know how to respond. Practicing simple conversations can help your child feel more comfortable interacting with others.

The most important social script your child needs to know involves greeting people. Many shy children look away or refuse to respond when someone greets them because they feel self-conscious. Use role playing to help your child practice greeting others by saying "Hi" and including the other child's name to make the greeting personal. Encourage your child to smile and look at the other person while saying the greeting. If your child has trouble looking people in the eye, suggest looking at the bridge of their nose, which may be less scary but still seems friendly. In some cultures, children are taught not to make direct eye contact with elders or with members of the opposite sex, but this is generally less of an issue between same-sex children.

If you have no difficulties greeting others or making conversation, you may feel frustrated with your child's struggles in these areas. Be careful not to overwhelm your child by pushing too hard. Also, don't correct your child in public. Your goal is to help your child feel more comfortable in social situations rather than pressured or embarrassed.

Once your child has mastered greetings, here are some other social scripts you can practice. These are very basic but critical for children who tend to feel awkward when people talk to them. They do not constitute interesting conversation, but these simple scripts can help these children handle a lot of routine interactions and get past their initial discomfort. As with the greetings, encourage your child to smile and make eye contact while asking or responding, if this fits your cultural practices. Your child may also be relieved to know that the best conversationalists are good at getting *other people* talking. If your child doesn't know what to say, asking an open-ended "how" or "what" question is a way to pass the conversational ball.

"What's new?" "Not much. How about you?"

"How's it going?" "Pretty good. How about you?"

"How's school?" *(question from an adult)* "Good. We're studying [topic] in [subject]."

"Bye!" "Bye! See you later!"

"How was your game?" "Great! We won." *or* "Not so good. We lost."

"What are you doing this weekend?" "Not much. How about you?"

"What did you do last weekend?" "I had a game." *or* "We visited my grandparents."

"What did you think of the math test?" "It was okay." *or* "It was pretty hard."

Find After-School Activities That Fit Your Child's Style

After-school activities are a great way to make friends because they create shared interests and experiences. Also, because they tend to be directed by adults, they may feel safer to children who flounder in unstructured settings. There are many opportunities available for kids today, so you can definitely find something that fits your child's style. A sports team can provide an instant community. If your child is not athletic, there are many other possibilities, including taking an art class, joining a choir, volunteering at an animal shelter, or participating in a reading program for younger children. You may need to present a few options and insist that your child select one. Start small, with just one activity, for a limited time period. Your goal is to help your child build up confidence rather than feel overwhelmed.

Play with Voice Recordings

Some very quiet children seem almost afraid of their own voice. Playing with audio recordings of their voice can help them feel more comfortable speaking up. You can use a digital recorder or an old-fashioned tape recorder. Let your child create a play or talk with different accents or make sound effects. Have your child interview family members. Take turns adding comments to create a silly story. Your child will have fun and also get used to the sound of his or her own voice.

AMALIA: FEELING REJECTED BY PEERS

"What's *that* supposed to be?" Amalia asked snidely. Patricia ignored her.

"It looks kind of like a horse, but you drew the neck too short," Amalia persisted. Patricia covered her paper and moved closer to Pria.

"Go away, Amalia," Pria said. "Nobody cares what you think."

"I can stay if I want to. You don't own the table," Amalia replied. "I want to draw, too."

Amalia reached to grab some markers. Pria and Patricia leaned over the table, covering their papers and the markers.

"We were here first!" Patricia insisted. "Go away! You always ruin everything!"

"Yeah, Amalia!" Pria added. "Go away!"

"I'm telling!" Amalia said. "You guys are being mean!"

Bright children are sometimes very critical of others. It's as if they feel duty bound to point out imperfections in the world. When something is Not Right, they feel compelled to announce it publicly. They seem to expect approval for their discernment, but what they usually evoke is irritation, and they make others dislike them. Amalia's criticism comes across as an unprovoked attack rather than a bid for connection. Patricia doesn't even try to defend her less-than-perfect drawing. She just moves to shut Amalia out.

Amalia feels like the victim in this interaction. She's hurt by the other girls' rejection and completely oblivious to her own role in eliciting that rejection. Michael Thompson and his colleagues have a wonderfully apt phrase to describe this bias that children often have in understanding conflict: "It all started when she hit me back."

How Kids Are Mean

As much as we try to prevent it, kids are often mean to each other. Psychologist Steven Asher and his colleagues conducted an elaborate study in which they used tiny microphones and remote cameras to study the social interactions of third- through sixth-graders while they were at lunch, recess, and gym. They recorded the children from October to June during one school year, and came up with a cringe-worthy list of thirty-two kinds of rejecting behavior. Some forms of rejection were physical, such as hitting, kicking, or throwing something at the rejected child or wrecking possessions; others were verbal, such as mimicking the rejected child, saying that the child was bad or naughty, or insulting the child's friends or family. Rejection was also sometimes expressed with no words or direct actions, just ignoring. Some rejections were quick, such as whacking a child on the back and saying something mean, then continuing to walk past; others involved protracted arguments ("Nuh-uh!" "Uh-huh!"). Some were one-on-one ("I don't like you!"); others were group oriented ("You can't be in our club!").

Although most forms of rejection were blatant (for example, loudly refusing to let a child sit at a lunch table), some were ambiguous. For instance, refusing an offer to share food could stem from concern about getting "cooties" or merely not wanting that food. Calling someone a name could be an insult or just friendly teasing.

Research says that children who are disliked by their peers are more likely to be the targets of rejection, but Asher's study found that even kids who consider themselves best friends sometimes reject each other cruelly. Impulsivity, immature problem-solving skills, difficulty managing feelings, limited perspective-taking ability, following the crowd, or just experimenting (What would happen if . . . ?) are all factors that could lead kids to do mean things.

Asher's research also suggests that the way children respond to rejection can make things better or worse. Some children were able to diffuse rejection by ignoring it or using humor or playfulness to get past it. In contrast, the kids who became very upset, who tried to extract revenge, or who desperately tried to get approval from the rejecting children made things worse. Asher mentions one example of a child who actually encouraged the other kids to hit her butt with a ball, in a sad and ineffective attempt to win them over. Repeated whining and pleading are also unlikely to lead to acceptance and may even encourage further rejection, by making the rejected child seem like an easy target.

Seeing All Sides

For parents whose child is being rejected, it's easy to focus on (and fume about!) how mean the other kids are, but that's usually not the whole story. We have seen some cases where children were victimized through no fault of their own (for example, they are new to the school, they are smaller or younger than their peers, or they are from a different culture than the majority of their classmates), but more commonly, children do play some role in eliciting or perpetuating rejection. *In no way does this justify or excuse meanness.* No child deserves to be treated cruelly, no matter what he or she does. However, at a practical level, it makes sense to intervene, when possible, to help kids become less of a target for rejection. If we can figure out how a child is contributing to a problem, addressing that could be an important step toward diminishing the problem.

Parents often wonder whether a child who is experiencing a lot of rejection would be happier at another school. A fascinating study by John Coie and Janis Kupersmidt suggests that a move might not help. Using peer ratings, these researchers identified fourth-grade boys who were generally disliked, and placed them in a new playgroup with three other boys who were either classmates or strangers to each other and the first boy. The playgroups met once a week for six weeks. Within three sessions, the boys who were disliked by their school peers became similarly disliked by the kids in their new playgroup—even when the other kids started out as strangers who didn't know the boys' school reputations. Both the familiar and the unfamiliar playmates saw them as troublemakers who caused fights. Somehow, these boys recreated their bad reputations in the new groups.

So what might rejected children do to contribute to their problems? Research has yielded a pretty clear picture of how rejected boys behave. About half of rejected boys are aggressive. They hit, kick, or shove more than other boys and tend to be more disruptive and argumentative. Videotape recordings from the playgroup study showed that the disliked boys were more likely than the other boys to interact in hostile and aggressive ways.

However, not all rejected boys are aggressive. Another 13 percent are shy, withdrawn, and uncooperative. Still others are neither aggressive nor shy, but their peers describe them as socially awkward. These boys are oblivious to general social expectations. They may have poor hygiene, unusual habits, or immature behavior that other kids find off-putting.

Girls are less likely than boys to be physically aggressive. Observations of disliked girls show that compared to other girls, they tend to be more bossy, to express more negative emotions, to talk more about breaking rules, and to have poorer conflict resolution skills. There's also some indication that rejected girls are more likely than other girls to be aggressive in indirect ways, such as by spreading rumors or trying to convince others not to like someone. Disturbingly, indirect aggression can start as early as preschool.

Bullying Prevention and Beyond

Recently, schools, scientists, and the media have been paying a lot of attention to bullying. Bullying involves deliberately hurtful actions that are persistent or severe, cause significant distress or harm, and involve a power difference between the bully and the target. Bullying isn't just meanness; it's intimidation, harassment, and abuse, and it can have serious long-term consequences.

Many schools have bullying prevention programs. This is heartening to see, because research says that the best way to combat bullying is through comprehensive, systemwide programs that foster awareness and an intolerance for cruelty. Bullying usually occurs when no adults are around, so it's important to motivate and inspire child bystanders, who are not directly involved in the bullying, to speak up rather than laugh or turn a blind eye. It often helps to offer children a discreet or anonymous way to express concern to adults about troubling situations that are too hard for them to handle directly. Perhaps because of bullying prevention initiatives, a recent national survey showed a marked decline in reports of physical bullying from 2003 to 2008.

But we can't stop there. Our schools, communities, and families need to do more than cut down on cruelty. We also need to create caring environments where all children can thrive. Innovative, research-supported programs, such as Responsive Classroom, focus on creating school communities that emphasize social and emotional growth as well as academic learning. They are woven into the fabric of everything that children do in school, rather than simply tacked on to a busy schedule. Children involved in Responsive Classroom express greater enjoyment of school, their teachers, and their peers, and they also show greater improvements on reading and math scores.

STRATEGIES TO HELP YOUR CHILD AVOID AND DEAL WITH REJECTION

Supporting the ongoing, long-term efforts of your child's school to create a caring community for all children is important, but you may need to take direct action to improve the social situation for your particular child *now*. All kids get rejected sometimes, but if your child is regularly teased or excluded by

peers, talk with your child's teacher, school counselor, and prin-
cipal, and work with them to find ways to help your child be safe
and fit in. If the rejection is very distressing for your child; if your
child is showing signs of stress, such as headaches, stomachaches,
and reluctance to go to school; or if worries about peer problems
are interfering with your child's ability to do schoolwork, we
strongly urge you to seek help from a psychologist or other counselor. Here are some additional ideas that you can use to help
your child avoid and deal with rejection.

Develop Alternative Friendships

Shifting friendships are the rule, not the exception, with children, so one of the best things parents can do is to provide
children with the opportunity to make a variety of friends in a
variety of settings. Having even one friend can mitigate the pain
of rejection. Having several friends can be especially helpful for
weathering the ups and downs of peer relationships. That way,
if certain friends are being unkind on a particular day, your child
has other social options at school, or can at least feel consoled
by the thought that his or her "real friends" are elsewhere. Play
dates and after-school activities can help expand friendship
options.

Often we've heard children complain about a particular
friend who is nice one day and mean the next. This can be very
confusing. Explain to your child that some friends are steady and
some run "hot and cold." These latter friends may have exciting
ideas that make them fun playmates, but they're unpredictable.
It's usually easier to choose consistently kind friends, but it's fine
to enjoy hot-and-cold friends when they're being nice, and to
look elsewhere when they're not. If they're being unkind, your
child should just say, "This isn't fun for me." If the meanness
continues, your child should calmly walk away and find someone
else to play with.

Stay Near an Ally

Children who are picked on have a hard dilemma: often the situation is more than they can handle on their own, but if they tell an adult, they violate the unwritten child code against being a tattletale, which could lead to further rejection. If your child does need to tell an adult, warn your child to do it discreetly. There's no need to announce, "I'm telling!"

However, a good prevention strategy is simply to stay near an adult or friends during unstructured times, such as recess or before and after school. This makes your child less of an easy target and ensures that there are witnesses or people available to intervene if anything untoward happens.

Practice Bored Responses to Teasing

All kids get teased. Those who respond emotionally—in effect rewarding the teaser with a big reaction—tend to get teased repeatedly. You may need to help your sensitive child come up with and practice uninteresting responses to teasing. These responses could be nonverbal, such as looking bored, glancing heavenward in disgust (tell your child only to do this with other kids, never adults!), or calmly walking away. They could also involve a brief, bored statement, such as "So what?" "Whatever," or "Tell me when you get to the funny part." Responses to teasing don't have to be clever. Your child just needs to remain (or at least pretend to be) unaffected by the teasing.

Try role playing using the nonsense insults here to help your child practice responding to teasing. The nonsense words ensure that the practice is not upsetting for your child, and they also underscore that teasing is meaningless.

"You're such a nurgle! You have grimzy murfs!"

"You're kiffy and flug! You're not even labbish!"

"Hah, hah, you brizbill!"

"You gilly pop!"

"You even rupnick your tuggy twaps!"

Harmonize with the Group's Emotional Tone

Conversations are like melodies, with each person adding harmonious notes to carry the tune forward. New comments need to blend with the emotional tone of the ongoing conversation. Otherwise they're like unpleasant discordant notes.

For example, if all the other kids are complaining about how hard a test is, your child needs to pipe in with a further complaint ("Yeah, the essay was a pain!" or "There were a million multiple-choice questions!"). Piping in with "I thought the test was easy" disrupts the conversation and comes across as annoying. Similarly, if the other kids are talking enthusiastically about a sports team, your child needs to express similar enthusiasm or at least interest. Saying "Sports are stupid" won't go over well.

You may want to practice "conversational harmony" with your child. Try making two emotionally similar comments about a topic, and see if your child can add a third comment that has the same the emotional tone and carries the tune of the conversation forward. Possible topics to use for practice include opinions about a class, a collectible, a TV show, a video game, or a musical group.

Identify Behaviors That Attract or Repel Friends

Being able to predict others' responses is an important part of social skills. Get two magnets and let your child experiment with how the opposite ends attract and the same ends repel. Explain that how we act around others can attract or repel friends. In general, *kids want to be around kids who are happy and having fun*.

Go over the behaviors in the boxed list and see if your child can predict their likely impact. Have your child explain why other kids would respond that way. How would the actions make the other person feel? What impression would the actions create about the person who does them? For the repelling behaviors, what would be a better choice? Encourage your child to choose an attracting behavior or a positive alternative to a repelling behavior to try during the next school day.

Predict Whether These Actions Are Likely to ATTRACT or REPEL Friends

Yelling "Nobody likes me. Everyone is mean to me." (R)

Saying "No fair! You cheated!" when you lose a game. (R)

Asking someone, "How was your weekend?" (A)

Telling someone, "Nice catch." (A)

Telling the teacher that someone isn't following directions. (R)

Offering to let someone use your colored pencils. (A)

Helping someone clean up a mess, even though you didn't make the mess. (A)

Refusing to answer and looking away when someone is talking to you. (R)

Calling someone a name, then saying, "Just kidding!" (R)

Greeting someone by name (for example, "Hi, John!). (A)

Bumping into people because they are in your way. (R)

Snatching the ball away from some kids who are playing a game, to get them to chase you. (R)

Quitting a game because you are losing. (R)

Telling someone, "You're doing it wrong!" (R)

Saying "It's your fault. You made me do it!" (R)

Saying "Nothing good ever happens to me." (R)

Saying "This is boring!" (R)

Pay Attention to Hygiene

Many children go through a "hygiene is optional" stage. We've known a lot of kids who've gone to elaborate lengths to create the impression of cleanliness without cleaning themselves. For example, they might wet their hair in the shower but not use shampoo, or they might dab toothpaste on their tongue but not brush their teeth.

Good hygiene is a foundational social skill—a daily shower won't *directly* lead to your child making friends, but skipping that shower (especially as your child gets older and smellier) could prevent other children from getting close enough to realize what a great kid your child is.

You may want to use "Our Hygiene Rap" as a playful way to inspire your child to use appropriate cleanliness habits. You could post it in a strategic place in your home or use it to start or continue a conversation with your child about the importance of self-care. You may also want to share this rhyme with your child's teacher so that the cleanliness message can be reinforced at school. We've noticed that fifth-grade teachers are particularly enthusiastic about "Our Hygiene Rap."

> *Our Hygiene Rap*
>
> Shower and deodorant,
>   Clean shirt, too—
> They're a social obligation,
>   And a daily to-do!
>
> Charming personality
>   Won't work well,
> If we don't remember hygiene,
>   And we just plain smell!
>
> Brush with toothpaste twice a day,
>   Wash with soap—
> That's just necessary hygiene,
>   So we're ready to cope!

Bodies clean and odor-free,
   Looking neat—
We create a good impression
   With whomever we meet!

In a few years, your child will spend excessive amounts of time in the bathroom cleaning and grooming. For now, you may need to institute a policy of "trust but verify." If your child has camel breath, insist on a return to the bathroom to try again, even if your child protests, "But I already brushed my teeth!"

Remember Happy Connections

Being aggressive can elicit rejection, but the flip side is also true: being rejected makes it more likely that kids will behave in aggressive ways because they feel angry or hurt and want to "get back" at whoever rejected them. An intriguing set of studies of college students by Jean Twenge and her colleagues show that a brief, friendly interaction with an adult, or writing about a family member, friend, or even a favorite celebrity can break through the typical tendency to behave aggressively after being rejected. By extension, doing something fun together, or even just helping your child vividly remember happy interactions with favorite people, could take some of the sting out of rejection, create a sense of belonging, and lessen the impulse to strike back.

Develop Self-Awareness About Unkindness

Kids can readily report instances when other children have been mean to them, but because their eyes point outwards, they may not recognize times when *they've* been less than kind, or they may dismiss these incidents as somehow unimportant. The following questionnaire is one we've used in bullying prevention programs. Have your child consider the questions, and emphasize that he or she does not have to tell anyone the answers. The point of this exercise is to increase awareness and to encourage kind choices in the future, not to force children to admit guilt.

Some Honest Self-Reflection About How We Treat Others . . .

For each question, decide whether the answer is "Never," "Sometimes," or "Often." Be honest. You will NOT have to share your answers.

1. Have you continued "joking" when you could see that someone was getting upset?

    Never   Sometimes   Often

2. Have you laughed or joined in when you saw someone being picked on?

    Never   Sometimes   Often

3. Have you said things about boyfriends/girlfriends that made someone feel uncomfortable?

    Never   Sometimes   Often

4. Have you laughed at someone who made a mistake or was struggling?

    Never   Sometimes   Often

5. Have you told people that you "hate" another kid?

    Never   Sometimes   Often

6. Have you deliberately called someone a silly name, even after being asked to stop?

    Never   Sometimes   Often

7. Have you made fun of how someone looks, dresses, acts, or talks?

    Never   Sometimes   Often

(continued)

8. Have you said mean things about others behind their backs?

Never   Sometimes   Often

9. Have you written or passed notes with mean comments about others?

Never   Sometimes   Often

10. Have you said, "Oh, no!" or complained when you've had to work with a certain student?

Never   Sometimes   Often

11. Have you told another kid, "Nobody likes you"?

Never   Sometimes   Often

12. Have you done unkind imitations of how another kid acts or talks?

Never   Sometimes   Often

Note: If you answered "Never" to every question, you're probably not being honest. Everyone makes mistakes and does unkind things sometimes. What's important is to recognize when this happens, try to make it right if you can, and promise yourself you'll do the kind thing next time.

Wrap Up Past Bullying Episodes in a Story

Parents often worry that having been bullied will do lasting damage to their children. This is less likely if (1) the bullying *stops*, and (2) the child develops a positive narrative that allows him or her to move past the unhappy incidents.

We humans are meaning-making creatures, and the stories we construct about our experiences describe and influence the meaning of those experiences. Kids can cope with a lot, as long as there's a happy ending.

Here's a story you might want to use or adapt if your child has been (and is no longer!) the target of bullying.

> You went through a terrible time. What those kids did to you was wrong. I wish I had known about it earlier. I wish you'd never gone through that. But as awful as it was, I'm glad that you now know that you're the kind of person who can have a serious problem, and speak up to get the help you need, and move past it. That's a pretty cool thing to know about yourself when you're only nine.

SHOW THE WAY

The importance of friendship doesn't lessen when we leave school. Friends make stressful times more bearable and fun times more enjoyable. The best thing you can do to help your child develop a healthy perspective on friendship is to demonstrate it in day-to-day life.

Make Time for Friends

Everyone is busy these days, trying to juggle paid or volunteer work, house chores, and a plethora of children's activities. Amid this hubbub, it's easy to let friendships slip to the bottom of the priority list. Allowing this to happen diminishes us and sets a poor example for our children.

Let your child see you setting aside time to get together with friends, even though you're busy. Get-togethers don't have to be elaborate to be fun. Call a friend and invite her to come along when you do a nighttime run to Target for construction paper. (She probably has a few things she needs to pick up, too.) Invite another family over for pizza. Meet a friend for breakfast. Over the summer, organize weekly outdoor potluck gatherings for families in your neighborhood, meeting in a different backyard each time.

Reach Out to Neighbors

Look for ways to be kind to neighbors, and let your child participate. Cook double to bring dinner to a family with a new baby or a spouse who is traveling. Introduce yourself to someone who has just moved in and bring a list of local service providers and their phone numbers. Offer to drive an elderly neighbor to the store and help with the shopping. Care for a vacationing neighbor's cat. Send a card to a neighbor who has been ill. These small acts of kindness build community and connection.

Treat Family Members with Kindness

Familiarity can breed insensitivity. Too often, we treat strangers in kinder and more respectful ways than we do family members. Of course we want to be able to relax at home, but the people we love and live with deserve our best behavior, not our worst. Children also tend to do what they see. So if your home is filled with sarcasm, put-downs, yelling, or worse, chances are these will carry over into your child's peer relationships. If your family members usually show warmth, interest, and kindness toward each other, it won't guarantee that your child will be nice at school, but it can help, because that's what your child will think is "normal." Experiencing lots of examples of kindness at home—as both a giver and a receiver—will increase the odds that your child will reach out to other kids in friendly ways.

Learning to connect with peers is complicated. Some children seem to do it effortlessly, whereas others struggle. They may come on too strong and irritate peers, or they may hold back from interacting with other kids. They may have trouble picking up on social cues, predicting or interpreting others' reactions, coming up with appropriate strategies, or implementing those strategies. This chapter emphasized ways to help children see, think, and do in social situations.

In the next chapter, we look at ways to help children manage their own strong emotions.

CHAPTER 3

MANAGING SENSITIVITY

How Does Your Child Handle Criticism, Conflict, and Disappointment?

 Does your child

- Have strong emotional reactions?
- Cry frequently, even in public?
- Become upset when someone else is upset?
- Seem to feel things more deeply than other children?
- Overreact to minor events?
- Have difficulty adjusting to a change of plans?
- Have "meltdown" tantrums at an age when most kids no longer do?
- Seem thin-skinned and easily hurt?
- Feel wounded by criticism?
- Readily perceive injustice or betrayal?
- Act intolerant of others' mistakes?
- Too quickly decide, "They're not my friends anymore"?
- Worry about tragedies and global crises?

Some kids seem to be born with their emotional volume set on high. Their reactions are longer, more frequent, and more intense than average. They are never just a little bit upset, because they readily become completely distraught. They feel deeply wounded by events that other children shrug off. For these sensitive children, emotions seem like a tidal wave—a crushing onslaught over which they have no control.

THE IMPACT OF SENSITIVITY

When children lack the skills they need to cope with their emotional reactions, it hurts them both personally and socially. They spend too much of their lives feeling miserable, because they are easily overwhelmed by minor frustrations. Other kids tend to avoid them. It's just not fun to be around someone who frequently becomes upset. Crying or raging around peers can also make children the targets of bullies who try to provoke their outbursts for entertainment.

Overexcitability

Some theorists have argued that emotional "overexcitability" is an intrinsic part of high ability. We think that's a cop-out. Although we've certainly seen a lot of bright children who struggle with emotional sensitivity, to shrug and say, "Oh, well, that's just the way they are" is to consign these children to a lifetime of misery. Children who tend to react more intensely and more frequently to upsetting events *can* learn ways to soothe themselves, and they have a greater need to do so. Being able to manage discomfort and disappointment in constructive ways is a necessary part of growing up. Some children just have to work harder than others to learn this.

Coping Rather Than Venting

Our focus in this chapter is on coping, not venting. Parents have asked us whether they should help their sensitive children "get their feelings out" through yelling, kicking, or punching pillows. The answer is no. There is absolutely no empirical evidence for any benefits of pure venting. Although it's undoubtedly better for a child to pound on a desk than to pound on a classmate, neither strategy is likely to improve the situation or to help the child feel more in control. Pounding, stamping, or yelling, while thinking about how they've been wronged, only serves to rehearse negative feelings. Moreover, other children are likely to avoid or ridicule kids who vent in public.

Feelings are not things to be "gotten rid of." They are a source of information about our environment and ourselves. We get upset when we perceive that something bad has happened that threatens us in some way. Teaching children how to cope with feelings isn't a matter of getting them to "let distress out." Instead, it involves helping them understand their reactions, alter their interpretations of the situation, tolerate unavoidable frustrations, know when and how to take a tension-relieving break, and respond to problems in productive ways.

Emotion Coaching

Psychologist John Gottman at the University of Washington has done some fascinating research on what he calls "*emotion coaching*." Emotion coaching involves empathizing with children's emotions *plus* actively teaching children how to cope with negative feelings. He contrasts emotion coaching with either (1) dismissing children's feelings or (2) being warm and accepting, but essentially leaving children on their own to figure out how to deal with their feelings. In one study, Gottman measured parents' emotion coaching when their children were five years old. He found that parents who did more emotion coaching had children who, *even three years later*, were better at self-soothing and had higher academic achievement, better peer relationships (assessed by teachers), and better physical health.

In the spirit of emotion coaching, this chapter describes many ways that you can teach your child to cope with negative feelings. This is an essential skill, because life is never trouble free. This chapter offers strategies that you can use to help your child learn to tolerate and manage distress. It describes self-soothing techniques as well as exercises in understanding other people's perspectives and communicating feelings effectively.

 ## MARIO: PERCEIVING BETRAYAL

Mario turned his back on the other boys and stalked off toward his bike.

"Mario, are you leaving?" Kenji called. "What's the matter?"

"You guys were laughing at me."

"We weren't laughing at you. It was just funny. You should have seen the look on your face when you fell!" Kenji chuckled.

"Well, it wasn't funny to me," Mario insisted. "I could have gotten hurt!"

"But you didn't get hurt," Kenji pointed out.

"Well, I could have."

"Oh, come on, Mario. Let's just go finish the game."

"No, I don't want to. I don't feel like it anymore. I'm going home."

Laughing when someone falls isn't a warm and compassionate response, but it's also not the crushing betrayal that Mario perceives. The other boys laughed because they were surprised when he fell and because he probably did look funny. Their laughter doesn't mean they don't care about Mario or that they wish him ill. It was just a brief, spontaneous reaction, but for

Mario it was enough to end the game and maybe even the friendships.

Perfectionism Turned Outward

Mario is very upset about the other boys' laughter because he interprets it as intentionally hurtful. In his mind, other people's behavior is always deliberate, and it's either right or wrong. He sees the boys' laughter as intolerably wrong. Mario's reaction is a kind of perfectionism turned outward, and it's a recipe for hurt and disappointment.

Some children are prone to righteous indignation. They have very specific ideas about how people ought to behave, and they don't know how to handle it when people fall short of their standards. Instead of sticking around to work things out, they storm off in outrage. Wounded, but clinging to their principles, they sever the relationship, insisting, "They shouldn't have done that!"

Tempering Idealism with Understanding

Bright children often develop abstract thinking abilities before their peers, and this can lead to misunderstandings. While they aspire to lofty ideals of friendship involving emotional connection, their age-mates might still be thinking of friends in concrete terms as "people to play with." They feel hurt and disappointed when peers just don't "get" their expectations. Moreover, because their cognitive maturity may not be matched by comparable emotional maturity, their ideals tend to be rigid. Yes, it's important to look for friends who are kind, loyal, and understanding, but it's also important to recognize that no one shows those qualities 100 percent of the time. Mistakes, disagreements, and misunderstandings are an inevitable part of any relationship. Most of the time, mistakes by friends should be met with understanding and forgiveness. They don't have to mark the end of a friendship.

STRATEGIES TO HELP YOUR CHILD HANDLE CONFLICTS WITH PEERS

Children like Mario need to temper their "you're either with me or against me" thinking about relationships. They need to become more tolerant and to develop appropriate ways of handling disagreements.

When your child feels wronged by a friend, respond first by empathizing. Acknowledge the feelings, *without* agreeing or implying that the other child is a horrible monster. You could say something like, "It hurt your feelings when she said that," "You're mad that he made other plans," or "You felt left out when they didn't include you." There is no point offering suggestions while your child is riled up, because when children are flooded with feelings, they are less able to think clearly or solve problems effectively. After you've expressed understanding for your child's feelings, *and given your child time to calm down*, then you can guide your child toward a more caring and responsible view of the situation. Here are some strategies you may want to try.

Consider the Other Child's Viewpoint

Empathy can temper outrage. If you can help your child understand the other's point of view, your child will be better equipped to respond with compassion, in ways that maintain or improve the relationship. Role playing is a useful technique for doing this. Talk about the problem, with you playing the role of your child, and your child playing the role of the friend. Encourage your child to vividly imagine what the friend is thinking and feeling.

Kids who are often angry assume too readily that others' actions are motivated by malice. But deliberate cruelty is not the only or even the most likely motivation. Help your child to consider more likely explanations. Was it an accident or a misunderstanding? Was there something about the situation that caused the misdeed? Did the friend simply not realize that the action would be hurtful? Was it just a mistake that the friend now regrets? During the role play, tell your child, "Let's assume that your friend wasn't trying to be mean. How might your friend explain what happened?" See if your child, speaking as the friend, can come up with a possible benign explanation.

Emphasize the Interpersonal Dance

Talk with your child about the saying, "It takes two to tango." Your child is likely to insist that the disagreement is entirely the other child's fault, but every conflict involves at least two people, even if one person is less "at fault."

You may need to help your child consider some of the less obvious ways of contributing to a problem. For instance, has your child

- Overreacted emotionally to being "wronged"?
- Ignored the other child's repeated requests to do or not do something?
- Failed to apologize for past actions that still bother the other child?
- Refused to accept an apology or let go of past grievances?
- Refused to speak to the other child?
- Harshly judged the other child for a minor or understandable mistake?
- Tolerated upsetting behavior from the other child, without politely requesting a change?
- Gossiped about the problem to other children not involved in the conflict?
- Tattled on the other child, instead of working out the problem?

Being able to identify one's own role in a conflict is an important step toward maturity and responsibility.

The beauty of the "two to tango" rule is that it means either person has the power to change the interaction for the better. Help your child brainstorm different and healthier ways of responding to the problem to break through the pattern of an unhappy interpersonal dance.

Encourage Relationship Repair

Because of their inexperience and their tendency toward black-and-white thinking, some kids may not understand that it's possible and usually desirable to work through conflicts in order to preserve a relationship. Explain to your child that being a good friend means taking active steps to repair relationships when there has been a rift. Here are some options your child may want to consider singly or in combination:

Acceptance and Forgiveness   Sometimes being a friend means accepting other people's foibles and forgiving their mistakes. Your child might have plenty of ideas about how another child could "improve," but real friends accept each other the way they are. Help your child understand that conditional liking, along the lines of "I'll only be your friend if . . ." or "You're not my friend if . . . ," is arrogant and ungenerous. It's not realistic to expect others to be perfect. It's also not realistic to demand a personality overhaul. To have friends, your child needs to accept other children, quirks and all.

Acceptance and forgiveness don't require a public declaration. In fact, telling another child, "I forgive you for being thoughtless and inconsiderate" or "I accept that you're just not as caring as I am" *won't* go over well. Acceptance is an inner decision, which your child should act on simply by being friendly. Suggest that your child smile, greet the other child, or invite that child to join in an activity. These simple actions show your child's willingness to mend the rift.

Friendly Assertiveness   Sometimes other children don't realize that what they are doing upsets your child. In that case, you may want to help your child come up with a clear but friendly way to communicate feelings. The following is a good formula to practice using:

"I feel _____ when you _____. Please _____."

Here are some examples:

"I feel annoyed when you call me Kimbo. Please use my real name."

"I feel mad when you use my ball without asking. Please ask me first."

This formula takes appropriate ownership of feelings with an "I" statement, identifies a specific problem behavior (rather than a personality flaw), and describes the desired remedy. It's a polite request, rather than a condemnation.

Requests for change are more likely to be effective when they involve asking someone to *do* something rather than to *stop* doing something. So help your child phrase the "Please _____" part of the formula in positive terms. It's easier for another child to hear "Please move over" than "Please stop being so annoying."

One important caveat is that children should only discuss their feelings with people who care about them. "I" statements are great for repairing or improving a relationship with a friend, but it's not a good idea to tell a bully, "I feel hurt when you call me names." The bully is likely to respond, "Good!"

Apology A final relationship repair strategy that your child should consider is apologizing. As we discussed in the section on the interpersonal dance, your child probably contributed to the problem in some way, so there's probably something your child can apologize for in order to reconnect with the other child.

Offer your child this rule of thumb: the person who is least wrong should apologize first. It's easier for that person to take the first step, which in turn makes it easier for the other person to apologize. Remind your child that once apologies have been offered, the event is over, and your child shouldn't bring it up again.

Emphasize Reasonable Doubt

A more general strategy to help your child avoid overreacting to minor slights is to talk about how our judicial system assumes that people are innocent until proven guilty. Tell your child that judges specifically instruct jurors that if there is a reasonable doubt about whether the accused committed the crime, they should not convict the accused. Also, the law distinguishes between premeditated and accidental crimes. Encourage your child to explain the rationale behind these laws. What would happen if the justice system presumed that people were guilty until proven innocent? Which would be more damaging to our society: to wrongly convict or to wrongly acquit someone? Would it be fair to judge people only on the outcome of their actions, regardless of intent?

Here are some examples of "kid crimes" with harsh judgments about why they occurred. As practice in allowing reasonable doubt, see how many benign explanations your child can come up with for these misdeeds. Have your child list possibilities, by saying "Maybe . . ."

Kid crime 1: Raul says, "Jason bumped into me on purpose and made me drop my books!"

Examples of benign explanations:

Maybe Jason didn't see Raul.

Maybe the floor was wet and Jason slipped.

Maybe someone else bumped into Jason, which made him fall on Raul.

Maybe Raul wasn't looking, and Raul was the one who bumped into Jason!

Kid crime 2: Kathy says, "Cara played with Aparna at recess because she doesn't like me anymore!"

Kid crime 3: Nikko says, "Stephen took my pencil! He deliberately stole it!"

Kid crime 4: Carla says, "Marissa deliberately ignored me when I said 'Hi' to her because she's stuck up!"

Discuss Different Kinds of Friendship

Your child may have only one model of friendship—soul mates for life—but it's possible to have many different kinds of friends. Your child could have a friend to sit with in music class, a friend from the neighborhood to play with after school, a friend from scouts, a friend to work with on school projects . . . These children aren't soul mates, but they are casual friends, and that's fine. True soul mates are a rare and wonderful gift. Most of us will only have a handful across our entire lives. In the meantime, and in addition, it's great to have a network of casual friends as companions. Help your child understand the value of these casual friendships.

You may want to encourage your child to make a friendship map that emphasizes varieties of friendships. Put your child's name or picture in the center of a large piece of paper. Then draw lines, coming out from the center, to the names or pictures of different friends. Your child may choose to place some friends closer to the center and others farther out, but emphasize that all friendships have value. For each friend, have your child note one or more favorite shared activities.

 JESSICA:
BALKING AT
CONSTRUCTIVE FEEDBACK

"It looks good, Jessica," her dad said. "I just didn't understand this one paragraph. Maybe you can expand that a bit, so it's clearer."

"Well, I think it's clear enough," Jessica insisted. "What don't you get? It's obvious."

"It may be obvious to you, but your reader would probably find it clearer if you gave a couple of examples."

"Just forget it. You always hate my papers."

"Honey, I think you're a wonderful writer. I'm just suggesting a minor change to make things clearer."

"Just leave me alone!" Jessica said, blinking back tears. "I shouldn't have even let you look at my paper!"

Some children are extremely sensitive to criticism. Parents often see this kind of sensitivity when they try to offer constructive feedback and their children respond with defensive anger or hurt tears. When Jessica's father offers a suggestion for improving her paper, her pride is injured. She sees his remarks as a personal attack. Although her father's comments are very mild, she feels wounded by them. She completely ignores the fact that he started out saying, "It looks good." Somehow, for Jessica, that initial, overall positive reaction is erased by the fact that there's room for improvement.

Seeing Criticism as Rejection

Because bright children are used to being praised, anything less than a stellar review stands out with glaring significance, and they are apt to take it very personally. For children whose self-worth is tightly tied to their ability to perform, negative feedback feels unbearable. When a parent or coach suggests improvements or in any way implies that their performance is less than perfect, they interpret this as evidence that "They don't like me!" If these children get a disappointing grade, instead of thinking, "Hmm . . . What do I need to do differently?" they immediately jump to the conclusion that "The teacher hates me!" They see no distinction between who they are and what they do, so having their work criticized feels like a personal rejection.

Sharing Versus Improving

Another possible explanation for the downhill spiral in the inter-action between Jessica and her dad might be a misunderstanding about why Jessica was showing him the paper. Maybe her father thought she was looking for suggestions for improving the paper, but Jessica just wanted to share it with him. Maybe Jessica asked for his suggestions, but realized only after she heard the feedback that that's not what she really wanted.

As we discussed in Chapter Two, feedback from a parent can be emotionally loaded for children, so you may want to leave it to your child's teachers and coaches to offer pointers. Yes, your child needs feedback to improve, but that feedback doesn't nec-essarily have to come from you. You definitely shouldn't feel obligated to give routine or unsolicited feedback.

If your child specifically asks you to look at a paper or project, clarify beforehand what your child wants from you. Ask, "Are you showing this to me because you want to share it with me or because you want suggestions for improving it?"

If your child chooses the "just sharing" option, you need to respect that. Bite your tongue to refrain from offering any tips. Don't make any evaluative comments—not even positive ones, because those are still judgments, and that's not what your child wants from you. Share your interest or make observations acknowledging your child's effort. You could say something like, "I didn't know there were so many varieties of jellyfish," or "I can tell you spent a lot of time on this picture," or "You must have worked hard to find so many references."

If your child chooses the "suggestions for improving" option, you may need to ask more questions to make sure that is really what your child wants. Before you even glance at the paper or project, say, "If I look at this, trying to find ways to improve it, I'm going to find some. With any project, there's always room for improvement. Are you sure that's what you want?" You could also ask, "Do you have the time and energy to make changes?"

or "Are you going to be able to hear my suggestions without getting upset?" If there's any doubt, steer your child toward the "just sharing" option.

STRATEGIES TO HELP YOUR CHILD COPE WITH CRITICISM

Nobody enjoys being criticized, but it's an unavoidable part of work life. Children like Jessica need to develop strategies for coping with constructive feedback. This involves helping them accept that no one performs perfectly all the time and also teaching them ways to manage distress and respond appropriately when they get negative feedback. The strategies in this section can help your child learn to tolerate criticism by keeping it in perspective, so it feels less overwhelming.

Tread Softly with Feedback

If your child insists on receiving feedback from you about a paper or project, clarify what kinds of suggestions your child wants. Younger children may want you to focus on spelling or punctuation. Older children might want you to offer ideas to enhance organization or clarity. You also might ask if there's a particular section that your child wants to improve. Having children explicitly communicate what they want from you makes it more likely that your interaction over the paper will go well. If children have specifically agreed to a particular kind of feedback, they are prepared for it and will be better able to tolerate it.

Before making any suggestions, remind your child that choosing to receive your feedback means listening without arguing. Your child can decide what to do with your feedback, but by asking for it, your child is agreeing to listen to it without debating it.

Set the stage by pointing out several things that you think your child did well in the paper. Children very easily slide to "all good" or "all bad" thinking. Starting with some positive observations can temper this tendency and also makes the criticisms easier to tolerate. Be as specific as possible. "You give lots of vivid details. I can picture in my mind what you're talking about." "I see you backed up your idea with three facts." "Your topic sentences are very clear. I understand exactly what you mean." "That's a nice strong verb."

When you state your suggestions, do so in a gentle and constructive way and concentrate on what your child could do to fix the problem. "This is what your character said, so you need quotation marks." "I had trouble understanding this sentence. Can you think of an example you could include?"

Less is more when it comes to feedback: it's better to offer just a few suggestions that your child can accept and use than to overwhelm your child with every possible tip to make things perfect. Remember that your child's paper or project is a learning tool rather than a permanent work of art.

If your child starts to get upset, revisit the question about whether your child really wants feedback from you. Maybe your child can't tolerate any more suggestions right now. Maybe that really wasn't what your child was looking for from you. Leave the decision to stop or continue in your child's hands. If your child still insists on more feedback, suggest a quick break, for a drink of water or a trip to the bathroom, before continuing, just to give your child a chance to calm down. When you continue the feedback session, keep it short, even if it means not mentioning all of your tips.

After the feedback session, however long or short, open ended or limited it was, acknowledge your child's courage in seeking and hearing suggestions for improvement. You could say, "Listening to criticism is a hard thing. That was very brave of you to be able to hear my comments without getting upset."

Some people might argue that going through all of this is coddling children. In the real world of school and work, nobody will be this gentle with your child regarding criticism. Don't kids have to learn to be tough? In our opinion, it is completely reasonable and appropriate for parents to treat their children with greater understanding and compassion than others would. That's just part of being a loving parent. The issue isn't making these kids "tough" but helping them develop coping abilities. By handling many instances of gentle feedback, children can gain confidence in their ability to tolerate well-intentioned criticism. In contrast, being subjected to harsh judgments could lead them to fear and avoid even minor feedback.

Focus on the Intent

Children instinctively cringe when they get back a paper that's covered in red ink. We've heard that some education books specifically recommend that teachers use pens of other colors. But the problem isn't the ink color—it's the interpretation that children attach to the marks. Kids see the marks and assume, "The teacher doesn't like me" or "The teacher thinks I'm no good."

Help your child understand that giving feedback is a sign of caring. It's much easier for a teacher to just scribble a grade at the top of a paper. Comments take effort and thought. A teacher who takes the time to write comments is invested in helping your child learn. That teacher believes in your child's ability to grow and improve. Tell your child to take a deep breath, then carefully read and take in the teacher's thoughtful messages.

Sometimes smart kids object to criticism by saying that their work is already better than that of some of their classmates, so why should they have to do more? Explain to your child that the teacher's job is to help every student move forward. What another child does or doesn't do is irrelevant to your child's progress.

Focus on the Content

When children feel threatened by criticism, they instinctively react by either defending themselves or running. By helping your child focus on the specific content of the criticism and the steps required to remedy the problems, you can help diffuse this fight-or-flight reaction.

Accepting feedback requires three steps: (1) understanding what the teacher wants, (2) figuring out how to address the teacher's criticisms, and (3) committing to taking appropriate action. With younger children or when there are only a few comments, you can talk through these steps. For each teacher comment, have your child answer the questions, "What's the problem?" and "What do I need to do to fix it?" Then encourage your child to make the correction either mentally or on paper, if the teacher wants to see corrections. When children know exactly what they need to do, the solution usually seems manageable.

If your older child feels overwhelmed by extensive revision requests from a teacher, it may help to write out these steps. Divide a piece of paper into three vertical columns and label them "Problem," "Solutions," and "Difficulty." Help your child briefly note the first teacher criticism in the Problem column. Tell your child, "Don't argue; don't defend; just write it down as though you're summarizing impersonal facts. Your job is just to list the teacher's impressions and suggestions." Next, brainstorm about specific strategies for addressing this criticism and jot them in the Solutions column. This is a thinking exercise, not a writing assignment, so tell your child to write just a few key words or phrases in the Problem and Solutions columns. Finally, in the Difficulty column, have your child label the solutions as easy, medium, or difficult. Do this for each criticism.

The point of this exercise is to slow down your child's automatic "I can't!" or "My teacher shouldn't!" reaction. Summarizing the teacher's comments forces your child to acknowledge and understand them. Focusing on specific ways to address the comments prevents your child from fleeing or dismissing them. Considering each comment in terms of problem, solutions, and difficulty allows your child to see the teacher's criticisms as manageable instructions, many of which can be addressed easily.

Even if addressing a particular problem is difficult, at least your child has a plan. Tell your child that teachers like kids who try, and responding appropriately to criticism is one of the most important ways of trying and learning.

SAMIR: CHAFING AT A CHANGE OF PLANS

"But you said!" Samir wailed. "You told me this morning that we could go to the store and get the new game for my Nintendo DS!"

"Well, that was the plan," Samir's dad replied, "but sometimes plans change."

"I saved up my own money to get it. You said I could get it today! Why can't we go to the store now?" Samir whined.

"The store is closed now. We'll try tomorrow or on the weekend."

"I really wanted that game *today*," Samir insisted.

"I know, but your aunt and cousins came over, so it just didn't work out today. You had a good time playing with your cousins, didn't you?"

"Well, I wouldn't have if I'd known it meant I couldn't get the game. You lied to me! You always do that! You said we could get it today!"

Samir is on the brink of a serious meltdown. His reaction seems out of proportion to the disappointment of a delay in getting the game he wants. There's a rigidity and a moralistic tone to the way Samir interprets the situation. Instead of seeing the delay as an ordinary and minor setback, he views it as a disaster and a gross injustice. Samir is so focused on his upset that he refuses to hear any of the reasonable responses his father offers.

Indirect Communication

A not-so-fun part of being a parent is that we often bear the brunt of it when our kids are unhappy. Samir's provocative accusations (for example, "You lied!") seem intended to infuriate his father. He's angry, so he's lashing out, and his dad is a handy target.

Children often communicate their feelings indirectly by acting in ways that elicit comparable feelings in their trusted adults. This kind of indirect communication is *not* deliberate or even conscious, but it is quite common. For instance, when children are feeling frustrated, they might obstinately refuse to cooperate, so that their parents feel equally frustrated. If they feel hopeless, they might reject every suggested solution until their parents also feel hopeless. In Samir's case, he feels angry and wronged, and his accusations are likely to evoke exactly those feelings in his father.

The key to handling these interactions is not to get sucked in. This is easier said than done. Yes, it's obnoxious and offensive to be called a liar. At some point, in a calmer moment, Samir's father should definitely say something like, "It's not okay to call me names, even when you're mad. That's not how we treat each other in this family." However, responding at all to these accusations in the heat of the moment will only shift the conversation in an unproductive direction. If Samir's father tries to argue or defend himself by saying, "I am not a liar! How dare you say that!" Samir will respond, "Yes, you are! You always lie!" But Samir's father's truthfulness is not the issue. The issue is that Samir is upset, and he needs to cope with that.

Sensory Overload

Another contributing factor to Samir's meltdown could be sensory overload. The visit with his cousins was undoubtedly noisy and exciting, and then it suddenly ended. Samir's meltdown may have little to do with the video game and a lot to do with his difficulty settling himself after the high level of stimulation.

Some children are especially sensitive to stimulation. They are very reactive to loud sounds, bright light, smells, texture, activity, and rapid changes. At the more extreme end, these children may be diagnosed with sensory integration disorder, but we have seen many children who don't qualify as having a full-blown disorder, but are definitely prone to overstimulation. If this describes your child, two excellent books on this topic that you may want to consult are *The Highly Sensitive Child*, by Elaine Aron, and *The Out-of-Sync Child Has Fun*, by Carol Kranowitz. In general, coping with this kind of sensitivity involves being aware of the types of situations that are difficult and helping your child cope by offering warnings, allowing breaks when needed, and supporting the development of self-calming strategies.

STRATEGIES TO HELP YOUR CHILD RECOVER FROM AND PREVENT EMOTIONAL OUTBURSTS

Children like Samir need to learn practical strategies for managing distress and preventing or minimizing outbursts. They need to accept that life is never problem free and that some frustration is inevitable. They need to understand the importance of self-control and to realize that this is an area that requires extra effort for them. Here are some ideas about how you can help.

Acknowledge the Feelings but Not the Intensity

When your child seems to be headed toward an outburst, often simply acknowledging the feelings can help your child calm down. Calmly but warmly say something like

"You're disappointed that . . ."

"You feel frustrated because . . ."

"I can understand how . . . would be annoying for you."

"You're mad about . . ."

These statements may feel awkward to you at first, or they may seem like things only a therapist would say, but practicing them is worthwhile, because they're surprisingly effective. With these statements, you're not necessarily agreeing that your child's feelings are reasonable; you're just acknowledging that they exist. When kids know that someone has heard and understood how they are feeling, they tend to relax. You may need to make several such statements until your child feels fully heard. You'll know when that happens because your child's body will visibly relax, and his or her tone of voice will become softer and slower.

The alternative strategy—insisting that your child is being unreasonable and shouldn't feel that way—is likely to backfire. Kids tend to get louder when they don't feel heard.

Sometimes parents respond to children's upset by immediately trying to solve the problem. If the problem is minor and easily fixed, this might work. More likely, in the throes of upset, your child will stubbornly refuse to be satisfied with or even consider any possible solution.

Acknowledging feelings first can help your child calm down enough to be able to consider solutions. But don't feel pressured to solve every problem that comes your child's way. Some problems are simply unavoidable. Just knowing you understand may be all that your child needs. When kids feel heard and understood, they can often come up with their own solutions.

Set Limits on Behavior

Sometimes kids who are prone to outbursts essentially hold their parents hostage. Their parents are so afraid of triggering another tirade that they tiptoe around their children and go to elaborate lengths to prevent or fix any possible disappointment. This is giving children excessive and inappropriate power within a family. It's not healthy for either kids or parents when children rule the family.

Your child needs to know, without question, that you are not afraid of your child's feelings, and that you're willing and able to set limits on inappropriate behavior. Make sure that tantrums don't "work" to get what your child wants. Speak up calmly and firmly when your child's behavior crosses the line. For instance, you could say, "I know you're angry, but it's not okay for you to scream at me or throw things. You need to take a break in your room." Don't be afraid to act to enforce your words. This could mean escorting your child to a bedroom, walking out of a store, or canceling a fun outing. For everyone's sake, you can't afford to be imprisoned by your child's emotional outbursts. No matter how bright they are, children lack the maturity, perspective, and judgment that come with adult experience, so they can't possibly do a good job running the family.

Teach Calming Self-Talk

When your child is feeling calm, try using a balloon that hasn't been blown up to demonstrate the effects of thoughts on feelings. Explain to your child that we all talk to ourselves in our heads, and the way we talk to ourselves affects how we feel. Sometimes self-talk makes us feel more tense and upset. Say the following statements (or your own variations) in a frantic tone of voice and blow into the balloon after each statement.

> This is awful!
> It's horrible!
> It's the worst thing ever!
> It's unbearable!
> I can't stand it!
> Nothing ever goes right for me!

Point out how the balloon is now full and tense and maybe even ready to burst.

We can also talk to ourselves in ways that help us feel calmer. Say the following statements in a soothing tone of voice and let a little air out of the balloon after each statement, until the balloon is completely deflated.

> "I don't like it, but I can stand it."
> "It's not the worst thing in the world."
> "I've dealt with harder things before."
> "It's not going to kill me."
> "I'll get through it. It won't last forever."
> "It's not what I want, but I can handle it."

Point out how the balloon is now relaxed. Do the exercise again, with your child supplying the frantic and calming statements.

You may want to help your child come up with a list of calming statements to use when the need arises. Keep in mind that the calming statements must be *believable* to be effective. In other words, it won't help to tell ourselves, "This is great!" when it really isn't, but telling ourselves, "I'll get through it" can feel reassuring.

Plan Distress Tolerance Strategies

It's much easier to prevent outbursts than it is to deal with them after they occur. Help your child come up with a variety of self-soothing strategies. Your child may want to draw pictures of these strategies on a poster or on a set of index cards that can be stapled together to make a booklet, where they can be easy references. Remind your child to use these strategies *early* because they work best when distress levels are still fairly low. They are unlikely to work in the middle of an emotional outburst.

Here are some of our favorite self-soothing strategies for kids. See which ones appeal to your child. What may be soothing for one child may be irritating for another. Be sure to explain to your child that it can sometimes take twenty minutes or more to completely calm down, so your child shouldn't use a strategy for a few seconds and conclude, "It doesn't work."

Calming Box   Get a cardboard box large enough to hold a pillow. Have your child decorate the inside with calming pictures from magazines, favorite stickers, or happy drawings. Place the box on the ground, with the opening facing sideways, and put a comfortable pillow on the bottom. Have your child lie on the pillow (head inside the box). The calming box can be your child's special retreat when things start to feel overwhelming.

Water   Many children find water soothing. For younger children, playing with a sink full of water and some measuring cups can be calming. A squirt of dishwashing liquid adds the extra fun of soap bubbles. Older children may enjoy a shower or bath. Water activities can be something your child does when irritation starts to rise, or they can be part of a regular schedule, to make transition times easier. We know one family in which the son routinely takes a shower right after school. This gives him a chance to unwind from the day and makes the evening more pleasant for the whole family.

Feathers   A kid-friendly way to do slow, calming breathing is to use feathers. Get soft, colorful feathers from a craft store. Keep some in envelopes in strategic places in your home. Have your child practice blowing softly to tickle the fronds of a feather without making any noise. Your child might also enjoy gently stroking the feather or rubbing it across his or her face.

Bubble Blowing   If the weather is warm, your child can try blowing bubbles outside using a small wand and bubble liquid. Encourage your child to use long, slow exhales to make a stream of bubbles or one large bubble.

Rhythmic Motion   Just as rocking can soothe a baby, it can also help older children regain their composure. Your child might enjoy using a rocking chair, swing, or real or stationary bicycle as a calming strategy.

Heavy Lifting   Some children find it steadying to carry moderately heavy objects. Formal weight lifting is usually not appropriate for young children, but with your guidance and appropriate safety precautions, maybe your child could rearrange the books on a bookshelf, carry some items to or from the basement, stack firewood, or help shift boxes in the garage.

Lotion   For some children, rubbing on a bit of hand lotion can be a way to slow down and essentially massage themselves into a calmer state.

Music   Music can have a strong effect on our moods. In fact, psychologists use carefully selected pieces of music in experiments involving mood induction. Advertisers use music to influence how consumers feel about their products. Producers also use music to set the scene in movies. Even with our eyes closed, we know when something good or bad is about to happen in a movie because of the background music.

Help your child select some favorite "mood music," and get it in a format where your child can easily access it—a tape, a store-bought or homemade CD, or an MP3. Your child may want to have some lively, happy pieces as well as some slow, soothing pieces.

Reading   Reading is another powerful way to influence mood. A favorite story is engrossing and can give your child a break from upsetting circumstances. Humorous collections, such as "Calvin and Hobbes" cartoon books, can also lighten your child's mood.

Create a Sensory Item Collection

Kids love collecting things, so your child might enjoy developing a collection of soothing sensory items to play with as a calming strategy. Consider all five senses, and help your child choose or create an appealing collection. Playing with sensory items can provide a crucial break that allows your child to step back from a situation for a few minutes and calm down. Here are some possibilities:

Touch: a collection of squeezable stress balls; play dough; moon sand; a texture card, which is a piece of cardboard with a variety of fabrics of different textures (for example, velvety, satiny, prickly, furry) glued on it

Smell: perfume sample cards from magazine ads, scented markers (draw, then smell), unlit scented candles

Taste: Tic Tac candies in a variety of flavors (Have your child concentrate on only sucking, not biting, the candy, to make it last as long as possible.)

Sight: a small photo album with special pictures or postcards of animals, castles, paintings, beaches, or other favorite objects or scenes

Hearing: a music box collection

Plan a Stopping Strategy

If your child tends to act impulsively or aggressively when upset, plan ahead to come up with something to do instead of acting out. For instance, your child might want to cross arms in front and squeeze tightly, like a self-hug, then gradually relax arm and shoulder muscles while keeping the arms crossed. Similarly, your child could clasp hands tightly and then relax the hand muscles. Just sitting on hands is another way to slow things down so that your child won't do something regrettable. Older children may prefer a less visible stopping technique, such as imagining their feet taking root into the ground, anchoring them firmly; imagining that they are moving slowly through deep water; or pretending that their tongue is stuck to the roof of their mouth.

Sometimes the best stopping strategy is to leave the situation temporarily. Talk with your child about when this might be a good choice. At home, you may want to use a "time-out" signal when family members need a short break because interactions are headed in a not-so-good direction. You may need to remind your child that this strategy is for cooling off, not for avoiding necessary tasks or conversations.

Conduct a Postgame Review

If your child has a meltdown, it's sometimes a good idea to review what happened afterwards, when your child is feeling calm, to help your child come up with better ways of coping. Explain to your child that athletes often review video footage of their games so that they can learn how to play better. Acknowledge that your child was very upset and that it's hard to think clearly under those conditions. A postgame review will help your child figure out what happened and how to handle things differently next time. Try to get your child to do most of the talking. Your manner should be calm, matter-of-fact, and mildly curious. Ask your child,

> What happened just before the meltdown?
>
> How were you feeling?
>
> What could you have done that would have been a better choice?
>
> What can you do now (or soon) to make things better?

The last question is the most important. Keep the discussion short. You don't necessarily have to cover every question. Resist the temptation to lecture. The point is *not* to force your child to admit to mistakes, but rather to encourage thinking about coping alternatives and to help your child move forward.

Sometimes children are extremely hard on themselves after an emotional meltdown. You may find that as you try to conduct a postgame review, your child says things like, "I'm such an idiot. I was just stupid. There's nothing to talk about. I'm just a jerk, okay?" No, it's not okay. Tell your child this has nothing to do with being "stupid" and everything to do with learning to manage negative feelings. Express your confidence that your child will be able to manage frustrating situations in a way that works out better for everyone, but that it will take time and practice. By thinking through the situation that didn't go so well, your child will be better able to handle it next time. Learning some skills will come easily to your child; learning others will take effort and practice. Handling frustration falls into the latter category.

Play "It Could Be Worse!"

If you and your child are enduring difficult circumstances together, you could try engaging your child's imagination and humor by playing "It Could Be Worse!" For instance, if you are waiting in a long line, say, "It could be worse: we could be standing in line outside, in a blizzard." Alternate with your child, repeating previous "worse" conditions and trying to top them. "It could be worse: we could be standing in line outside, in a blizzard, wearing our bathing suits, surrounded by twelve people with really bad body odor." The "worse" conditions can be as silly or outrageous as you want. By the time you are done, your present circumstances will seem quite mild.

Only use this game with *shared* adversity. Saying that your child's circumstances could be worse can come across as dismissing your child's concerns.

Distinguish Between Controllable and Uncontrollable Conditions

During a calm moment, discuss with your child how some things are controllable and some are not. Help your child come up with some examples of each. (See the following box for possibilities.)

Things I CAN Control	*Things I CAN'T Control*
How I act.	How other people act.
How quickly and well I do my homework.	Whether I get homework.
How I treat my siblings.	Whether I have siblings.
How I respond when I'm frustrated.	Whether frustrating things happen.
Whether I invite a friend over.	Whether that friend can come over.
Whether I forgive a friend.	Whether a friend forgives me.

The reason it's important to distinguish between controllable and uncontrollable conditions is that they require different coping strategies. When problems involve controllable conditions, we can make plans, try hard, ask for help, try new strategies, and actively change the situation. When problems involve uncontrollable conditions, we need to work on tolerating and accepting what can't be changed.

You may want to help your child come up with some phrases to acknowledge when a situation is uncontrollable. Some possibilities are "It is what it is," "I have to deal with what is," or "It's out of my hands."

If your family is religious, you may want to teach your child the Serenity Prayer, which directly addresses this issue. Here's the original version of that prayer, written by Reinhold Niebuhr:

> Father, give us courage to change what must be
>   altered,
> serenity to accept what cannot be helped,
> and the insight to know the one from the other.

COLLIN: SHOULDERING THE WORLD'S WOES

"Mom, I can't sleep."

"Collin, are you still up? It's so late! What's wrong, sweetie?"

"It's the war. I can't stop thinking about the Afghani children. I mean, they didn't do anything wrong. But they're getting hurt and even dying. And their parents are dying, too. Who's going to take care of them?"

"Did you see or read something that has you especially worried?"

"No. I was just thinking. But now I can't sleep. It's just not right that the kids are suffering."

Some children are extremely softhearted. They may cry when another child is hurt or scolded at school. They become distraught over scary or tragic movies. It's as though these kids have an extra-strong sense of empathy that causes them to suffer when they see or imagine others suffering.

A Gap Between What They Know and What They Can Handle Emotionally

Children like Collin sometimes become aware of harsh realities before they are ready to cope with them emotionally. Their peers are oblivious to or disconnected from such issues as world hunger, ozone layer depletion, child abuse, drunk driving, or war, but these children feel deeply and personally responsible for worrying about these adult-size problems.

Unfortunately, there are children who really do have to contend with awful circumstances, but some sensitive children become preoccupied with extreme difficulties even when they have no direct experience with them. They may learn about these problems because of their advanced reading skills, or they may just happen to hear or see information that they somehow take to heart. Collin has never been to Afghanistan, and he certainly hasn't experienced war, but the suffering of the Afghani children is very real and very troubling to him.

Cognitively, Collin can understand big issues, but emotionally, he's too young to deal with them. He hasn't developed the ability to protect himself from this kind of pain and fear.

Developing the Capacity for Healthy Cognitive Distance

Although empathy is important and valuable, being able to step back and get some emotional distance from others' distress is also essential. We've known some children like Collin who feel it isn't right for them to be happy when other children are suffering. These kids can't sufficiently separate their own experience from that of others. They feel deeply, but they don't yet have the ability to take a step back when they want or need to do so. This is a skill that develops with maturity. It's why an older child can watch *Bambi* and be sad but not devastated by the mother's death, whereas for a younger child, the death scene is completely overwhelming.

STRATEGIES TO HELP YOUR CHILD COPE WITH BIG WORRIES

Children like Collin don't need "toughening up." Their compassion is an endearing quality that should be respected. At the same time, to minimize their own suffering, they need to learn coping strategies for managing distress. They also need to understand that it's okay for them to be just a kid and, at least sometimes, to leave the big issues to the grown-ups.

Limit Exposure to Upsetting Material

No children benefit from exposure to violence or gore, but if your child has a gentle soul, you may need to be particularly mindful about limiting exposure to media that other people in our society consider "no big deal." Just because every other kid in the class likes "Goosebumps" books doesn't mean your child should be forced to read something he or she finds frightening. If you know your child will be upset by the violence in a new hit movie, support your child in choosing not to see it, even if all the other kids think the scene where the villain's head is cut off is "cool."

The Web site www.kidsinmind.com is a practical resource that offers detailed descriptions of the sex, violence, and language in movies, so you can make informed decisions about whether a movie is right for your child. If you have an older child, you may want to read over the descriptions and decide together whether a particular movie is something your child can handle.

You may need to help your child develop appropriate self-advocacy skills. Plan and practice phrases that express your child's preferences without judging other children's reactions. Possibilities include "I don't like scary movies," "I'm not into that kind of movie," "May I be excused? This is too scary for me," or "I like comedies better."

You may also need to be careful about your child's exposure to the news. Television news, in particular, often contains images that are frightening to young and sensitive children. It's great for your child to know what's going on in the world, but you need to make informed decisions about how much and what kind of information your child can handle at a particular age.

Consider both content and immediacy. By immediacy, we mean how vivid and personal the information is. For instance, suppose there is a news story about forest fires. Hearing you (a trusted adult) say calmly that there are bad fires in another state is less immediate than reading a detailed description of the fires, which is less immediate than seeing photos of burned-out homes, which is less immediate than seeing video footage of a burn victim sobbing as she describes how her children died in the flames. Most children could tolerate simply hearing about the fires. Few could tolerate the video footage, nor do we see any benefit in exposing children to such vivid and upsetting information. You decide what level of information is right for your child, keeping in mind that this will change over time, as your child matures.

Illustrate Who's in Charge of Safety

Sensitive children may become especially frightened by world events because they feel both personally threatened and personally responsible. Here's a caring way to emphasize that there are many layers of protection surrounding your child.

Draw a small stick figure at the bottom of a piece of paper. Tell your child, "This is you. Let's talk about who's in charge of keeping you safe." Draw additional stick figures above your child to represent parents. Have your child name more people in charge of safety, as you represent them in additional rows of stick figures. The final picture could include rows for relatives, friends, neighbors, teachers, community workers, and government officials. The goal is to depict many layers between your child and danger.

We like to use drawings with children whenever possible. Neither of us is particularly artistic, but the aesthetic quality of the drawing doesn't matter. We've found that a vivid image often gets through to kids better than a lot of adult words.

Take Positive Action

Most of us feel better when we can *do* something about a problem. So another way to help a child who is concerned about a big issue is to find an appropriate way for that child to take some

Who's in charge of keeping you safe?

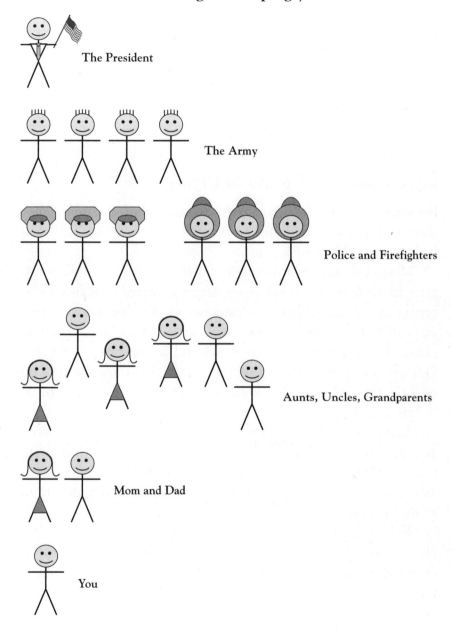

The President

The Army

Police and Firefighters

Aunts, Uncles, Grandparents

Mom and Dad

You

kind of action toward solving the problem. For instance, your child might want to write a letter to an official or an article for the school newspaper. Other possibilities are helping select which charity your family will support or participating in a family service project. Acknowledge to your child that none of these actions will come close to solving a world problem, but every little bit of help counts, and lots of little bits from lots of people can really add up.

Make Plans to Try to Avoid Crying in Public

For some sensitive children, crying becomes almost a habit. They react to big issues, but they react with equal intensity to small issues. No problem seems minor to them.

Most children cry at home from time to time, but once children reach first or second grade, there is often a social cost to crying in public. Although classmates might respond in caring ways to very occasional tears, especially if they are related to physical injury, they tend to avoid and sometimes even mock kids who cry a lot. Other children's (and sometimes even caring adults') sympathy tends to dwindle when they say or think, "Chris is crying, *again*."

Sadness can lead to tears, but frequent tears can also lead to greater sadness. When children spend a lot of time crying, that's time that they're not learning or playing or chatting or doing other fun and interesting things. Fewer tears could translate to greater happiness for them.

Telling tears-prone children, "Don't cry" doesn't help. It's also not a realistic or compassionate message, because everyone cries sometimes. What these children need is to have replacement behaviors—other things they can do when they're feeling upset—so that they have less need to resort to crying.

Creating an illustrated list of possible coping strategies can help your child manage distress and avoid crying in public. Slow, deep breathing is one possibility that's easy to use in many situations. (Remind your child to do this silently.) Distraction is another strategy that often works well. Your child might want to count floor tiles, go through math facts, or make a mental list of relatives or people who live on your street or kids who came to last year's birthday party, until the urge to cry passes. Calming self-talk (described earlier) can also be helpful. As a last resort, your child may need to take a quick trip to the bathroom to calm down. Once your child is feeling less upset, it's easier to use problem-focused coping strategies, such as fixing whatever is broken, making a different choice, or asking for help.

If you know your child is heading into a situation that often triggers tears, you may want to talk beforehand about what to do. For instance, if your child routinely cries during soccer games, work together to identify the specific circumstances that might trigger tears (for example, a teammate fails to block a goal) and plan specific coping options (for example, tell the teammate, "Nice try" or remember that it's more important to be a good sport than to win the game). If your child tends to burst into tears at school when the teacher's directions aren't clear, have your child prepare to cope by practicing raising a hand and saying, "I don't understand. Could you please explain what I need to do?"

Be sure to acknowledge the times when your child is able to refrain from crying in public about a minor situation that has evoked tears in the past. You could say something like, "That shows a lot of maturity to be able to hold it together, even though you were disappointed. How did you manage not to cry?" Also acknowledge change over time in moving past the crying habit. For instance, you could say, "Mrs. Murphy says you haven't cried at all this week in school! You're getting good at managing problems without letting them get to you! How are you doing this?" Knowing that they can do more than cry can be empowering for children.

SHOW THE WAY

Our children watch and learn from how we handle our feelings. Unless we demonstrate the ability to manage our own temper, we can't possible teach our children to manage theirs. Unless we show the courage and empathy required to resolve a disagreement with a friend, we can't expect our kids to learn to work things out with their peers. So think carefully about how you can model for your child healthy ways of coping with feelings.

Demonstrate Compassion

If someone is rude to you—maybe a stranger cuts in front of you in line, or a store clerk is surly—talk to your child later about what happened. Admit that you didn't like it, but offer some possible explanations for the rude behavior. "Maybe she didn't see me." "Maybe he was tired or having a bad day."

Give Yourself a Time-Out

The next time you feel furious with your child, announce, "I'm too mad to talk about this right now. I'm going to take a break to calm down before I say something I'll regret. We'll deal with this situation when I'm feeling calmer."

Choose Appropriate Confidants

Because bright kids' questions and vocabulary seem mature, we can sometimes forget that they're still just kids. If you are coping with serious difficulties, such as marital problems, health problems, or job instability, be careful what you say in front of your child. You don't necessarily need to keep the issue a secret, but you need to make careful judgments about how much information to share. Your child doesn't need to know all the details or every bad thing that might happen. If you need to talk things over with someone, choose an adult confidant and wait until your child is out of earshot. Beware of kids eavesdropping.

Share Stories of Your Struggles

Think of times when you've faced difficulties in the past. Talk with your child about how you coped, what you learned, and what it took to get through the hard times. You may also want to share stories about struggles that your parents or grandparents faced. These kinds of "family legends" can be inspiring to children. They make it clear that everyone faces challenges, and they also send important messages about courage, perseverance, and grace under adversity.

Some children tend to have strong emotional reactions. For these kids, learning to cope with feelings is especially important. Often this involves understanding the connection between thoughts and feelings. When children are able to perceive events and actions in a less judgmental or more compassionate way, they are less likely to become intensely upset. Coping with feelings also requires strategies for tolerating frustration and solving problems. When kids know how to soothe themselves and communicate effectively with others, they are better equipped to handle whatever life throws at them.

In the next chapter, we look at ways to help children cope with winning, losing, and working together with their peers.

$$\boxed{\text{CHAPTER 4}}$$

HANDLING COOPERATION AND COMPETITION

How Does Your Child Fit in a Group?

 Does your child

- Have trouble compromising?
- Tend to boss other kids around?
- Dismiss other children's ideas or wishes as "stupid"?
- Annoy others by turning everything into a competition?
- Avoid even mildly competitive activities?
- Feel extremely anxious before competitive events?
- Behave like a sore loser?
- Act disdainful of peers' efforts?
- Refuse to work in the areas where a sibling or parent has been successful?

Imagine a group of kids playing tag. First, they have to cooperate to agree on the rules. How far can they run? Is there a base? What happens after someone is tagged? Then they compete to decide who will be It. But they need to cooperate to agree on the decision process. Will it be the last person to yell "Not It," or will they use "Eenie Meenie Minie Mo"? Then there's competition as the players run away from the tagger. The game won't work unless everyone tries hard to win. But there might be cooperation as players rescue each other. Also, if someone is It for too long, another player might volunteer to be the tagger or the tagger's helper, to make the game more interesting. The game is fun for everyone only if the competition is fairly even.

Cooperation and competition are interwoven in a lot of what children do. These are among the most important and most difficult skills kids need to learn. Although cultural background can influence which of these two skills is harder for a particular child to master, children from all backgrounds need to learn to handle both. On the one hand, kids who veer too far in the aggressive, "Me! Me! Me!" direction will quickly find themselves on the outside of a group. On the other hand, kids who are afraid to venture beyond the group may have trouble finding their own path. Helping children learn to slide easily back and forth between cooperation and competition is key for enabling them to work and play with others.

PROVING THEIR WORTH

For many bright children, cooperation and competition are particularly difficult because they attach too much meaning to how well they do. This makes the stakes too high. They can't participate in games or projects in a relaxed way because they think they constantly have to prove themselves. They can't just play a game for fun, because victory seems vitally important and defeat feels crushing.

The Social and Emotional Costs of Excessive Performance Focus

When bright children focus too much on performance, it can give them a one-dimensional view of both themselves and others. They live as if there were a giant and very public scoreboard rating their performance at all times. They make things harder on themselves because they have trouble asking for or accepting help. They crave recognition, but they're constantly on guard against the shame of failure. To them, performing poorly isn't just a temporary setback; it feels like a humiliating exposure of weakness or a scary loss of control.

Performance-focused kids often extend their harsh judgments to others. They dismiss less capable children as "stupid" or "useless." They're intolerant of others' mistakes, especially when they see these as jeopardizing their own work. They're apt to elbow other children aside in order to do things their way, so peers resent them. On the flip side, they often feel jealous of rivals whom they see as threats.

Activities involving cooperation or competition tend to evoke strong negative emotions for these children: intense anxiety, self-righteous rage, disdain, dejection, envy, bitterness, shame . . . In contrast, their satisfaction with victories is fleeting— their imagined scoreboard is still there, and the score could change in a downward direction at any moment.

Some bright children find group activities so painful that they actively avoid them. But that's not really a good option, because both cooperation and competition are part of life.

Doing Well and Doing the Right Thing

So, what can parents do to help children cope? How can we help them find the line between healthy ambition and unhealthy preoccupation with performance?

Because cooperation and competition tend to bring up intense emotions in bright children, it's often hard to get them to try or even consider alternative responses. When they see another child only as a threat or a source of irritation, they tend to dismiss all suggestions about getting along.

We believe that the answer lies in helping smart kids balance their focus on doing well with an emphasis on doing the right thing. This involves cultivating their awareness of other people's feelings and the impact of their behavior on others. It's not always possible to "win," but we always have the option of behaving in ethical, respectful, responsible, and compassionate ways. We make our mark on the world, not just through our accomplishments, but also through how we treat others whose lives we touch. As Richard Weissbourd, author of *The Parents We Mean to Be*, points out, "Achievement is only one theme in the larger composition of a life." Seeing cooperation and competition in a broader context can enable bright children to approach these tasks in a more relaxed and competent manner. Having a caring view of others can also open the door to being less hard on themselves.

 ## STEVEN: INSISTING ON HIS WAY

"No! That's not how it should be!" Steven yelled.

Mrs. Armstrong hurried over to the table where Steven and three other classmates were making a model of a dinosaur. "What's the problem here?" she asked.

"Steven says we have to use *his* dinosaur legs," Martha complained. "He won't let anybody else help make the dinosaur. Since there are four legs and four kids, we should each get to make one."

"That doesn't even look like a dinosaur leg!" Steven insisted. "And who ever heard of a dinosaur with four different legs? That's just stupid."

"You're not the boss of us, Steven!" Martha insisted.

"Steven, this is a group project," Mrs. Armstrong interjected. "You need to work together as a team."

"But they want to wreck it!" Steven wailed. "We're supposed to be making a model of Diplodocus, and that leg doesn't even look like a Diplodocus leg. It looks like it belongs on a chicken!"

"What would be a fair solution?"

"I just want to do my own dinosaur!" Steven moaned.

❦

Bright children tend to have strong views about how things *should* be done. Steven is correct in that, ideally, a dinosaur's legs should match. However, the artistic and anatomical ideal is not the only issue in this scenario. Steven also needs to consider the other children's feelings and the situational context, which is an assigned group project. Working with fellow students who are less capable can be frustrating for smart kids. However, to survive in school, work, and life, they need to learn how to work with others.

The Challenge of Group Work

Teachers tend to talk about group work romantically, enthusing about how incorporating everyone's ideas will result in a more wonderful product. To bright children, these comments seem absolutely false. They are convinced that they could do a better job on their own, and they're probably right.

Smart kids tend to believe in meritocracy, but they often lack the maturity to temper this belief with compassion. Their focus is on having *the best* person produce *the best* product, and they believe everyone else should just stay out of the way. Although their words may come across as mean or arrogant, that's usually not their intention. In most instances, these remarks stem from a narrowness of focus. Because they see the quality of the product as the only goal, they overlook or dismiss other considerations, so they're apt to treat less able classmates as obstacles. Like a horse wearing blinders, they charge single-mindedly toward their goal. They truly expect adults and peers to be delighted by their product, and they're baffled by the negative reactions their behavior elicits.

Focus on Process as Well as Product

Bright children need to learn that *a good product can never make up for a bad process*. Even if Steven manages to produce a museum-quality dinosaur replica, his classmates and teacher will be unhappy with him because he elbowed his teammates aside. You may want to explain to your child that in the adult workplace, if employers have a choice between a brilliant worker who upsets other employees versus a less brilliant worker who gets along with everyone, they will *always* choose the one who gets along. That may not seem fair, but employees who make others unhappy are costly to a company.

If your child tends to complain about having to work with others, sympathize about the difficulty of working in a group, but also emphasize the importance of getting along. This is a critical life skill. Group projects give your child a chance to learn and practice it.

STRATEGIES TO HELP YOUR CHILD LEARN TO COOPERATE

Group work doesn't come naturally for most kids. Being part of a group requires being able to recognize and respond appropriately to other people's needs. It also sometimes means putting the good of the group ahead of their own wishes. This takes maturity that children achieve only gradually. Here are some strategies you can use to help your child learn to cooperate.

Encourage Thinking About Fair Play

Elementary school children talk and think a lot about fairness. If you watch children on a playground, you'll see that a great deal of their play involves discussions about what is or isn't fair. Often these discussions take up more time than the actual game! The focus on fairness represents an early stage of moral thinking. It can prompt a tempering of self-interest, as children learn to balance "What I want" versus "What's fair."

Sometimes it helps to frame the conflict clearly. If you hear your child arguing with a sibling, neighbor, or friend, you could say, "You want this. They want that. What could you do that would be fair for everyone?" Stating both positions is important, because it recognizes and gives legitimacy to both perspectives.

You may need to be persistent. Your child is likely to respond to such statements by insisting more adamantly on the rightness of his or her perspective. Acknowledge the vehemence of your child's opinion, but restate the problem in terms of fairness. You could say, "You feel very strongly that it should be done that way, but they feel equally strongly that everyone should be able to participate. What would be a fair solution?" or "Yes, I can understand how it would be easier to just do what you want, but right now we need to figure out a solution that's fair to everyone." If either party suggests a solution, say to the other person, "I know that's not exactly what you want, but can you accept it?" If that child says no, ask, "Then what's your suggestion for a fair solution?" If the children still can't come up with any alternatives, you can ask leading questions, such as, "If you want that, what can you offer them?" "What would be a way to divide it?" or "How could you take turns?"

Whenever time permits, be willing to tolerate the healthy struggle as your child first balks at the need to consider others' wants, then resists letting go at all of what he or she wants, then wrestles with considering possible compromises. It may be more efficient to simply tell children, "Fine. You do this. You do that," but doing so deprives them of the learning opportunity of coming up with their own solution. The mental thrashing needed to accept the necessity of compromise and to negotiate alternatives is an important exercise in moral thinking that supports moral development. So, when possible, try to act as a mediator rather than as an arbitrator.

Once the kids arrive at a fair solution, be sure to acknowledge the difficulty of resolving disagreements. "Compromising is hard. That took a lot of maturity to come up with a solution you can all accept."

Describe Ways to Contribute to Group Morale

There are many ways to contribute to a group. Coming up with ideas and actually carrying out the work are ones that bright children tend to do readily. However, children like Steven are often unaware of another essential aspect of group participation: contributing to group morale. This means ensuring that each member of the group feels valued and also making the work as enjoyable as possible for everyone.

The following checklist describes ways to contribute to group morale. Which strategies has your child tried? Which strategies has your child seen other kids do? Encourage your child to pick one or two to try out in school and observe how others react. Specific plans about when and with whom to try these will make it more likely that they'll actually occur.

◎　Ask other children's opinions. "What do you want to do?" "What do you think?"
◎　Listen carefully to other children's comments without arguing.
◎　Agree with other children's suggestions. "Good idea!"
◎　Thank other children for their effort. "Thanks! You did a lot of work on that!"
◎　Work cheerfully without complaining.
◎　Offer to share the most fun parts of the project. "Let's do that together."
◎　Express enthusiasm for the project. "This is fun!"
◎　Offer to compromise. "How about if we do it partly your way and partly my way?"
◎　Give in graciously if others disagree. "Okay, if that's what you all want, that's what we'll do."
◎　Ignore others' small mistakes or minor imperfections.
◎　Ask permission before correcting other children's work.
◎　Compliment other children's work. "That looks great!"

Emphasize Kindness and Human Dignity

If you don't talk to your child about the importance of kindness and the fact that every human being deserves to be treated respectfully, who will? This is a moral issue. Parents sometimes feel awkward discussing morality, but bright children need to hear this message. High ability does not confer the right to step on others by being rude or cruel. Smart kids need to learn from caring adults where the lines are. Tell your child, "It's not okay to call him stupid and say his work is bad," or "It's not kind to complain publicly about having to work with them."

Identify "Team-Busting" Behavior and Alternatives

Ask your child, "What's the difference between a team and a group?" Your child might mention a shared goal or mutual support. Explain to your child that whether a bunch of people is a team or just a group depends on how each person acts. The figure shows four examples of kids who act as team-busters. These aren't bad kids, but they haven't learned critical team-work skills. Read each character's comments aloud and see if your child can predict the impact of those remarks on the other group members. Have your child suggest what the characters should do instead that would be team building rather than team busting.

Seek Alternatives to Arguing

Dale Carnegie once wrote, "You can't win an argument . . . if you lose it, you lose it; and if you win it, you lose it." See if your child can explain what that quotation means. What do people lose when they win an argument? How does the loser of the argument feel? How does it affect the relationship?

Bright children who are very verbal often relish arguing. They seek to overpower others with their words, by talking faster, louder, or more forcefully. Focused purely on the "rightness" of

How does the way these characters act affect team members? What should they do instead?

Negative Ned

"That's a dumb idea."
"It'll never work."
"This is so stupid."
"I hate doing this."

Lumpish Louise

"Whatever."
"I guess so."
"I don't know."
  (Sighs and rolls her eyes.)

Bossy Bert

"Okay, I'm in charge. You do this! You do that!"
"My way is best!"
"You have to, or I won't be your friend."
"I'm telling!"

**Glued-Together
Gail and Greta**

"We only want to work with each other."
"No, we're going to do our own thing."
"We're our own team."
"After this, we're going to do something
  really fun without you."

their position, they dismiss or fail to notice the resentment their steamroller tactics generate.

There are certainly times when it's important to stick to our principles regardless of popular opinion. When we know something is ethically wrong or contrary to our personal values, it doesn't make sense to just go along with the crowd. But these situations are rare, particularly in elementary school.

So what can your child do instead of arguing? Here are three possibilities:

1. *Ask questions.* Conflict means that two people see a situation differently. Genuinely trying to understand how another person views a situation not only diffuses hostility but also can pave the way toward solutions. Asking questions like "What do you want to do?" "What's most important to you?" or "Which matters to you more?" might help your child understand the other child's perspective.

2. *Suggest a compromise.* Explain to your child that a compromise means doing partly what you want and partly what the other person wants. It respects the wishes of both people, but neither one gets exactly what he or she wants.

3. *Give in graciously.* Sometimes, to preserve a relationship or out of caring for the other person, the right thing to do is to just give in. "Okay, since this matters to you a lot, we'll do it your way." Giving in can be an act of generosity—a gift to a friend.

Teach Dispute Resolution Rituals

When people work or play together, disagreements are inevitable. Fortunately, children have a lot of rituals for handling disagreements. Flipping a coin, playing Rock-Paper-Scissors, picking a number between one and a hundred, and using "Eenie Meenie Minie Mo" are all examples of this kind of ritual. Practice these at home so that your child is familiar with them and can use or even suggest them to resolve disputes with peers.

Discuss True Leadership

Many bright children love the idea of being a leader. However, they tend to have an immature fantasy of leadership as issuing orders and having others leap to obey. Their peers are not likely to go along with this view for long, if at all.

Talk to your child about the characteristics of true leaders listed here. See if your child can come up with examples of true leaders he or she has met—perhaps a teacher, coach, scout leader, or peer who demonstrates these qualities. Ask your child for examples of these qualities or tell about leaders you've known. You may even want to read biographies about great leaders together and look for instances of these qualities. Ask how your child could apply the leadership qualities to a current group situation.

◎ *True leaders are good at building a connection with others.* People follow leaders who understand and care about their concerns. True leaders know that in order to lead, they first have to join with the group. The relationship is the source of their influence.

◎ *True leaders listen before they speak.* Listening carefully to others enables leaders to have more informed responses. They recognize that they can build upon others' observations and suggestions.

◎ *True leaders ask good questions.* Often, the most effective way to influence people is to ask the right questions so that they come to the answers themselves.

◎ *True leaders value others' contributions and bring out the best in others.* When people feel that they are contributing to a solution, they have a greater investment in making it work. True leaders are good at spotting and drawing upon others' capabilities, which makes people feel like valued members of the team.

◎ *True leaders work at least as hard if not harder than their followers.* Leaders who roll up their sleeves and dive into the collective work can inspire others by example. They demonstrate through their actions, "We're in this together."

ANITA:
BEING A SORE LOSER

"1 . . . 2 . . . 3 . . . 4! Sorry! Your guy has to go back to start!" Carmen gloated.

"No fair! You're mean!" Anita complained.

"Well, you landed on my guy just a few minutes ago!"

"Yeah, but you didn't have to get me! You could have moved your other guy."

"But you're winning!" Carmen protested. "I have to try to catch up. That's how you play!"

Anita shoved the game board, knocking over all the pieces.

"Hey, why'd you do that?" Carmen yelled.

"I don't want to play this anymore. It's a stupid game."

Many children have trouble handling winning and losing. Developmentally, children can't grasp the idea of "playing by the rules" until they are around five years old, and most children aren't reliably capable of being gracious losers until about age nine. However, by first or second grade, winning-and-losing games are a big part of children's interactions.

Why Is Losing So Hard for Kids?

Losing is hard for kids because it makes them feel powerless. They tried, they hoped, they thought they would win . . . but they didn't. Losing is like not getting their way on something that matters. They feel hurt, angry, and unjustly deprived. Like Anita, children who are sore losers cry, "No fair!"

Because children generally live in the present, the disappointment of losing can feel unbearable. That's why Anita knocked over the game. Cheating, arguing, tantrums, changing the rules midgame, and quitting all seem like reasonable strategies to a child who believes that losing is intolerable. Kids reach an important milestone in learning to handle defeat when they realize that both winning and losing are temporary states.

For some children, losing is painful because they attach too much significance to it. They quickly jump from "I lost" to "I'm no good." Adult reassurances that "It's just a game!" don't penetrate. To them, the loss feels like a judgment that they are somehow flawed and undeserving. Their struggles with losing don't usually translate into empathy when they are victors. Children who have a hard time being gracious losers usually also have trouble being gracious winners.

Parent Reactions to Children's Winning and Losing

How we, as parents, react to our children's competitions can influence their perspective on winning and losing. If we care too deeply about whether or not our children win, the weight of our feelings can make it harder for them to take competition in stride. If we respond by feeling embarrassed or annoyed when our kids cry after losing a game, we may add to their upset by making them feel our criticism on top of their own disappointment. If we try too hard to protect our children from disappointment by avoiding all situations involving winning and losing, we communicate that competition is dangerous. Being able to tolerate losing is a skill that emerges gradually for most children. Ideally, we need to strike a middle ground between accepting our children's distress about losing while also helping them learn to cope with that distress.

STRATEGIES TO HELP YOUR CHILD COPE WITH WINNING AND LOSING

Children need to learn how to respond appropriately to winning and losing. Explain to your child that we can't always win the game, but we can always win the fun. Winning the fun means staying calm no matter what the outcome of the game, and just focusing on enjoying the other player's company. Here are some ideas about how to help your child cope with competitive activities.

Recite a Verse About Winning and Losing

If your child is eight or under, try reciting "The Winning and Losing Poem" together. You may even want to help your child memorize it. Make the recitations fun by speaking dramatically or inventing silly movements to go with the words. You could also type up the verse, have your child decorate the paper, and post it on your refrigerator as a reminder.

> *The Winning and Losing Poem*
>
> I wish that I'd won, but I'll handle the loss.
> I'll finish the game up without getting cross.
> We spent time together and did something fun.
> It just doesn't matter which one of us won.
>
> Like quick summer breezes that gust and blow past,
> Both winning and losing are things that don't last.
> I'll try again next time and maybe I'll win.
> For now I'll just tell you, "Good game!" with a grin.

If your child won't participate, you can still wander around reciting it enthusiastically yourself or try teaching the verse to a younger sibling. Hearing it often enough—willingly or unwillingly—will cause the verse to stick in your child's head. Your child will at least know the expected response to a game, even if he or she can't always follow through.

Teach Good Sportsmanship

Here is a list of sportsmanship mistakes. See if your child can suggest a better way to handle each situation. Ask your child to explain why these aren't good choices and what the person should have done instead. Encouraging children to think through situations helps them process the ideas more deeply than if they are just told the answers.

Examples of Bad Sports—What Should They Do Instead?

1. Marvin knocks the board game, scattering all the pieces, because he's losing and doesn't want to play anymore.
2. Brendon says "Hah, hah!" every time Mike's game piece gets sent back to home.
3. Chen doesn't like the card she picked, so, even though it's against the rules, she puts it back and picks another one.
4. Kevin argues that the four-square ball was on the line, even though it was really out, because he wants to continue playing.
5. Jose is losing, so he accuses Miguel of cheating.
6. Natalie says to her friend, "I'm a lot better than you are at this game." When her mom says, "That's not a nice thing to say," Natalie insists, "Well, it's true!"
7. Quentin wants to change the rules in the middle of the game so that he won't be behind.
8. Sasha starts crying when Maria takes her ace during a card game of War. She says Maria is mean.

Read Books About Sports Together

Whether or not your child is interested in playing team sports, fictional books about sports can be a great resource for learning about cooperation and competition. These books convey the excitement and fun of competition, the value of cooperating with teammates, and the importance of being a good sport. They are a vicarious way for your child to work through issues of winning and losing. They are also a way to familiarize your child with popular sports, which can be important for relating to peers.

Reading these books together can prime your child's interest in sports and also provide opportunities for discussion. Remember to ask more than you tell in order to get your child thinking. Be careful not to let the discussion diminish the pleasure of the story. Some books to try are those by Matt Christopher or Mike Lupika. These cover a wide range of sports, from common ones like baseball and football to more unusual sports like gymnastics and horseback riding.

Gradually Increase Tolerance for Losing

The best way to help your child learn to handle winning and losing is to give your child lots of practice doing so. If your child is sensitive in this area, proceed gradually. Use what you know about your child's current coping abilities to decide at which of the following steps to begin. Your goal is to increase your child's tolerance rather than to elicit lots of upset.

Step 1: Play "Beat Your Own Record" Introduce your child to the pleasure that can come from taking on a challenge, by creating opportunities for your child to beat his or her own performance. For example, you could use chalk on a sidewalk to mark how far your child can jump and encourage your child to jump farther. You could also use a stopwatch to time your child doing some activity and encourage your child to try to do it faster or longer. The timed activity could be anything your child considers fun or interesting: holding his or her breath, running an obstacle course, jumping on a pogo stick, or doing math facts. Do this enough times that your child sometimes wins and sometimes loses at beating the record.

Step 2: Play Cooperative Games Choose games where you and your child have to work together to accomplish some goal that is not guaranteed. This allows your child to experience losing occasionally, but with the shelter of your company. It also gives you the chance to model acknowledging disappointment without being devastated by a loss. You could say something like, "Rats! We were so close! Oh, well. We can't win 'em all. Let's try again."

Family Pastimes (www.familypastimes.com) is a company that specializes in well-designed cooperative games. Two of our favorites are Harvest Time and Sand Castles.

Step 3: Play Small-Team Competitive Games   One option is to create two teams of one adult and one or more children, so that children have a parental ally to help cope with the game outcome. "Kids against the grown-ups" is another option that can be a lot of fun because this arrangement makes a loss less threatening and a victory more thrilling. If you don't have enough family members to create teams, invite another family over to play. Charades and Taboo are good possibilities.

Step 4: Play Short One-on-One Competitive Games   Short games allow your child to try again quickly. Choose games with an element of luck or give yourself a handicap, so that your child has an equal chance of winning or losing. Blink is a two-minute, fast-moving, and fun card game that works well for this. Kerplunk, Connect Four, and Jenga are also possibilities. If your child starts to fuss, put down your cards (or game piece), look disappointed, and say, "We can only play while you're being a good sport." If your child pulls it together, continue playing. Otherwise, if your child continues to fuss or fusses a second time, end the game and say calmly, "We'll try again another day." Don't let tears, whining, or shouted protests convince you to continue playing.

Don't allow your child to cheat. Calmly remind your child, "The rule is . . ." or "You need to play by the rules." Other kids won't put up with tantrums or cheating, so you'd be giving your child the wrong message about social expectations if you did.

Often, in order to avoid their kids getting upset, parents let them win. You may feel mean trying to beat your child at a game, but it's important that you try to win with kids ages six and up.

Playing against you is the safest possible context for your child to learn that losing is tolerable. It gives your child a chance to experience that the outcome of the game doesn't change your love.

Step 5: Play Longer Competitive Games and Involve More People   Have a family game night involving just your family or your family plus friends. Choose an active game without much waiting around, such as Uno Attack or Apples to Apples. If you have guests, you may want to let your child help choose whom to invite. Before game night starts, ask your child questions to review appropriate behavior (for example, "So, what will you do if you have to pick up a whole bunch of cards?" "What will you say if someone else wins?"). Let your child help plan a postgame treat for everyone.

Step 6: Involve Your Child in Sports   If your child has any athletic interest or ability, consider signing him or her up for a YMCA sports class or a recreational or travel league. Sports are a big part of many children's social lives. Baseball, soccer, and basketball are easy to practice in informal ways, with a minimum of equipment. Youth sports can teach kids about practicing hard to improve skills, doing better next time, and being part of a team. For example, if your child is on a hockey team, the coach will emphasize that players need to know when they should pass the puck rather than taking the shot themselves. The coach will also insist that players be supportive of teammates, especially when mistakes happen. Sports teams also usually have postgame rituals, such as giving everyone on the opposing team a high-five, that encourage good sportsmanship. You may want to talk with your child before each game to review coping strategies, so that your child is prepared to be a good sport.

Have a Frank Discussion About Academic Cheating

When winning feels critical and losing seems intolerable, cheating may feel like a viable alternative. Cheating at games can cause social problems, but cheating in school can have larger ramifications.

Statistics about academic cheating are alarming: roughly one-third of elementary school children admit to cheating. Cheating begins as early as first grade and escalates through middle school and beyond. In one survey, 80 percent of high-achieving high school students admitted to cheating on tests. Cheating among young children typically reflects impulsivity or a lack of clear understanding about what behaviors are against the rules. However, by age eight or nine, children are capable of deliberate cheating, so it's important to have some frank and specific conversations about this issue.

You may want to start by asking if your child has ever seen or heard about someone cheating. Your child will probably relish anonymously reporting other kids' crimes. This gives you an opportunity to talk about specific kinds of cheating. For instance, you might say something like, "A lot of kids don't realize that letting a friend copy their answers counts as cheating." See if your child can explain why cheating is not a good idea. Ask questions to help your child think of reasons besides "Because you'll get in trouble." For instance, you could ask, "How do people feel if they do well because of cheating compared to when they do well because of skill and hard work?" "How would other children feel if they found out someone had cheated?" "How does cheating affect learning?" "When people cheat once, does it make it more or less likely that they'll cheat again? Why?" "What would happen if everyone—plumbers, doctors, bus drivers, architects—cheated on tests?"

Sociologist Donald Cressey claims that three elements are necessary for corporate fraud to occur: (1) perceived opportunity, (2) perceived pressure, and (3) rationalization. These same elements are also very relevant for cheating. Teachers play a primary role in determining opportunity for cheating, but parents can help by drawing ethical lines regarding how much they help children with assignments. Parents can also influence how much academic pressure a child experiences by reacting mildly to successes and calmly and constructively to failures. However, the most important thing that parents can do to minimize cheating is to target rationalizations directly.

Explain to your child that a rationalization is an excuse for doing something wrong. Ask questions to help your child think deeply about typical rationalizations for cheating. With younger children, you may want to bring up just one or two excuses. For instance, you might say, "Some people say cheating is okay as long as you don't get caught. What do you think?" With older children, you may want to present some of the more sophisticated rationalizations listed here and see if your child can explain why they aren't true. Thinking these issues through won't guarantee that your child will refrain from cheating, but it can help your child be better prepared to resist temptation.

What's Wrong with These Rationalizations?

"Everyone cheats, so it's no big deal"

"Cheating doesn't hurt anyone."

"Since other people cheat, I have to cheat too, to keep up."

"The teachers don't care about cheating because they don't prevent it."

"I was just trying to help my friends by letting them copy."

"I'll just do it this one time."

"I don't care about this class, so it's okay to cheat."

"I don't like this teacher, so it's okay to cheat."

MISHA:
FEARING COMPETITION

"I hate Wednesdays!" Misha moaned to her mother. "I wish I could stay home from school every Wednesday."

"Why?" her mother asked.

"Wednesday is Math Around the World day. Two kids stand up, and they see who answers the math fact fastest. Whoever wins keeps going and has to try to beat the next person and the next person and the next person, and get all the way around the class. It's stupid. I hate it!"

"But Misha, you're good at math. I bet you can do very well at that game."

"Well, I hate everyone looking at me. And sometimes I get nervous and I forget, and then I have to sit down. And if I remember the math fact, then I have to do it again. And the other kids won't like me because I made them sit down. Once I beat Caroline, and she looked really grumpy when she had to sit down. And anyway, Leila usually wins, and she's always saying 'Easy peasy! Everyone knows that!'"

"How do the other kids in your class feel about Math Around the World?"

"Some of them like it. Some of them say, 'Yay!' when Ms. Martin says we're going to do it. But I hate it!" Misha started to cry. "I don't want to play it. It's a stupid game! Can you write me a note and say I don't have to play?"

Misha's pain is real, but no, her mother shouldn't write her a note to get her out of playing the game. Misha's mom could say something like, "Playing that game is hard for you" or "You feel very uncomfortable when you have to compete with your classmates." Telling her, "It's no big deal" or "That's silly; you shouldn't feel that way" won't help, because competition is genuinely anxiety provoking for Misha. Nevertheless, it's something she needs to learn how to handle. Allowing Misha to conclude, "I can't cope with competition" is much too limiting. She may not enjoy it, but she has to learn to tolerate it. Like it or not, competition is part of life.

Fear of Competition

Some bright children are competition-phobic. The prospect of being judged, and perhaps found wanting, is so anxiety provoking that they actively try to avoid even mild forms of competition. They may refuse to participate or refuse to try. Misha is afraid of both winning and losing. She dreads the possibility of losing, but she also worries that if she wins, she is being mean to the other child. This simple math contest has somehow taken on too much significance. It's as if it entails a choice between destroying others or being destroyed herself.

When Anxiety Interferes with Performance

Sometimes children become so anxious in competitive situations that they can't do their best. They freeze up. They feel exposed, and they just want to hide. These children view anxiety as a stop signal. If they feel at all anxious, they believe they should get out of the triggering situation as quickly as possible and avoid it at all costs in the future.

But a little bit of anxiety is actually helpful. It focuses our attention, marshals our strength, and prepares us to do something difficult. As parents, we want to help our kids be energized rather than immobilized by performance-related anxiety.

STRATEGIES TO HELP YOUR CHILD HANDLE FEARS ABOUT COMPETITION

Children like Misha need to learn strategies for managing the anxiety that competition elicits in them. They also need to gain perspective so that they can more comfortably accept competition and recognize its potential benefits. Winning helps children build confidence that they can succeed; losing gives them the opportunity to learn that they can cope with disappointment. The challenge of competition can also be fun, because it allows children to stretch themselves. Here are some strategies to help your child develop a healthier view of competition and lessen performance anxiety.

Explain the Anxiety-Performance Curve

To explain the relationship between performance and anxiety, tell your child to imagine a baseball player who is filled with a great deal of anxiety. You may even want to act out or have your child act out how that player looks. He's clutching the bat tightly to himself. His whole body is stiff and tight. He's staring with gritted teeth and wide-eyed apprehension at the pitcher. Ask your child, "What will happen when the pitch comes?" Because this player is so anxious, his arms will be too tense to get a full, strong swing.

Now have your child imagine a baseball player up at bat who has absolutely no anxiety. He's holding the bat limply, maybe with only one hand, resting it on his shoulder. He's gazing at the clouds or checking his fingernails, and not really paying attention to the game. What will happen with this player when the pitch comes? He'll either get hit by the ball or, at best, just bat the ball weakly with droopy arms.

What about a baseball player with a medium amount of anxiety? He's pumped! His body is poised, but not tense. Knees bent, leaning over the plate, he's alert, concentrating on the game. When the pitch comes, he's primed and ready to knock it out of the park!

The dark curve in the illustration shows the relationship between anxiety and performance. The small-dashed line shows that at high levels of anxiety, performance is poor—that's the first, tense baseball player. Similarly, at low levels of anxiety, performance is also poor—that's the second, bored baseball player. The larger-dashed line shows that the best performance (the highest point on the curve) corresponds to moderate levels of anxiety—that's the third player who was ready to hit a home run.

How anxiety affects performance:

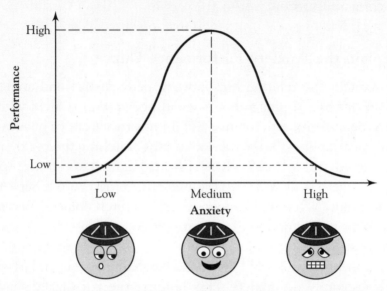

Research consistently shows that people who are moderately anxious about a task generally perform best on it. So when your child notices that she is starting to feel anxious, remind her that that's okay. It's just the body's way of getting ready to do something hard.

Put Worries in Perspective

Children's worries grow along with their imaginations. As they get older, children become more able to envision dire possibilities, which leads them to have more varied and complex worries. Preschoolers worry about ghosts or monsters. Five-year-olds worry about getting physically hurt. Eight-year-olds worry about their own competence. From eight onwards, children increasingly worry about how their peers view them. When children can vividly picture a terrible situation, they may believe that it's likely to happen. Worries can loom as powerful and frightening thoughts that bleach the joy out of life.

Being able to put worries in perspective can make them seem more manageable. If you hear or sense that your child is worried about a competition (or other situation), ask, "What's the worst thing that could happen in this situation?" If your child comes up with lots of possibilities, you may need to make a list. Next, have your child decide *how bad* and *how likely* each worrisome outcome is.

To judge "badness," encourage your child to consider how life altering the event is in a negative way, rather than how subjectively distressing it seems. The death of a loved one would be truly horrible and drastically life altering. Events that don't really change anything of importance aren't that bad.

To judge likelihood, ask your child, "How many people do you know who've had this happen?" or "How many times has this happened to you in the past?" If your child can't think of many examples of past occurrences, then the event probably isn't very likely, even if your child can vividly imagine it.

Problems that are either not that bad or not that likely are not worth worrying about. Dwelling on nightmare scenarios that probably will never happen is draining and discouraging. With practice, most children can learn to quickly assess "How bad?" and "How likely?" This can help them let go of unwarranted fears.

In Misha's case, it's quite likely that she'll have to sit down, because everyone in the class except the winner ends up sitting down (likelihood = high). But this outcome isn't particularly bad, because the only thing that happens afterward is that the whole class moves on to the next subject (badness = low). Misha might also express the worry, "Caroline won't be my friend anymore if I do better than she does." If they are close friends, this could be pretty bad (badness = medium), but good friendships don't dissolve easily, so it's not likely to happen (likelihood = low).

You may also want to help your child come up with strategies to make a bad outcome less likely. For instance, reviewing math facts the night before a contest would make it less likely that Misha would have to sit down right away or that her mind would go blank when it's her turn.

Notice Examples of Gracious Losers and Friendly Rivals

When children fear outperforming others, in part this represents empathy, but in part it involves a projection of their own fears: because they would find it devastating to lose, they expect that others will, too. Observing examples of people feeling disappointed but not destroyed by a loss can help provide perspective. In Misha's case, her mother might encourage her to notice how other children react to losing the math game. Although some may appear upset, most probably take it in stride. She might also notice that some children say something like "Rats!" but are grinning when they sit down. They seem to enjoy the competition even though they lost.

As you read the news, keep your eyes open for examples of friendly rivals. Whether it's two athletes, two scientists, or two bakers, you may be able to find some quotations that you can read to your child, in which the competitors talk about how their rival inspires them to do their best and how they enjoy the back-and-forth of winning and losing with their rival.

The concession speeches of politicians can also provide good examples of gracious losing. Invariably, these speeches talk about "the good fight" and "how much we accomplished even though we lost." They acknowledge disappointment but also express hope, gratitude, and respect for the winning candidate.

Seek Out Just-for-Fun Competitions

Most communities offer a variety of low-key competitions. You may find contests involving coloring a picture, creating a slogan, decorating a bicycle, or rowing a boat made out of cardboard. If your child is very anxious about competition, start by just observing some of these, so your child can see that even though only one person won, lots of people had fun competing. Point out that the kids didn't have to be in the contest, but they chose to enter, despite knowing that the odds were against them winning. They did it because there was a chance that they might win, plus they thought it would be fun to try their best.

Next encourage your child to enter some of these contests, "just for the fun of it." If it's too hard for your child to enter alone, start with a parent-child team competition, and work up to solo competition. Laugh, smile, and celebrate the effort regardless of the outcome.

Look for Winning Role Models

Some sensitive children need permission to win. Girls, in particular, may feel ambivalent about outperforming peers because they worry that it's not "nice" to do so. At some level, they may have bought in to societal messages that succeeding in competition is unfeminine.

Look for winning role models for your child. Older children whom your child likes and admires—perhaps a cousin or neighbor—can be particularly effective role models. The role model should be five or more years older than your child. This large age gap minimizes rivalry and makes it clear that the other child's performance is a possible source of inspiration, rather than a standard of comparison. For the same reasons, it's usually best to look for a role model who is not a sibling. You and your family may want to attend the older child's art exhibit, play, spelling bee, or sports contest to cheer that child on. Tread delicately. Be very careful not to say or imply, "Why can't you be more like that wonderful child?!" Your goal is to expose your child to possibilities rather than to force a particular path. Emphasize that your family is attending the performance to support that child's efforts, which is a kind thing to do.

If you have the chance, ask the older child questions to elicit experiences and coping strategies related to competition. Voice the concerns that your child won't. For example, you might ask a young actor, "How do you manage pre-audition nervousness?" "Have you ever tried out for a play and not gotten the part you wanted? What did you do then?" "Have you and a friend ever competed for the same part? What happened?"

Ideally, you should find several older kids to observe, so that your child can see examples of coping with competition in a variety of domains. Observing several winning role models is also helpful to ensure that your child gets the message, "Here are options" rather than "Here's the *right* way." Let your child draw his or her own conclusions about how the role models' experiences might be relevant. Actively promoting "lessons" will backfire. If you pipe in with, "That's just like what happened to you! You should try doing what Samantha does!" your child will actively resist the prescribed coping strategies.

If appropriate older children aren't available, you may want to look for a relevant celebrity whom you think your child might admire. Again, a light touch works best. Don't tell your child, "You could be just like this famous person if you only tried!" That's too much pressure. Instead, merely express interest in the role model's path, and look for quotations about winning and losing that might be inspiring for your child.

For girls, Silvia Rimm's book *How Jane Won* is a great resource. It contains stories describing the life journeys of fifty-five successful women in a wide variety of fields. The book is written for adults, but you may want to read some of the stories aloud to your daughter. Many of the women specifically talk about how they coped with competition—finding the courage to put themselves forward, gaining confidence from victories, and picking themselves up to try again after defeats.

CRAIG:
DEALING WITH
COMPETITION IN THE FAMILY

"Did you see these grades Craig brought home?" Craig's father exclaimed. "A C in spelling? A D in social studies? What's the matter with him?"

"I don't understand it either," Craig's mother said, looking over the report card. "Jeffrey never got anything below a B+ at that age. Craig is just as smart if not smarter. There's no reason he can't do as well as his brother in school."

"Is he studying?"

"He says he is."

"Well, he's obviously not studying enough! I never got a C in my life! And he's only in elementary school! What's he going to do when the work gets harder in middle school and high school? I'm going to talk to him about this. This is just not acceptable."

"Well, don't be too rough on him. You know how he gets."

❧

Craig is a bright boy who seems to be opting out of academics. There could be a lot of reasons for this, but one possibility is that he is refusing to compete with the long shadows cast by his academically successful father and brother.

The Family Context of Achievement

The meaning of achievement within a family can be complicated, and it's often fraught with spoken or unspoken comparisons. Parents hope their children do as well or better than they did. Children compare themselves to what they perceive as parental expectations and to the actual performance of siblings and classmates. When kids feel that they don't measure up in a particular area of achievement or that the cost of that achievement is too high, they're apt to turn their backs on it.

When children come from a high-achieving family, it can be harder for them to find a healthy, balanced perspective on achievement. Even when accomplished parents or siblings don't explicitly apply pressure, their mere existence is something that children need to come to terms with somehow.

Withdrawing from Competition

Some children, like Craig, seem to withdraw from competition before they even try. They see the costs of high performance outweighing the benefits, although they rarely say this directly. On the basis of their fears or observations, they worry that

- Even if they try hard, their performance won't be good enough.
- If they perform well, parents or teachers will expect even more.
- If they do well, other kids won't like them, or they'll be perceived as uncool.
- Doing well requires giving up all fun and free time.

Hypercompetitiveness

Other children respond to a high-achieving family by becoming extremely competitive. For these kids, competition can become all-consuming. They may become excessively preoccupied with performance, even sacrificing relationships and personal happiness in their quest to be The Best. Socially, they often act in arrogant and condescending ways. They tend to brag and frequently invite comparisons. "What did you get?" "What's your score?" They are apt to bicker about grades or quibble about rules in games. They tend to alienate both peers and teachers, not because they are personally ambitious, but because they see everything in terms of winning and losing. This can make them come across as insensitive, petty, and annoying. Their unremitting competitiveness makes others not want to be around them.

STRATEGIES TO HELP YOUR CHILD COPE WITH COMPETITION WITHIN THE FAMILY

Intrafamily competition is a very tricky issue to navigate. Inevitably, some siblings are going to perform better than others, and it's unlikely that a child will achieve exactly the same way parents did. As kids develop, they glean what competition means for them and develop their own way of responding. Here are some ideas about how you could smooth the way for your child.

Don't Voice Comparisons Between Siblings

If you have two or more of anything, you'll probably compare them. That's human nature. But if you have two or more children, be careful to keep those comparisons silent.

Sometimes parents think that comparing one sibling to another will inspire a child to do better. It *never* works this way. Comparisons hurt. They make the kid with the short end of the comparison feel resentful and determined to be nothing like the glowing example. Comments like "You could do well in school, too, if you did your homework every night like Meredith," may be meant as encouragement, but they come across as condemnation.

Even positive comparisons are dangerous. Saying something like "Well, you're good at reading, and your brother is good at math" carries a terrible weight. A child can interpret this as "You're not allowed to have anything to do with math. That's your brother's turf." That's not how parents mean it, of course, but that's what kids hear.

Avoid the Fairness Trap

Almost all parents have heard accusations of "That's not fair!" from their children. Even if you carefully count out M&M'S of different colors, one kid is likely to complain, "His green ones are greener!" Falling into the fairness trap of trying to make everything equal for your children is a no-win game. In fact, it tends to compound rivalry because it encourages comparisons and suggests that differences are intolerable.

If the "unfairness" is not of your doing, respond to complaints with empathy, but without stepping in to make things "even."

Tell your child, "That sounds very frustrating. Do you need a hug?" Offer unlimited hugs, but stay above the fray regarding who gets the yellow cup. If both kids are complaining, say, "I'm sure you two can figure out something that's fair to everyone." Then walk away.

If your child accuses you of loving a sibling more, agree that you *don't* love your children equally. You love each of your children in his or her own way, so of course you don't treat them the same. Why would you love them the same when they are different people? Resist the temptation to list all the nice things you do for each child, because you don't want to encourage scorekeeping. Besides, justifying your past actions is neither necessary nor relevant. Instead, if your child seems to be looking for reassurance, list the things you love about him or her in particular. Focus on qualities that aren't performance related. For instance, you might give your child a hug and say, "You are the only that I love in a special Claudia way. I love how your eyes sparkle when you smile. I love how you comfort your little brother when he cries. I love how you laugh when we watch movies together and keep me company when I go grocery shopping on Saturdays."

Plan Responses to Competitive Sibling Taunting

Sometimes taunting between siblings can take the form of incessant competition. Typically, one sibling is more outwardly confident and tends to make disparaging comparisons, such as, "Hah, hah! I got to the corner first! I beat you! I win! Oh, yeah, I'm the best!"

The other sibling then wails loudly, "It wasn't a race! No fair! You didn't say we were racing! I don't want to race!"

Typically, parents will respond to this kind of scenario by scolding the taunting child and trying to reassure the wailing child that the victory is meaningless. This rarely works, however, because the taunting child feels powerful from being able to stir up a big reaction (from sibling and parent), and the wailing child, perceiving the sibling's satisfaction, gets caught up in the drama of defeat and urgently wants to steal the victory by recruiting adult support. It's important to keep in mind that neither child is coping appropriately with competition.

A more effective approach is to coach the wailing child privately about how to diffuse the competition. Tell that child to say calmly, "Congratulations." Practice this together so the wailing child is prepared for the next episode of taunting.

"I got there first."

"Congratulations."

"I got more."

"Congratulations."

"Mine is bluer."

"Congratulations."

When the big reaction fails to appear, the taunting child will find this game less entertaining. Meanwhile, the wailing child will experience a sense of strength and satisfaction from knowing how to handle the taunts and being able to refrain from getting sucked into meaningless rivalries.

Emphasize Being "Smart Enough"

Children's worlds are small, so their only standards of comparison are family members and classmates. This can lead to a distorted view of themselves. For instance, we know a family in which the younger child has an astronomical IQ—well over 160. His older sister has an IQ of "merely" 140. That's in the 99th percentile, but compared to her younger brother, she doesn't feel smart.

Help your child understand that comparisons are relative. Start by talking about physical size: Is your child big or little? The answer is, bigger than a toddler and smaller than a teenager, but *big enough* to do his or her favorite activities. Is your child's bedroom big or little? It's bigger than a closet and smaller than a gymnasium, but *big enough* to hold your child's bed, clothes, and favorite possessions. So size is not a yes-or-no question.

The same is true for smartness. Your child is definitely smarter than some people. However, the world is a very big place, so the odds are that there are at least ten people who are smarter than your child. Maybe a sibling is one of those ten people. Maybe your child won't meet any of those ten people until high school or college. It doesn't matter. The existence of those ten people doesn't change your child's abilities any more than the existence of gymnasiums changes the measurements of your child's bedroom. The important thing is that your child is *smart enough* to learn whatever he or she wants to learn. Ask your child, "What is it that you want to learn?" That's a much more interesting and important question than "Who is smarter?"

Discuss Similarities and Differences Within the Family

Siblings try to strike a balance between feeling like part of the family and having their own individual identity. One danger is that children might define their differences too sweepingly. For instance, a child might decide, "My sister's a good student, and I'm a good athlete," implying that school success is impossible for him and sports are impossible for her. So, for parents, the goal is to convey the message, "You belong" as well as the message, "You are special," and to help children define their differences in ways that are not too limiting.

One strategy for doing this is to get a large sheet of paper and, with your child's help, list family similarities and differences. Start with similarities and then discuss differences within those similarities. Your child's contributions will probably be trivial: "We all have brown eyes." "We all like pizza." Your contributions should be strategic: you want to assign ownership of important qualities to *all* family members, while allowing for individual expression of these core values. Think theme and variation. Below are some examples of family traits you may want to claim:

We all are smart (but we may show it in different ways).

We all like people (but we have different friends and like different kinds of social gatherings).

We all enjoy being active (but we have different hobbies).

We all are curious (but we wonder about different topics).

We all are kind (but we show our caring in different ways).

Encourage Siblings to Have Fun Together

The best antidote to sibling rivalry may be sibling fun. The opposite of sibling warmth isn't conflict but indifference. When siblings see each other as sources of fun, they're likely to feel less threatened by each other's successes. Toys and games that require more than one person can give your children a chance to interact in enjoyable ways. If your children aren't used to playing together, you may need to be involved in the game at first, but then pull out and let the kids continue. Having kids compete together against parents can also build sibling solidarity.

If your older child is going through an ornery stage, you may want to try hiring him or her to babysit a younger sibling (while you're around, doing something else) or to teach a younger sibling some skill. Pay a nominal amount (for example, $.25 per fifteen minutes), but emphasize that the older child will get paid only if the younger child has fun. This can bring out a kinder side to the older sibling, which will be reinforced by the enthusiasm of the younger sibling. It can also help the older child feel happy rather than threatened by the younger child's success.

Share a Fable

Rivalries within a family are often hard to talk about. Your child may be aware of resenting a sibling or "hating" a certain activity at which a parent or sibling excels, but be unable to articulate the reasons for these feelings or know how to cope with them.

Reading this fable to your child might help provide enough distance to see the issues clearly.

THE WEAVER'S SHADOW

Once there was a town that was famous for its weaving. People came from far and wide to buy the beautiful fabrics created by the townspeople.

Now in that town lived three sisters, who were the granddaughters of the most talented weaver the town had ever known. Their grandmother had long since passed away, but her weaving still held a place of honor in the town hall, where it was admired by one and all.

All three girls had been taught to weave by their beloved grandmother. They enjoyed weaving and worked hard to learn their craft, which is what everyone expected from them, as the granddaughters of the town's most famous weaver.

It was the custom in the town that when young people came of age, they would present a masterwork. The masterwork was a showcase of the young weavers' skill, and everyone would gather in the town hall to admire it.

When the oldest of the three sisters approached the age of presentation, she thought to herself, "I will create a weaving as beautiful as my famous grandmother's!" She studied the colors and patterns in her grandmother's work. She experimented with dyes, trying to get just the right shades. She wove, unwove, and rewove trying to get exactly the right interplay of threads.

On her birthday, she spread her weaving before the townspeople who had gathered to see it. "What lovely colors! What delicate stitching!" the townspeople exclaimed in delight. "Why, it's very similar to your grandmother's creation!" But the oldest sister didn't hear their praise. She looked at her weaving where it lay next to her grandmother's fabric, and she saw only the ways that it fell short of her model. She would not allow the townspeople to display her masterwork. Instead, she took it home and pulled it apart. After that, the oldest sister continued to weave, but in her heart she felt bitter. When people complimented her work, she only shook her head and said, "It could be better."

The next year, it was the second sister's turn to present. She saw the unhappiness of her older sister and vowed, "For my masterwork, I will create something that is nothing like my famous grandmother's weaving!" She too studied the colors and patterns in her grandmother's work, but she did so to ensure that she included not a single thread or stitch like her grandmother's.

On her birthday, the second sister spread her weaving before the townspeople who had gathered to see it. "What unusual colors! What unique patterns!" the townspeople exclaimed in delight. "It's so different from your grandmother's creation!" But the second sister also didn't hear their praise. She looked at her weaving where it lay next to her grandmother's fabric, and it seemed harsh and coarse to her. She had tried so hard to be different, but she'd ended up excluding all of her favorite colors and the delicate designs she had loved as a child. The second sister turned her back on her masterwork, and from that day forward she refused to weave. Although she sometimes felt sad when she thought about how she'd given up the weaving she used to love, she told herself it was worth it to avoid being compared to her grandmother.

Years passed until finally the youngest sister came of age. Like her sisters before her, she too studied her grandmother's work. She noticed that certain colors and patterns drew her eye, and she thought, "These I will make my own." She looked also at the vivid colors and dramatic patterns of the second sister's weaving and thought, "Here too is beauty that I can make my own." As she went about her day, she noticed the curve of a rock smoothed by the river, the glow of sunlight through leaves, the pattern of petals in a flower, and from all of these she drew inspiration. She worked long and hard on her masterwork, but she sang as she worked, and her mind was filled with images that she wanted to bring into her weaving.

On her birthday, the youngest sister spread her weaving before the townspeople who had gathered to see it. "How beautiful! It's just like your grandmother's work!" some of the townspeople exclaimed. But others said, "No, the loveliness of the weaving lies in how different it is from your grandmother's!" The townspeople argued back and forth. Was it the same? Was it different? Finally, they turned to the third sister to ask how she thought her work compared to her grandmother's. But the girl wasn't there. She wasn't interested in the debate. She'd already gone off, her head filled with ideas, to start her next weaving.

You can use this fable to open a conversation about comparisons between family members. Ask rather than tell, to help your child think through the issues. The questions here may help draw out relevant themes. Don't feel as though you have to ask every single question. Your goal is just to get your child thinking.

What does the title mean?

Why did the first sister try to do work just like her grandmother's?

Why did the second sister try to do work unlike her grandmother's?

Do you think the second sister made the right decision to give up weaving? Why or why not?

Which sister seems happiest? Why?

What advice would you give to the two older sisters?

The fable can also be an opportunity to share with your child your own experiences regarding comparisons. How rigid were the expectations in your family when you grew up? To what extent did you feel that you had to live up to a certain standard or reputation created by others? How did you discover your own path? An honest description of the wishes, worries, and struggles you had while growing up may help your child acknowledge feelings about being compared to family members. It's also a chance to offer reassurance that your affection doesn't have to be earned, because you love your child uniquely and unconditionally.

SHOW THE WAY

Cooperation and competition are issues that are relevant throughout life. In the best scenario, parents lead by example, demonstrating effective coping for their children.

Model Good Sportsmanship

What messages are you giving your child about the rivals and collaborators in your life? Do you talk respectfully about the contributions of the other committee members, or do you grumble that they are morons and you have to do everything yourself if you want it done right? Are you gracious when you lose, mentioning that you enjoyed or learned a lot from trying, or do you complain that the victor had unfair advantages? Are you and your spouse a good example of teamwork? How do you get along with your adult siblings? Your child is watching and learning from what you do.

Underreact to Your Child's Victories and Defeats

Make sure that your responses to your child's victories and defeats are smaller than your child's. Strong emotion from parents deflects attention away from children's experiences and make it harder for children to recognize and cope with their own feelings. That's not being supportive; it's upstaging your child. If you are ecstatic at the 100 percent grade on a test, it doesn't allow room for your child to be pleased. If you are angry at a poor performance, your child's reaction is eclipsed. Instead of saying, "I'm so proud!" or "I'm disappointed," comment on your child's feelings: "You must be very proud" or "I can see you're disappointed." It's your child's reactions that matter for moving forward.

Similarly, take a step back if you catch yourself worrying about your child's upcoming test, game, or performance, or "sizing up the competition" for your child. Children develop at different rates and in different ways. Long term, it really doesn't matter if your child is the best trumpet player in fourth grade. What matters more is your child's sense of satisfaction and determination to improve. Barring death, nothing that happens in childhood is an end point. Each victory or defeat is only a step along a child's life path, and we can't accurately predict where that path is going.

Have Interests Unrelated to Your Child

Of course we want to be loving, supportive parents, but a certain amount of benign neglect is good for kids. It gives them room to figure out how to solve problems and to discover their own feelings. It gives them freedom to move forward in some direction without constantly having to feel responsible for their parents' reactions.

Think carefully about what brings you a sense of personal satisfaction and let your child see you pursuing that interest. It could be work you find rewarding, a hobby you enjoy, or volunteer work you find meaningful. Living your own dreams makes it less likely that you will inadvertently live through your child.

Don't Measure Yourself by Your Child's Performance

We parents generally put a lot of effort into raising our children. We work hard and sacrifice so that our kids can do well; it's understandable that we'd want to see evidence that our efforts are paying off somehow. But this is a very dangerous train of thought, because it removes our children's ownership of their accomplishments and places it in our hands. Moreover, it creates an unstated expectation of payback that unfairly burdens our kids.

The hard reality is that there is absolutely nothing we can do to guarantee that our children will be successful. Not reading to them. Not paying for piano lessons or signing them up for soccer. Not checking their homework or providing tutoring. Not sending them to a special school. Each of these may be valuable in some circumstances, but ultimately our children's success will be influenced by many factors, including a lot of things that are outside of our control, such as our kids' peer relationships, mentors, personal choices, and luck. That's why this book emphasizes helping children develop coping skills, so that they are equipped to handle whatever life throws at them.

By all means do things for your children, but do them as a loving gift, not as an investment. The real rewards from raising children can't be measured in external accomplishments that impress the neighbors. Instead, they involve more subtle but profound benefits, such as experiencing the joy of giving to them, the tenderness of comforting them, the delight of shared laughter, and most of all the pleasure of watching and discovering how they bloom in their own unique way.

Cooperation and competition are entwined in most group activities. Children need to learn to develop a healthy perspective on these by learning to balance doing well with doing the right thing. They need to recognize and respond appropriately to other children's feelings, so that they can focus on process as well as outcome. Kids also need to learn ways to make a positive contribution to a group. Children are better equipped to cope with competition when they don't fear it, and they understand that winning and losing are temporary conditions. Competition within the family can be complicated. Parents need to communicate to children both "You are special" and "You belong."

In the next chapter, we look at the challenges that bright children face in dealing with authority figures.

CHAPTER 5

DEALING WITH AUTHORITY

How Does Your Child
Respond to Those in Charge?

 Does your child

- Fail to recognize the status difference between adults and children?
- Unintentionally irritate adults by assuming, "They shouldn't care what I do!"?
- Dig in her heels and refuse to cooperate when an adult wants her to do something she doesn't feel like doing?
- Frequently and inappropriately argue with adults?
- Fret about an adult feeling angry?
- Worry about not following the rules exactly?

The word *authority* conjures up many associations and varied feelings. An authority is someone with knowledge and expertise, which is admirable. But authority also means "power," and that's where the ambivalence comes in. We'd all like to have the authority to make decisions or do what we want to do, so we have qualms about being subject to other people's authority. We respect great leaders, but leaders require followers, and we're not so keen on being followers. In fact, some of our greatest heroes are people who challenged authority or helped overthrow unjust rulers.

Yet we recognize that some forms of external authority are necessary to avoid chaos. Although we prize autonomy and independence, we also choose to submit to authority when we follow traffic rules, pay taxes, and do the job that our boss at work expects us to do. We go along (more or less) with these requirements because they're for the greater good or they fit with our long-term goals, but we tend to complain about them. Given that adults have such conflicting feelings about authority, it's no wonder that so many children struggle to find healthy ways to deal with authority figures!

DEVELOPING DIPLOMACY

Children need to know how to build positive relationships with those in charge. This is a kind of diplomacy. It requires understanding interpersonal power and influence, being able to gauge other people's wants and expectations, and being able to respond in ways that create positive connections.

Many adults bemoan office politics. They see it as somehow underhanded or manipulative. Saying someone is "very political" is usually not a compliment. But that's not what we're talking about in this chapter.

Diplomacy is an awareness of social context, and it's necessary for being able to move smoothly and effectively in the world. Without this understanding, children proceed blindly and can unwittingly offend others and undermine their own ability to get where they want to go.

Being Smart About Dealing with Authority Figures

Some children are very adept at getting teachers, coaches, and other adults to like and respect them. They seem to have an intuitive understanding of roles and expectations, and a natural ability to elicit support from those in charge. They've learned how to figure out what makes the boss happy, which is a skill that will serve them well throughout their lives.

Other children routinely manage to rub authority figures the wrong way. Often these children blame adults for their difficulties. They complain that the adult in charge is mean, stupid, or boring, or just doesn't like them. However, even when children don't respect a particular person in a position of authority, they need to be savvy enough to realize that that person has the power to make their lives pleasant or unpleasant. This means it's worth trying to figure out a way to get along.

Dealing with authority figures in an effective way requires sophisticated thinking. It involves recognizing who's in charge, understanding one's own place in a hierarchy, deducing (often unspoken) expectations, anticipating others' reactions, weighing short-term versus long-term goals, considering individual versus collective needs and wants, and consciously choosing a response rather than reacting impulsively. Children who have not yet developed this multifaceted awareness and judgment struggle to get along with those in charge.

How Kids Struggle with Authority Figures

There are three main ways that we've seen bright children have trouble with authority figures:

1. Some are simply oblivious to social roles. These kids tend to be idealistic, but also somewhat inflexible and naïve. They focus on what is Right or True in a heartfelt but uncompromising way. They run into problems with authority figures mainly because, in their zeal, they don't recognize or acknowledge status differences.

2. Other children are directly confrontational and tend to become embroiled in power struggles with adults. They question everything and openly balk if they feel that an adult is trying to control them. Authority doesn't make

sense to them. Why should they have to listen to someone just because they're older? These children have trouble accepting that, like it or not, the adult is in charge.

3. Still other children, at the opposite extreme, are overly fearful of authority figures. At school, these kids are angels, but their parents see what lies behind that angelic behavior: the tears and frantic worry about following the rules, doing things right, and avoiding any criticism from teachers.

The theme that's common to all of these children is the rigidity of their "shoulds." Their unbending beliefs about how the world *should* be, what they *should* be able to do, or how they *should* behave makes them blind to the actual responses of those in charge. Too often, this inflexibility ends up making them miserable, because they either elicit or anticipate negative reactions from adults. In this chapter, we look at practical strategies to help kids learn to relate in healthier ways to authority figures.

 ## LISA: BEING BLIND TO AUTHORITY

"That's not true!" Lisa objected.

"Lisa, you need to raise your hand and wait until I call on you," Mrs. Franklin said.

"But what you're saying is wrong!" Lisa insisted. "We aren't born with all the brain cells we'll ever have! The brain has stem cells that can form both neurons and glia. The brain can even repair itself under some circumstances."

"That may be, Lisa, but I've asked you not to interrupt—"

"I have a whole book about the brain. What you're teaching us is what they used to think. It's not true!"

"Lisa, if you want to bring your book in to show me, that's fine. But it's not okay for you to interrupt the lesson. And if you continue to be disruptive, I'll have to call your parents again."

"It's not fair!" Lisa muttered. "Why should I get in trouble when I'm right?"

❧

Lisa is clearly an expert on the brain. She has read about it and studied it deeply enough to have facts at her fingertips. Her enthusiasm for learning about the brain is admirable, but the way she expresses herself gets her in trouble. Her words, her tone, and her correcting the teacher in public all come across as disrespectful.

Some people might read this scenario and conclude that the teacher's response was less than ideal. Surely she could have found a way to support Lisa's thirst for knowledge while also maintaining order in the classroom. From your own experience, you know that teachers—and bosses—are not always perfectly kind, thoughtful, or even reasonable. But you don't want your child to be a hothouse flower that can only thrive under optimal conditions, so it's important to help your child find ways to relate to many different kinds of authority figures. This is usually more effective than hoping that the adult will change to accommodate your child's style of relating.

Understanding Hierarchy

If we pulled Lisa aside and pointed out that her comments were rude, she would respond with surprise and defensiveness. She wasn't trying to be obnoxious, and she's genuinely puzzled about why her comments elicited such a negative reaction from the teacher. Lisa is so focused on The Truth that she's blind to the social context of her remarks and their likely impact on others. Her final comment, "Why should I get in trouble when I'm right?" clearly indicates what she doesn't understand: that some relationships are hierarchical.

In a classroom setting, the teacher is in charge. By aggressively contradicting the teacher, Lisa disrespects the teacher's authority and even puts herself above the teacher. The other students, most of whom accept the teacher's authority, are likely to find this uncomfortable or even annoying to watch. A teacher who repeatedly encounters this kind of challenging behavior from a child is likely to feel furious. It's hard for authority figures to like a child who seems persistently disrespectful. An adult's instinctive response to this kind of provocation is to want to put the child "in her place."

Children like Lisa don't even realize they have a "place." They see themselves as being on equal footing with adults, so they frequently overstep. They argue or criticize, oblivious to the fact that they are presenting a challenge to the adult's authority. They then feel surprised when adults are offended and respond angrily. Lisa realizes that her teacher is mad, but because she's unaware of hierarchy, she doesn't understand why the teacher is upset or what she did that was unacceptable.

Losing Versus Saving Face

When someone "loses face," it means that they lose status or dignity or somehow appear less worthy of respect. Erving Goffman was a pioneering sociologist who studied the ways that people enhance, maintain, or threaten each other's public identity in everyday interactions. He viewed *face* as a positive social position that people claim for themselves in a particular context. Face is maintained by consensus, because other people do things that acknowledge and communicate acceptance of an individual's social role. For instance, students show respect for Mrs. Franklin's role as the teacher by addressing her by a title and her last name rather than by her first name, following her instructions, and waiting to speak until she calls on them. Lisa's public and aggressive criticism threatens Mrs. Franklin's face by undermining her authority. It's as if Lisa had shouted, "You don't deserve to be the teacher! I refuse to accept the validity of your claim to that role!" Depending on their severity, threats to face can induce feelings of embarrassment or rage, and they strongly motivate efforts to restore status, thereby saving face.

Empathy for Authority Figures

Lisa's comments show a lack of empathy for Mrs. Franklin. She blurts out her criticism without stopping to think how that might make the teacher feel. She doesn't see the teacher as a real person with her own hopes, fears, and sensitivities.

Kids need to realize that it's at least partly up to them to create a good relationship with those in charge. At school, this involves anticipating the teacher's reactions. For example, complaining about a classroom activity by saying "This is boring" comes across to the teacher as "You are boring." It's unlikely to elicit a positive response, especially when the teacher spent time and effort planning the lesson. In contrast, expressing genuine enthusiasm or interest makes the teacher feel validated. To predict a teacher's reaction, children need to pay attention to and remember the teacher's past responses and imagine how the teacher might feel.

Lisa is not a cruel girl; she's just not attuned to the feelings side of interactions with her teacher. She probably doesn't even realize that she should pay attention to the feelings of those around her. Although it isn't Lisa's job to take care of the teacher, she does have a responsibility to try to get along. Not infuriating those in charge also has pragmatic survival value.

STRATEGIES TO
HELP YOUR CHILD WORK
EFFECTIVELY WITH THOSE IN CHARGE

Children like Lisa need help seeing themselves as part of a layered social community and gauging how adults perceive their behavior. They need to be able to think purposefully about ways to create and maintain positive relationships with authority figures. Here are some ideas about how you can help your child develop these skills.

List the Teacher's Pet Peeves and Pleasures

Explain to your child what a pet peeve is: a minor annoyance that an individual finds particularly aggravating. Mention some examples involving family members. For example, maybe it drives you crazy when your child leaves dirty socks in the family room. Maybe it drives your child crazy when you sing along to the radio. See if your child can tell you his or her teacher's pet peeves. What happens when someone does something that is one of the teacher's pet peeves?

Next ask your child what things the teacher particularly enjoys or appreciates. You may want to write down a list of what your child has noticed. Ask your child, "Why is it important to figure out your teacher's pet peeves and pleasures?" The answer is that it's a sign of caring to notice what matters to others, and knowing these can help your child build a more positive relationship with the teacher.

If your child hasn't noticed any of the teacher's pet peeves and pleasures, suggest being a good detective over the next week and trying to discover some of these. Ask your child what the teacher might say or do that would provide clues.

Inductive Versus Deductive Reasoning

When bright children rely too heavily on deductive reasoning, they can end up going down the wrong path in social interactions. Deductive reasoning is theory driven: it starts with a general premise that is then applied to specific situations. For example, in dealing with authority figures, children might believe, "I should be able to . . . ," "She shouldn't care if I . . . ," or "He should . . ." Unfortunately, the combination of their idealism and inexperience means that their theories are often unrealistic.

One boy we know balked at suggestions that he try to write more neatly. He insisted that because he worked hard to do the writing, his teacher should work hard to read it. His belief that "handwriting shouldn't matter" was misguided. There was a lot of evidence that the teacher *did* care about his work being legible: she expressed irritation with his messy assignments, and she made him rewrite them. She told him repeatedly that his papers had to be legible and that she wasn't going to struggle to read them. However, because he relied on deductive reasoning, he overlooked or dismissed evidence that contradicted his belief.

The opposite of deductive reasoning is inductive reasoning, which is data-driven: it involves drawing general conclusions by looking at the data from specific instances. This is much more likely to lead to accurate conclusions.

Explain the difference between deductive and inductive reasoning to your child. Then, when you hear your child carrying on about how things *should* be, say, "That's the way you want things to be, and I can understand why you'd like that, but let's try some inductive reasoning. What evidence do you have about how things actually are?" If your child continues to rail about how things ought to be, respond with understanding but emphasize reality. You could say, "It's frustrating when things don't work the way we want them to work. I can see why you'd wish . . . Unfortunately, we all have to deal with what is, not what should be."

Look Ready to Learn

Respect for authority involves more than just refraining from aggressive arguing. It also involves nonverbal behavior.

KIPP schools are independently run public charter schools that are deliberately located in impoverished neighborhoods and are achieving remarkable results. Students entering KIPP schools are typically one, two, or more years behind academically, but the majority who stay in the schools end up outperforming district norms. KIPP schools employ a wide range of approaches, including more time in school and greater contact between the school and families, but for our purposes, one of the interesting things they do is train students in how to behave in a classroom. They use the acronym SLANT:

Sit up straight.

Look and Listen.

Ask and Answer questions.

Nod your head.

Track the speaker with your eyes.

Show your child this list. Which of these does your child do regularly? See if your child can explain why these behaviors might be helpful. How is the teacher likely to respond? What impact might these behaviors have on your child's learning? If your child doesn't normally use these behaviors, suggest an experiment: use SLANT for one week and see how the teacher reacts.

Teach a Formula for Dealing with an Angry Adult

Some children, when they do something that makes an adult angry, say things that make the situation much worse. They argue, defend, accuse, and shift blame in ways that adults find infuriating.

If your child frequently gets in trouble, you may want to teach him or her our formula for dealing with an angry adult. This formula enables children to step back from the conflict so that they can move forward in a positive direction. Many children are intrigued and relieved to learn that they have the power to respond to angry adults in a way that can help diffuse the adults' anger.

Formula for Dealing with an Angry Adult

"You're right."

"I should have _____."

"I'll _____ now (next time)."

The first line of the formula ("You're right") gets the adult's attention and stops the scolding for a moment. Explain to your child that it's not necessary to agree with everything the angry adult is saying. The adult may be going on about "You never do this" and "You always do that" and "If you keep doing this there will be dire consequences," but somewhere in the whole tirade is a kernel of truth. That's the piece that your child needs to find and express agreement with.

Adults tend to lecture until they feel heard. The second line in the formula ("I should have _____") demonstrates that your child has understood the adult's concern and acknowledges responsibility for the problem in some way. This makes the adult feel less need to continue scolding.

Finally, actions speak louder than words, so it's important for your child to demonstrate a willingness to take action. Ideally the action will be immediate ("I'll _____ now"), but if that's not feasible, your child should commit to action as soon as possible (for example, tonight, next week, next time).

Explain to your child that this formula is powerful because it enables your child to dramatically reduce or even stop an angry lecture. We've never known it to fail as long as (1) the child remembers to use it right away, (2) the child uses it exactly as written (no ad libs, because children who need to learn this formula are apt to embellish it only in ways that make it less effective), and (3) the child does follow through on the promised action.

Help your child practice using the formula through role playing. You be the angry adult, and have your child respond to the tirade with the formula. Here are some scenarios you could try.

> TEACHER: You've wasted half the period talking to your neighbor. You're supposed to be doing research for your report. Have you found any books on your topic? You're not making a good choice about how you're using your time. Do I have to separate you?
>
> YOUR CHILD: You're right. I should have been looking for books. I'll do my research now.

> TEACHER: Where is your homework? Don't tell me you forgot. It's your responsibility to write the assignments in your agenda and check it. Next year you're going to be in X grade, and then what will you do? They're not going to be as understanding about missing homework.
>
> YOUR CHILD: You're right. I should have written the assignment in my agenda. I'll write the assignments down today.

> TEACHER: Put that book away. We're doing science now. You need to be helping your group and recording the results of the experiment, not reading a book.
>
> YOUR CHILD: You're right. I should have been paying attention to the experiment. I'll put my book away now.

Teach a Formula for Questioning a Rule Politely

School is filled with rules that can seem pretty arbitrary, although they often have an educational or practical rationale. For example, teachers often tell students, "All paragraphs should have five sentences." The reason for this rule is that the teacher wants students to learn to back up their topic sentences with examples. However, if you open any book, it's obvious that paragraphs come in many sizes. This is the kind of contradiction that often irritates bright children. "The five-sentence rule is stupid!" they protest.

Explain to your child that people never respond positively to being told that they or something they are doing is stupid.

Your child has three choices when faced with an unreasonable rule:

1. Refuse to follow the rule, and accept the consequences.
2. Go along with the rule because it's not important or not worth enduring the consequences of disobeying.
3. Challenge the rule politely.

To challenge a rule politely, the first step is to understand the rationale for the rule, even if your child doesn't agree with that rationale. Then your child can suggest an alternative that addresses the concern that prompted the rule. Here's a useful formula:

Formula for Questioning a Rule Politely

"I understand that you want me to [rule] because [rationale].

Would it be okay if I [alternative that addresses concern of rationale]?"

This formula is most likely to work if your child uses it privately, in a one-on-one conversation with an adult, without an audience. The first line communicates that your child understands the concerns of the authority figure and is not simply protesting for the sake of protesting. The second line is a polite request that respects the adult's concerns and also acknowledges that the adult has the power to make decisions regarding the rule.

For example, to politely question the five-sentence rule, your child might say, "I understand that you want me to have five sentences in every paragraph because you want me to back up my ideas with facts. Would it be okay for me to write paragraphs of different lengths if I make sure that at least three paragraphs in my essay have five sentences?"

This formula is about developing negotiation skills. It may not work—the adult could say no despite the respectful tone of the request—but the formula represents your child's best shot at changing the adult's mind. If used judiciously, it's also unlikely to anger an authority figure. If the adult says no, your child needs to let the matter go. Further argument will only make the adult more adamant. Your child still has the choice of either complying or ignoring the rule and accepting the consequences.

Consider Options for Responding to Others' Mistakes

Many bright children assume that if someone makes a mistake they *must* set the record straight immediately and publicly. They even expect to receive praise for being clever and catching the mistake. They don't realize that correcting others publicly comes across as impertinent and can make them seem like an inconsiderate know-it-all. Cultivating empathy can help temper this behavior.

Ask your child to think of a time he or she made a mistake. How did your child come to recognize the mistake? Did anyone comment on the mistake? How did that make your child feel? How would your child have felt if the mistake had been broadcast in the school's morning announcements? Some children will answer that they wouldn't care. If your child says that, you'll need to explain that most people would feel embarrassed or angry.

Explain to your child that correcting someone, especially an adult, should be done privately and respectfully. Your child should broach the topic in terms of seeking clarification or sharing information. For instance, your child could say, "Could you please help me understand something? You mentioned ____, but I thought ____," or "I read something that I thought you might find interesting."

Your child should also be open to the possibility that he or she might be wrong or that there is more than one answer. For instance, ask your child how many continents there are. This seems like a straightforward, factual question, but it turns out the answer can be anywhere from four to seven, depending on how people count them. (See www.countriesandcities.com/continents/.) None of these is more correct than the others.

Also talk with your child about the possibility of letting a mistake slide without commenting. Often, in the name of kindness and civility, this is the best option. Before correcting someone, especially an adult, your child should consider these questions:

Is the mistake hurting anyone?

Will the person feel embarrassed if I mention the mistake?

Will the person feel embarrassed if I don't mention the mistake?

Can I mention the mistake without drawing everyone's attention to it?

Examine an Organization Chart

Showing your child a chart depicting the hierarchy within an organization is one way to help your child learn about different roles and responsibilities. You could use the organization chart of your company, a local recreational sports league, your regional scouting organization, your state or county library system, or your religious community leadership.

Most kids love the idea of being at the top of the chart and being able to order everyone else around. Discuss what qualifies individuals to be at the top of the chart and what responsibilities come with that role. Children (and young adults) often have very unrealistic expectations about being able to become "the boss" quickly and easily. You may want to do some research about the top person's qualifications or career path.

Emphasize that even CEOs are answerable to their board of directors, and entrepreneurs are answerable to their customers. Ask questions to help your child think through how organizations function. What happens if people ignore the "chain of command" and everyone decides, "I'm going to do it my own way, and I don't care what you want me to do"? Why do people accept being in positions that are not at the top of the organization chart? (Possible answers: because they haven't earned a higher position yet, because they recognize that people in higher positions have more knowledge or experience, because they recognize that not everyone can be chief, and they believe in the mission of the organization . . .) Talk about how all the positions are necessary to make the organization work.

See if your child can create an organization chart for his or her school. You may want to help your child go online to see how that chart fits within the organization of your whole school district.

Model Respect for Your Child's Teachers and Coaches

Inevitably, your child will have some teachers and coaches that you like more than others. There may even be some that you strongly disagree with either practically or philosophically. This can particularly be a problem if you yourself are an educator, or if the teacher is covering something in your area of expertise.

You might be tempted to explain to your child how the teacher is getting it wrong. Don't. If necessary, you can speak with the teacher privately, but nothing good will come from disparaging the teacher in front of your child. Your child might even view your criticism as license to be rude and disobedient to the teacher.

Be careful also not to accept as the whole truth everything that your child reports regarding what the teacher said or did. Your child's description may be incomplete, mistaken, or out of context.

If you do decide to speak with the teacher, make sure that your approach is collaborative and respectful of the teacher's training and experience. Give the teacher the benefit of the doubt. Recognize that the teacher has many students to deal with and many competing educational obligations. Ask before you tell. Share rather than argue. Offer to help, and ask for the teacher's suggestions. Say "we" more than "you." Acknowledge the teacher's efforts. Teachers, like mothers, are easy targets for criticism and receive far too little appreciation.

NICHOLAS: MAKING EVERYTHING AN ARGUMENT

"Nicholas, how many times do I have to tell you? Don't leave your papers all over the kitchen counter!" his father said. "How am I supposed to make dinner?"

"Well, you can just work around my papers," Nicholas replied.

"I don't want to work around your papers! They don't belong here."

"Yes, they do," Nicholas insisted. "That's where I like to keep them. That way I won't forget them."

"You're not the only person in this family. There are four people who want dinner, and your papers are in the way."

"Well, you have some of your papers on the kitchen counter."

"I have the list of emergency phone numbers. It takes up very little space. Your stuff is spread all over. You have a bedroom. You have a desk. These things belong in your room."

"If I put them in my room, I'll forget them. This is the only way I can remember them."

"Nicholas, just move your papers! I have to make dinner, and they're in the way. Why does everything have to turn into a big argument with you?"

"I'm not the one who's arguing."

Nicholas has an answer for everything. He is absolutely convinced that his way is right, so he dismisses his father's objections. There's even a certain logic to his arguments, although his conclusion—that he should be able to claim the entire kitchen counter as his turf, and other family members should just work around him, regardless of the inconvenience—is unreasonable.

Relishing the Argument

Parents of children like Nicholas often say that their kids will make great lawyers someday, but in the meantime, they're hard to live with. These verbally precocious children seem to relish arguing. It's their automatic response to almost every adult utterance. No issue is too small for them to debate. No loophole is too obscure for them to find. They are masters at following the letter of their parents' edicts while stomping on the spirit of those instructions. "But you didn't *say* I couldn't . . . ," they object with feigned innocence and a slight smirk. Their ingenuity in bending, twisting, and challenging the rules is impressive, but the relentlessness of their arguments is wearing and exasperating for adults.

So why do these children turn everything into an argument? There are several reasons:

1. *Because they can.* Do you remember when your child was first learning to pull up into a standing position? She probably practiced standing all the time: whenever you set her down, while you were changing her diaper, when you tried to get her in her car seat, even in the middle of the night. Psychologists call the drive to learn and practice new skills the *developmental imperative*. Your child's current tendency to argue is not unlike that earlier determination to stand. Her growing brain enables her to muster unlimited counterarguments, to imagine arcane exceptions and caveats, and to formulate an unending supply of

clever retorts. Of course she wants to try out these new skills at every opportunity!

2. *Because it's fun for them.* Nicholas's father was focused on getting dinner on the table. For him, the argument was an irritation that impeded his goal and left him feeling disrespected. For Nicholas, this was an enjoyable interchange—an entertaining contest of wit and will. It would have taken him ten seconds to move his papers, but it was more fun for him to engage his father in extended banter. He doesn't quit, because he doesn't want to lose the game. He thinks his smart-alecky remarks are clever, so he ignores his father's growing anger.

3. *Because sometimes it works.* Everyone knows that slot machines are rigged to favor the casino, but people still play them, despite the odds, because every now and then their efforts pay off in a big way. Many people figure it's worth a shot to play. This is called intermittent reinforcement. It's extremely difficult to get people to stop doing behaviors that are reinforced only occasionally, at unpredictable times, because they keep trying, expecting the next effort to pay off. Kids are deeply familiar with intermittent reinforcement, also known as "trying to wear a parent down." It sounds like this: "No. No. No. No. No. Okay, fine! But just this once!" Children assume they have nothing to lose by continuing to argue, and if they keep trying, sometimes they win.

What Nicholas doesn't understand is that the constant arguments do cost him something: they annoy his father, which increases the likelihood that his father will respond more harshly to his next minor misbehavior and less warmly to his next request. The arguments also add to the general strain and tension in the home. It's just not pleasant to be around someone who is always arguing.

Having a habit of arguing also hurts children outside the family. If you, who love your child with all your heart, find the constant arguing exasperating, imagine how teachers or coaches, who don't love your child, react to it.

"You're Not the Boss of Me!"

In our practices, the most common complaint we hear from parents is that their kids "don't listen." Parents often hope that we can say something to their children to convince them to listen. Unfortunately, the best we can do is to help guide parents in asserting their own authority in firm but compassionate ways. This is a difficult middle ground for parents to walk.

A common pattern we see is parents giving in, giving in some more, trying to be nice and understanding, perhaps making some halfhearted requests or oblique complaints, then suddenly reaching the end of their rope and exploding in anger at their children. They wonder bitterly how their children can be so obnoxious after all they've done for them. Their children feel bewildered and sometimes frightened by these explosions. "All I did was . . . ," they protest. What the children see is only the final step—their parent "losing it" in response to their most recent provocation—and not their contribution to the buildup that preceded the explosion. After the explosion, these parents tend to feel guilty, so they return to their pattern of appeasing their children despite their growing resentment, and the cycle begins again.

Other parents seem to have a very sensitive hot button when it comes to issues of authority and respect. When kids say, "You can't make me!" or "You're not the boss of me!" they feel furious and helpless. In an effort to combat these feelings, they clamp down hard on their children, by yelling, threatening, and sometimes even hitting. These parents are prone to getting into head-to-head power struggles with their children that feel like battles to the death, where there can be only one victor. Unfortunately, the harder they push, the more their children dig in their heels. Conflicts quickly escalate, as both parties try to be as hurtful as possible in order to force the other to back down. Over time, when power struggles are frequent, parents and children learn to

skip the preliminaries and go straight to harsh attacks and coun-
terattacks. The bitterness and resentment that follow these
battles mean that no one ever really wins the power struggles.

A parenting pattern that can be especially toxic for children
is the "mean parent–nice parent" dynamic. One parent is very
firm (perhaps overly so) and the other parent is very soft (perhaps
overly so), but the biggest problem is that both parents work to
undermine the other's authority. The firm parent disparages the
soft one as weak and ineffectual, which unintentionally gives
the child permission to ignore or disrespect the soft parent. The
soft parent tries to "make up for" the harshness of the firm
parent, which unintentionally tells the child that limits don't
mean anything, and it's okay to sneak to get around the firm
parent. No two parents are ever going to do things exactly the
same way, but parents do need to try to work together. They
need to support and respect each other, or their children will
be left with an unhealthy belief that they don't have to listen
to any adult.

Compassionate Authority

There's a lot of confusion about discipline nowadays. For instance,
we often hear harsh punishment justified by a desire to "teach
kids a lesson." But kids don't learn through suffering; they learn
by doing it right (whatever "it" is). Severe punishments don't
motivate children to contemplate the error of their ways; they
make kids focus on the "meanness" of the adult inflicting the
punishment. Logical consequences for misbehavior are sometimes necessary, but kids also need the chance to try again as
soon as possible. Moreover, preventing problems is a much more
powerful teaching strategy than creating consequences for problems after they occur.

Some parenting books advocate elaborate reward systems
that give kids the opportunity to earn prizes or privileges for

doing certain things. Clearly, it's more pleasant for all involved to focus on rewarding positive behavior rather than punishing negative behavior. Reward systems can work very well to help a child get over a temporary hump, but they're very hard to maintain long term. Few parents can keep up a reward system for more than a few weeks. Parents get sick of them, and kids get bored with them.

Besides practical difficulties, there are other less obvious potential problems with reward systems. First, they focus on compliance with external controls, when what we really want to teach kids is self-control that they'll maintain regardless of whether rewards are present. Second, reward systems can set up a mercenary pattern that doesn't belong in close, loving relationships. It induces children to demand, "What do I get if I do that?" Third, some children simply won't participate, saying, "Keep your reward. I don't care. It's not worth it." These children refuse to be "bought," and offers of greater rewards only elicit greater resistance.

If you do choose to use rewards, be careful not to reward every positive thing your child does, and keep in mind that nonmaterial rewards, such as getting to do something fun with a parent, are the most valuable to children. Also, your child needs plenty of positive attention from you that is not earned but given freely out of love.

When we're angry, it's easy to think of our children as "brats." We may even lash out at them, telling them how terrible they are, accusing them of being selfish or mean, of always doing this and never doing that. We may predict dire future outcomes: "If you don't shape up, you're never going to . . ." "If you keep going this way, you'll end up . . ." None of this is productive or kind. *We can't help children move forward by convincing them of their badness.*

In our view, authority is most effective when it's exercised with compassion. As parents, we need to set limits and establish realistic expectations, but we need to do this in a context of love

and empathy, of justice tempered by mercy. Our guiding questions should be, What is it that my child needs to learn, and how
can I facilitate that learning?

Just about every parenting book talks about the need for
consistency. It's certainly important that our children have a
sense that their world is predictable and that they know what to
expect from us, but we also need to be flexible.

In a family we know, the eleven-year-old son once became
extremely angry during an argument with his parents and ended
up throwing his plastic garbage can to the floor and breaking
it. His mother left the broken pieces lying on the floor, assuming, logically, that because her son had broken it, he ought to
pick it up and pay for a new one. For several days after this
episode, he refused to pick up the pieces. Every day he stepped
over them, barely glancing at them. Although he didn't
have any more outbursts, his mother noticed that he seemed
angry and ashamed. He refused to talk about what had
happened.

Then his mother did something very loving: she picked up
the broken pieces and threw them away, and she bought him a
new garbage can. He didn't deserve this. He knew it, and she
knew it, but she did it anyway, because she understood that he
was stuck. Rescuing children from the consequences of their
actions won't work as a general parenting policy, but in this case,
it was the right thing to do. That night he came to her and
apologized. His mother's caring gesture expressed her faith in her
son. By making the first move toward him, she enabled her son
to move forward.

STRATEGIES FOR EXERCISING COMPASSIONATE AUTHORITY

The best way to teach children to respond appropriately
to authority figures is for parents to be firm but compassionate
authorities themselves. This can be especially challenging when

our children have an aggravating habit of arguing with everything we say. We may feel tempted to lash out angrily at them, or we may give in resentfully because we just don't have the energy to fight with them *again*. However, it's not fair to be angry with children for failing to put limits on themselves. It's kids' job to test the limits; it's our job as adults to set the limits. For your own sanity, for your children's well-being, and for the sake of peace in your family, you need to insist that your children behave well enough that you enjoy their company most of the time.

Here are some strategies for exercising compassionate authority.

Help Your Child Know Where the Lines Are

A simple but surprisingly effective parenting strategy is simply to state expectations or limits briefly. Aim for fewer than ten words, because children tune out long lectures. "Coats go in the closet." "Homework before video games." "You need to . . ." "It's not okay to . . ." "It's your responsibility to . . ."

Make sure that your expectations are realistic. They should match what your child is already doing most of the time, or just slightly beyond that, rather than how you think an ideal child ought to behave. Unrealistic expectations are a recipe for frustration and shame.

State your expectations with the same calm certainty that you would say, "The grass is green." Keep your voice pitched soft and low so you sound in control of yourself. If your child argues, just repeat the limit or expectation using the same words, then stand there, waiting confidently for your child to comply.

Refuse to be drawn into a verbal sparring match. Sometimes when kids ask, "Why do I have to?" or "Why can't I?" they are genuinely seeking information, but usually these comments are not really questions but objections. You don't have to convince your child that your expectations are justified. They just are.

If your child grumbles but complies, ignore the grumbling and just say, "Thank you."

Address Back Talk

One form of misbehavior that tends to infuriate parents is children's talking back in disrespectful ways. This can be particularly upsetting for people who come from cultures that place a high value on respect for one's elders, but we've heard parents from many different backgrounds complain, "I never would have spoken to my parents the way my kids talk to me!"

We sometimes see families in which the child insults a parent or calls a parent names. This is a tricky problem, because if the parent yells, "You can't call me stupid!" or "Don't you dare talk to me like that!"—which is a very human response—it tends to escalate the battle. It also makes the parent seem helpless, because the kid already *did* say the disrespectful remark, so it makes no sense to say, "You can't . . ." It's not possible to shove the words back into a child's mouth *after* they've been spoken. All we can do is label the comments as inappropriate and prove that they have no power over us.

What we recommend in response to disrespectful comments is for parents to say, calmly and confidently, "It's not okay for you to speak to me like that" or "You know how to talk to me if you want me to listen." For younger children, a short time-out might then be appropriate. For older kids, it's usually best then to walk away. This is not giving in; it's asserting appropriate parental authority in refusing to accept or be drawn into a disrespectful interchange. Although it's tempting to rehash the exchange at a later time in order to explain in detail to your child how wrong the remarks were or how hurtful you found them, it's often better *not* to do this. You need to draw the line, but bringing up disrespectful comments again makes them seem too important and makes your child's words seem too powerful.

Empathize, but Don't Give In Just Because Your Child Is Upset

Some parents have trouble acting like authority figures because they hate the idea of their children being mad at them. Although it's important to recognize and acknowledge our children's feelings, that doesn't mean we always go along with what they want. Sometimes the answer has to be no, even if they don't like it. Being a good parent means sometimes having to endure our children's anger.

In their warm and sensitive book, *Parenting from the Inside Out*, Daniel Siegel and Mary Hartzell comment, "Parents need to be able to tolerate the tension and discomfort that a child may experience when the parent sets a limit. If a parent cannot tolerate a child's being upset, it is very difficult for the child to learn to regulate her emotions. If we always capitulate and give our child what she wants just to keep her from being upset, we will not support our child in developing a healthy ability to apply the brakes and redirect an activity."

Go ahead and empathize. Say, "You wish you could do that," "I can see why you like that," or "It's hard to stop when you're having so much fun." Acknowledging these feelings can make it easier for your child to accept the limit. But you still need to stick to your guns, even if your child isn't happy about it.

Post a Picture of the Effects of Increasing Requests

Kids who argue a lot tend to dismiss the impact of their arguing. They can see an adult's growing irritation, but somehow they just don't believe it's important, or they interpret it as a signal that they should argue more vehemently in order to convince the adult. Unfortunately, the more irritated adults feel, the less willing they are to listen, so more arguing only compounds the problem.

Show your child the set of pictures labeled "How Many Requests?" or sketch your own version with faces that look more like you. This is a simple representation of how adults feel when kids don't follow instructions.

How many requests?

 0 requests = **Delighted**

 1 request = **Happy**

 2 requests = **Annoyed**

 3 requests = **Exasperated**

With young children, ask, "Which Mommy is most fun to be around?" Point to the face next to "0 requests" and explain, "This is how I feel when you do what you're supposed to do without my asking. I'm delighted." Go on to explain the remaining faces in the picture. "This is how I feel when I only have to ask you one time to do something," and so on. Post the drawing on your refrigerator, then, whenever your child does something helpful or responsible after zero or one request, point to the picture and say enthusiastically, "This is how I'm feeling now!"

With older children, after you explain the drawing, you can comment that too often lately you've ended up feeling like the exasperated mom, which isn't fun for either of you. Has your child noticed this? You may want to propose a deal that involves you trying to make fewer requests, and your child making an effort to stay in the zero-to-one-request zone. If you post the picture on your refrigerator, you can also use it to give your child feedback about your feelings during an interaction. For instance, you could point to the picture and say, "I'm at two requests now, and I'm starting to get annoyed. Think carefully about what you want to do now."

Parents often tell us, "I have to ask my kid fifteen times to do something!" Unfortunately, this means that they've trained their child to ignore them fourteen out of every fifteen times, which is exasperating for any parent.

Don't ask your child to do something more than twice. If your child doesn't listen the first time, walk over, make eye contact, and perhaps put your hand gently on your child's shoulder to make sure you have your child's attention before repeating the request. Ignoring you is not an option.

If your child doesn't comply after two requests, you may need to escort your child toward doing the task. If you sense that your child feels overwhelmed by the job, you can say, "I'll help, but this has to be done." With older children, you may need to pause the computer or turn off the TV until your child is ready to listen. Tell your child, "When you [complete requested action], you can continue [desired activity]." It's hard, but it's especially important to keep your voice low and calm and to resist being drawn into an argument at this point. Yelling and arguing undermine your authority and make you seem more like a sibling than a parent. They also shift your child's focus to your "meanness" and away from the task your child needs to complete.

What if your child says, "I'll do it in a minute"? Use compassion, but be firm and follow through. Waiting for a commercial is reasonable. Waiting an hour for the end of the video game might not be practical, especially if your child is prone to "forgetting" adult requests. To avoid debates about how long you are willing to wait, you may want to set a timer or extract a written promise from your child regarding when the task will be completed.

It's also wise to approach your child with requests at times when the odds of compliance are high, in order to avoid unnecessary power struggles. If you see that your child is engrossed in an activity or is in a particularly crabby mood, you may want to postpone your request. This is not "giving in"; it's exercising good judgment as a parent.

If your request isn't that important or you don't have the energy to make sure your child carries through, then don't ask. It's better to do whatever it is yourself than to teach your child that it's not necessary to listen to your requests.

Address the Habit of Arguing

Some children argue purely out of habit. If this is the case with your child, you may want to talk about bad habits, such as biting nails or sucking on hair. What bad habits has your child observed? How do people react to them? Explain that bad habits are unattractive and off-putting to others. Comment that you've noticed your child has gotten stuck in the habit of arguing lately, which makes life unpleasant for both of you. See if your child has any ideas about how to break this habit.

Explain that when you ask your child to do something, the correct response is to say, "Okay" and then get up and do it. You may want to agree that your child is allowed to (but doesn't have to) ask one question after you make a request. This question could be to clarify what you want done or to find out if there is any flexibility in the request (for example, "Can I do it after dinner?"). Asking, "Do I have to?" would count as the one question, but it wouldn't be a very good use of that question because the answer will always be "Yes, you do." "Why do I always have to?" is also not a good choice for a question, because the answer will always be, "Because I love you" (or, if you have a joking relationship with an older child, "Because I want you to suffer").

Insist that you will not answer more than one question following a request.

If your child has additional concerns beyond the one question, suggest putting these concerns in writing, in a respectful way, and you will consider them. Most kids won't bother with this, unless the issue is very important to them.

Because habits are hard to break, you may want to agree on a nonverbal signal to remind your child not to argue.

Minimize Reactance

Reactance is a psychological term for the angry, resentful, defiant feelings that occur when people feel that their freedom is being restricted or threatened. Everyone experiences reactance sometimes, but some people are especially prone to it. We've noticed that some extremely contrary bright children seem to have antenna up for detecting when adults are trying to influence or control them, and they respond with intense resistance. They may even do the exact opposite of whatever it is that the adult wants them to do. Reward programs never work with these children, nor does punishment, which they endure like martyrs for a just cause.

Reactance is most likely to occur when demands are forceful and numerous, and when they're accompanied by threats. "Do it now, or else!" is very likely to inspire resistance. Even if you get outward compliance in that moment, your child will feel resentful and less willing to cooperate next time.

Exercising compassionate authority means recognizing that nobody likes to feel controlled. Here are some ideas to minimize your child's reactance and avoid power struggles:

- Pick your battles. If it won't matter a week or a month from now, let it go.
- Offer two or three acceptable options. This gives your child some decision-making power.

- Use an indirect or playful approach. Talk with a silly accent. Have a puppet make the request. Write your child a note and sign it "Love, Your Toothbrush."
- Ask for your child's ideas for solving the problem.
- Say, "Let's do it together."

Adele Faber and Elaine Mazlish's classic book *How to Talk So Kids Will Listen and Listen So Kids Will Talk,* is an excellent resource for learning to communicate warmly yet effectively with children.

Emphasize Values

Ultimately, we want our children to behave well not because we're somehow forcing them to do so but because they have incorporated our values. You can bring up values to stem your child's arguing. For instance, you could say, "That's a logical argument, but it's not a caring choice. I trust you to make a caring choice."

Think about the values that you would most like your child to exhibit. Then be on the lookout for times when your child demonstrates these qualities and comment sincerely about your observation. You could say,

> "That was kind of you to share your muffin."
>
> "You showed real perseverance by continuing to try, even when it was hard."
>
> "You sure are curious about that!"

Children are in the process of discovering who they are. Descriptive statements like these help them own certain desirable attributes. Research suggests that when children believe that they possess a particular personal characteristic, they are more likely to behave in ways consistent with that characteristic.

Enjoy Each Other's Company

The foundation of our authority with our children is the warm feelings that we share. Fan the flames of these feelings by spending time doing things together that you both enjoy. Reaffirming your closeness is especially important after you and your child have quarreled. Don't wait for your child to make the first move. Reach out.

STEPHANIE: FRETTING ABOUT ADULTS' ANGER

"Stephanie, you forgot to turn in your permission slip for the field trip. It's still here in your folder," her mother said.

"Oh, no! Mr. Ricardo said it was due today!"

"Well, just be sure to give it to him first thing tomorrow."

"But he'll be mad at me!"

"Mr. Ricardo is a very nice teacher. I'm sure he won't be mad."

"Yes, he will. It was supposed to be turned in today."

"Sweetie, there's nothing you can do about it today."

"Can we drive to the school to turn it in?"

"No, we can't drive to the school. It's 7:30 at night. Nobody is at the school. Besides, I have to get your brother to bed."

"But, Mom! He said it had to be in today!"

"The field trip isn't for two weeks. I'm sure it'll be fine if you turn it in tomorrow. Now go get in your pajamas."

"I won't be able to sleep because of the permission slip."

"Stephanie, let it go! You can't do anything about it until tomorrow, so there's no point in fretting about it tonight!"

"Now you're mad at me!"

"I'm not mad at you, I just want you to get ready for bed!"

"Yes, you are mad at me, and Mr. Ricardo is going to be mad at me, too!"

"Stephanie, enough already! This is *not* a big deal, and I'm *not* mad at you!!!"

"Then why are you yelling?"

Stephanie is an example of a child who fears authority. More specifically, she fears authority figures' being mad at her. This would make sense if her parents or teacher were harsh and punitive, but they're not. Her mother's comments are calm, not critical, in response to Stephanie's mistake. The teacher is nice. But Stephanie fears that that they will become angry with her. Ironically, she brings about exactly what she fears: she keeps insisting that her mother is angry, despite reassurances, until her mother finally does snap at her in frustration.

Trying to Ward Off Anger

No one enjoys being the target of an authority figure's anger, but for Stephanie this possibility seems unbearable. She's convinced that she must avoid angering adults at all costs. This belief is like a phobia—it's not rational. No amount of logical argument or reassurance alters it. In calmer moments, she might admit that she's overreacting, but she can't seem to control this fearful response. So instead, she works very hard to prevent the occurrence of anger. The strategies she uses to try to ward off adults' anger give her some sense of control, but they also make her miserable.

1. *Watching*. Stephanie is constantly on the lookout for signs of adult anger. A question, a comment, a lack of a comment, a furrowed brow, or just the absence of a toothy grin—any of these behaviors from adults can make her fret, "Are they mad at me?" Unfortunately, her vigilant readiness to detect anger often leads her to perceive anger when it's not (yet) present, which compounds her anxiety.

2. *Worrying*. Stephanie believes that if she worries about the occurrence of anger, she can prevent it. She is prepared to stay

up all night ("I won't be able to sleep") fretting about her teacher's possible anger, as if this will somehow keep the anger at bay. This is a bit like thinking that worrying about a plane crash, as a passenger, will help keep the plane in the air.

3. *Striving for perfection.* Stephanie has convinced herself that "If I can do everything perfectly, adults won't ever get mad at me." Children like Stephanie tend to be meticulous about following the rules, and they feel frantic if they don't understand the instructions. Trying always to be perfect is very stressful, and it's also an impossible goal. Mistakes are inevitable, but they feel intolerable to Stephanie, so she imagines that the adults in her life will respond angrily when she does something wrong. What she doesn't understand is that the harsh standards actually reside within her, not the adults.

Feeling Helplessness in the Face of Anger

If someone we care about is angry with us, usually the best thing to do is to acknowledge that anger and then do something to address the problem. But that's not even in the realm of possibilities that Stephanie considers. Her fear of anger paralyzes her and prevents her from taking positive action. She cries helplessly, "You're mad at me. I can tell you're mad at me," daring the adult to contradict her but refusing to accept any reassurances. She doesn't know how to move past anger.

As frightened as she is of adults' anger, we suspect that Stephanie is even more scared of her own anger. Kids like Stephanie tend to deny that they ever feel angry. They only feel hurt. It's as if they believe that anger involves destroying or being destroyed, so they can't bear it in either themselves or others.

STRATEGIES TO HELP YOUR CHILD DEVELOP A HEALTHY PERSPECTIVE ON ADULTS' ANGER

Children like Stephanie need help gaining a healthy perspective on adults' anger. They need to understand that most adults are not harsh judges ready to condemn them. They also need to understand that in a caring relationship, anger doesn't erase love. Anger is usually a temporary state that they can work through and get past. Teaching all of this takes patience, empathy, honesty, and perseverance. Here are some strategies you may want to try.

Don't Deny Your Own Anger

People who live together and care about each other are going to feel angry at each other sometimes. That's just part of being in a close relationship. If your child asks anxiously, "Are you mad at me?"—and you really are—don't fall into the trap of denying it in an effort to reassure your child. Also, don't dismiss your feelings by saying, "I'm not angry; I'm [annoyed, irritated, frustrated, miffed]." Gradations and fine semantic distinctions among forms of anger are irrelevant to a child who fears any anger. Your child will sense your anger and continue to fret, "Yes, you are mad at me!" Denying your feelings only adds to your child's conviction that anger is a terrible and dangerous thing.

Instead, tell your child, "Yes, I am angry. But that's okay, because you're strong enough, and I'm strong enough, and our relationship is strong enough to tolerate anger."

Acknowledge Your Child's Anger

To help your child feel less scared of his or her own anger, talk about it. Reflect feelings, "That must have made you mad." "You're angry because . . . I can understand that." "You're feeling furious about . . ." It's especially important to acknowledge your child's feelings of anger toward you, because this shows that you accept the feelings and aren't afraid of them.

Find Ways to Take Action

If your child feels frozen with fear when faced with actual or possible adult anger, finding ways to take action can reduce this sense of helplessness. Ask your child, "What can you do to solve the problem or at least make the situation better?" You can ask this whether it's you or someone else who is angry with your child. If your child can't do anything immediately, making a list of problem-solving options to be implemented later might help.

Focus on the Evidence

If your child is worried about the possibility of an adult being angry, avoid debating whether or not this will occur. It may seem obvious to you that the other adult won't be mad about your child's minor transgression, but "Yes she will," "No she won't" arguments will only cause your child to be more convinced that the adult is going to be furious.

It may be more useful to talk about whether the anger would be truly unbearable. Encourage your child to look at evidence from the past. Ask very specific questions:

"How many times has Mr. Ricardo yelled at you when you made a mistake?"

"How much blood have you lost due to Mr. Ricardo's anger?"

"Exactly how many of your bones has he broken?"

"How many times has he strangled you?"

"How many times has he hung you from the fluorescent lights by your shoelaces?"

Your questions can become increasingly absurd, until your child protests, "None of that is going to happen!" That's your opening to say, "Okay, so if Mr. Ricardo does get mad at you, it'll be unpleasant, but the odds look pretty good that you'll survive it." Be careful to say this with warmth and gentle humor rather than irritation or cold sarcasm.

Encourage Your Child to Ask for Help

Many children are afraid to ask adults for help because they expect to be criticized for not figuring things out on their own. However, most adults respond warmly to a polite request for help from a child. Asking for and receiving help is one of the best things children can do to see that adults are on their side. So if you see a need, try to convince your child to ask for help. Role playing can help your child practice doing this. With young children, you may want to e-mail the teacher or coach ahead of time to say that your child is trying to ask for help.

Emphasize Relationship Repair

Children who fear anger often need help recovering from angry interactions. If you were angry with your child, after you've cooled down, make a point of telling your child, "I'm not angry anymore," to signal the end of the incident and your willingness to move on.

If you said or did something you regret in the heat of the moment, don't hesitate to offer a brief but sincere apology. "I'm sorry I yelled at you. I was very angry when I saw . . . I realize now that it wasn't fair of me to . . . Would you like to tell me about your view of what happened?" Feeling heard and understood makes it easier for kids to let go of their anger. Remember not to undercut your apology by saying, "I'm sorry, *but* you should [shouldn't] have . . ."

Some kids hate rehashing an argument, and the best way to help them move forward is to say, "Come here," give them a big hug, and remind them, "I love you, no matter what." Other kids prefer more indirect relationship repair. Do a small, unexpected kindness for them, or leave them a note saying, "I love you. Let's try again" in a discreet place where they'll definitely find it. Trying again is what relationships are all about.

SHOW THE WAY

Dealing with authority is a lifelong task. You may find parallels between your child's struggles with authority and your own experiences. If anything, authority issues become more complicated for adults, because we have to contend both with being subject to others' authority and with being authority figures to our children. Parents often feel torn between their desire to get along with their kids and the practical necessity of being in charge of their kids. Here are some strategies for thinking and talking about authority issues in your life.

Reflect on Your Own Experiences with Authority Figures

Reflecting on our own experiences with authority figures, both as children growing up at home and at school, and as adults in work or volunteer settings, can help give us insight into our own special sensitivities, automatic reactions, or blind spots. It can also help us cultivate empathy for our children's struggles.

The way we were parented ourselves is our first example of authority, and it's one that adults tend to either accept as normal, embrace as desirable, or vow to be nothing like. Ask yourself how your parenting style compares with your parents'.

Looking for patterns in our workplace relationships can also help us understand our perspective on authority. Which bosses have you worked best with and why? Which bosses have you found hard to deal with and why? Most people say that good bosses are ones who give them enough guidance so that they can be successful, and enough autonomy to make decisions about how the work gets done, plus lots of appreciation for their efforts. To what extent would you say you're a "good boss" to your child?

Talk About Your Mentors with Your Child

Some bright children believe that they always have to be the smartest person in the room. What they don't understand is that most successful adults have had mentors along the way who have taught and guided them. Few have done it completely on their own.

Talk about your own mentors with your child. Describe how you learned from them and how important their support was to you. Emphasize that being smart means knowing how to learn from others, whether it's specific information or more internal strategies, such as patience or kindness.

Describe Things You Do to Get Along with Your Boss

If you work in a company, you know that part of your job is to make your boss look good. Smart kids tend to rely on impressing others as a way of connecting, but in the context of an organization, grandstanding and hogging credit are self-defeating strategies. Talk with your child about the things you do to get along with your boss. These could include responding promptly to requests, acknowledging others' contributions, or anticipating the boss's needs. Which of these strategies might be relevant for your child's school life? Explain to your child that these generous behaviors don't diminish your status; they contribute to your success and the success of your organization.

This chapter was about helping bright children who struggle in their relationships with adults. We emphasized ways to help these children exercise diplomacy. We focused on ways to address problems involving being oblivious, defiant, or fearful of authority. Learning to develop positive relationships with those in charge is an essential life skill.

In the next chapter, we look at how children can develop motivation to work hard and do what's necessary to succeed.

CHAPTER 6

DEVELOPING MOTIVATION
What Matters to Your Child?

 Does your child

- Dawdle and complain, dragging out homework that could be done quickly and easily?
- Defend poor performance by grumbling that school is boring or that teachers are unfair?
- Rush to finish and turn in sloppy or incomplete work?
- Involve you in battles about homework?
- Insist that certain work is "stupid," "pointless," or "too babyish," and refuse to do it?
- Only do work for favorite teachers?
- Promise to "do better" at school but somehow fail to carry out that resolve?

There are few things more frustrating to parents than bright children who don't seem to be trying. Parents wonder, "Why won't he just do what he's supposed to do?" or "How will she ever get anywhere in life if she just rushes through her work or doesn't even bother to do it or turn it in?" Children's motivation problems can be particularly puzzling and exasperating for parents who have earned their own accomplishments through hard work.

MOTIVATION MATTERS

Just because children are smart doesn't mean that they are automatically highly motivated to learn. In fact, some of the most disengaged students we've met have been extremely bright but unable or willing to be productive.

Motivation is critical for success in life. It's not enough simply to "have" ability. Children also need to use and develop their skills and talents.

The Benefits of Self-Discipline and Grit

Research clearly shows that motivation is important. One study of college students found that high self-control (which implies strong motivation) is linked to better grades, happier relationships, and better psychological adjustment. Two other longitudinal studies involving eighth-graders found that self-discipline is a better predictor than IQ of academic performance.

Achievement often requires sustained motivation over time. Angela Duckworth at the University of Pennsylvania uses the term "grit" to describe perseverance and passion for long-term goals. People with grit seem to be lit from within by an enthusiasm and determination to reach their goals. They are able to persist, despite obstacles or setbacks. Their determination stems not from grim, clenched-teeth drive, but from an inspired, personally embraced sense of purpose. Duckworth insists that grit is not just a matter of intensity of effort; it also involves consistency and duration of effort. Research by Duckworth and her colleagues has found that grit is associated with having a higher grade-point average, ranking higher in the National Spelling Bee, spending more years in school, and even persisting longer at the elite West Point Military Academy. Grit is not related to IQ—some bright children are very gritty and some aren't.

Children's Motivation for Schoolwork

Children vary widely in their motivation to do schoolwork. Some kids find it relatively easy to knuckle down and do their homework, whereas other, equally bright kids find it agonizing even to open their schoolbooks. Some children relish challenges, whereas others go to elaborate lengths to find an easy way out.

Bright children who perform poorly are often called "lazy" or "unmotivated." But there is no such thing as a truly unmotivated child. At some level, all children want to feel capable and to have the important adults in their lives think well of them. No child enjoys failing, but sometimes other factors get in the way of children's acting on their motivation to achieve.

Children who feel unmotivated to do schoolwork typically complain that the work is "boring." Unfortunately, "boring" is probably the least descriptive word in a child's vocabulary. It could mean anything. It could mean the work is too hard or too easy. It could mean the child is feeling scared, angry, helpless, inadequate, or disconnected. It could mean the child doesn't know how to do the work or doesn't see why the work is necessary. It could reflect fear of failure, fear of success, or fear of effort.

Parents who come to us concerned about their children's lack of motivation often feel frustrated, helpless, and scared. They've already tried arguing, warning, threatening, bribing, and cajoling, but nothing seems to get through to their children. The bad news is that there are no quick fixes for motivation problems. The good news is that understanding precisely how your child is stuck can suggest ways to move forward. In this chapter, we take an in-depth look at motivation and describe parenting strategies to help children find their passions, cultivate persistence, and translate motivation into action.

ETHAN:
AVOIDING SCHOOLWORK

"Dad!" Ethan called. "Take a look! I'm already up to Level Seven: Passage of Death on the new video game Aunt Nora gave me."

"That's great, Ethan."

"Yeah, and to get in here, I had to find the lost jewel and insert it into the eye of the idol, and then there was this huge explosion!"

"Uh-huh. Is your homework done?"

"Sort of. Now I have to find a way to get past the Viper Pit. It's really hard. I keep dying and having to start over."

"Ethan, you know the rule: homework before video games."

"Awww, Dad. Homework is boring. Just let me finish this level."

"Your mom says you've been on all afternoon. That's enough. Don't you have a social studies test tomorrow? You know, if you spent half the time on your homework that you do on those video games, your grades would be a lot better."

"Da-ad!" Ethan groaned.

Ethan demonstrates superb motivation for playing video games. He does it eagerly, of his own accord, persisting for hours, despite difficulty, frustration, and even virtual death. Ethan is not an unmotivated child. He just isn't motivated to do his schoolwork.

Intrinsic Motivation: Just for Fun

Intrinsic motivation is motivation that stems from our positive perceptions of a task. When we're intrinsically motivated to do something, we *want* to do it because we see the task itself as fun, interesting, or satisfying. When children are intrinsically motivated to learn, they tend to learn more and perform better than when they are extrinsically motivated to gain something outside the task, such as prizes, approval, or good grades.

Young children are avid learners, driven by intrinsic motivation. They have an eager curiosity about the world and an enthusiastic drive to master new skills. Maybe you remember your child as a toddler, engrossed in playing in a sandbox, or endlessly pouring water back and forth from one cup to another in the bathtub, or determinedly chasing Cheerios on a high-chair tray.

In elementary school and beyond, too often the drudgery of worksheets and tests seems to quash children's desire to learn. They may begin to see learning as a chore, driven by external demands from teachers or parents, rather than something they enjoy.

Research shows that there's a shocking progressive decline in American students' intrinsic motivation for schoolwork between third grade and eighth grade. As children move through upper elementary grades and toward middle school, their ratings of how much they enjoy school and how useful and important they consider academic activities steadily decline. It's not just that older kids are less motivated generally, because intrinsic motivation for nonacademic activities is fairly stable across these ages.

The more we can make work enjoyable and meaningful for children, the easier it is for them to feel motivated to do it. Not everything can be fun and exciting, but the experience of being enthusiastically interested in something prompts effort and adds zest to children's lives.

Sources of Intrinsic Motivation

Video and computer game manufacturers know all about intrinsic motivation. They systematically apply every factor that research tells us enhances intrinsic motivation. There's no denying the kid appeal of these games: children will readily spend long periods of time working diligently to solve problems or get to a higher level, without any external rewards. They do it because it feels fun and satisfying. No, we're not recommending that children spend more time playing electronic games, but we do think it's worthwhile to consider what makes activities appealing to children, and to look for ways to apply this knowledge.

Research tells us that there are four main sources of intrinsic motivation:

1. *Challenge.* In general, people prefer activities that are neither too easy nor too difficult, but allow them to stretch their skills.

2. *Curiosity.* Activities that hold surprise, arouse questions, and allow experimentation and exploration tend to be enjoyable.

3. *Control.* People prefer activities that give them some control over what they do and what happens to them.

4. *Context.* Activities that appeal to our senses and incorporate humor, movement, fantasy, or game playing tend to be enjoyable.

With a bit of effort and imagination, it's not hard to incorporate these four sources of intrinsic motivation into our children's daily lives. When we're able to be silly or playful with our children, when we encourage their questions and allow them choices, we not only make room for them to discover what they enjoy but also create a sense of closeness.

STRATEGIES TO SUPPORT YOUR CHILD'S INTRINSIC MOTIVATION

Fanning the flames of children's enthusiasm helps build a foundation for lifelong learning, even if it doesn't necessarily translate into high grades. In this section, we describe some strategies for developing and supporting children's intrinsic motivation to learn.

Encourage Exploration and Support Your Child's Interests

To discover their interests, children need opportunities to explore the world and try different activities. Take your child to museums, festivals, libraries, nature preserves, and performances. Let your child choose a club or class related to a possible interest. If your child resists doing any activities outside of school, you may need to offer three choices and insist that your child pick one. It's usually best to start small, with one or two short-term activities that leave your child wanting more. A greater number of activities isn't necessarily better.

Sometimes parents are concerned that certain childish interests have no long-term value. It's true that in-depth knowledge of the points and powers associated with each Yu-Gi-Oh! card is unlikely to translate into exciting career opportunities, but the experience of pursuing knowledge and being passionate about a topic might. You can show respect for your child's interests, even if you don't share them, by offering books, magazines, or activities related to these interests.

Supporting your child's interests doesn't mean allowing unlimited access to them. Children need parents to set appropriate limits. "Homework first." "No reading at the dinner table." "Lights off at 8:30." "No more than one hour per day of screen time." These types of limits are often necessary, and they will in no way diminish your child's interest.

Be careful not to take over your child's interests. If you are more enthusiastic than your child about the interest, or if you are working harder than your child to find opportunities to express this interest, you've gone too far. It's no longer your child's interest—it's yours. A positive but low-key stance allows your child to own the interest and manage the intensity of it.

Sometimes parents worry that their child hasn't found "a passion." That's developmentally normal. The elementary and middle school years are about exploration, not specialization.

Your child doesn't need a singular, intense passion. What can carry through across different interests is a sense of themselves as active, capable, and enthusiastic learners.

Don't Protect Your Child from Boredom

Contrary to your child's protests, no one ever died or even became seriously injured from boredom. The ability to manage boredom is a critical life skill and central to cultivating intrinsic motivation.

When your child comes to you complaining of being bored, resist the temptation to try to solve this. Acknowledge the feelings by saying, for example, "You're having trouble thinking of what to do. Nothing appeals to you right now," but avoid providing an answer. Your child will moan. Your child will groan. Your child will sprawl limply across the closest table or chair. Your child will complain that there is never anything to do in your home. You, of course, will be thinking of all the fascinating things you've done with your child and the large assortment of books, toys, and games your child owns. You will have a hundred ideas for possible activities. Don't mention any of this. Your child is likely to find fault with anything you suggest at this point, so save your ideas for another time. Also, offering suggestions of activities in response to your child's complaints sends the wrong message about who is responsible for managing boredom. If you can just hold out long enough, something wonderful will happen: your child will think of something to do.

Draw Connections Between Favorite Interests and Schoolwork

A common obstacle to children's interest in school is that the work often seems disconnected from their lives. Helping children insert their interests into assignments can increase their enthusiasm. For instance, if your son loves baseball, you could explain the math behind players' stats, or help him choose a baseball-related biography or novel for a writing assignment. If your daughter loves ancient Egypt, she might want to insert Egyptian names, items, or places as she writes out her spelling sentences.

Let Your Child Teach You

You can model curiosity and enthusiasm for learning by giving your child the opportunity to teach you. Choose a topic (academic or nonacademic) that your child enjoys and knows more about than you do. Ask questions and express interest in your child's answers. For instance, if your child is doing a report on polar bears, you could ask how they keep warm, what they do in the summer, if they live in groups, if the dads are involved in raising the babies . . . If your child has a favorite music group, you could look at a picture of the band and ask the names and roles of each member. You could ask if the band's style is changing over time. If you ask a question to which your child doesn't know the answer, don't push it. Suggesting, "Let's go look that up!" could turn a pleasant conversation into a chore. It's okay just to leave your child wondering. Be careful to express only genuine interest—children instinctively sense and react very negatively when adults fake enthusiasm.

JARED: COMPLAINING THAT SCHOOLWORK IS BORING

"Why do I have to write the capitals and color in the countries on this map? I mean, if I ever decide to visit Lithuania, I can download a map off the Internet for free."

"Just do your homework, Jared," his mother said, matter-of-factly. "If you sit down and do it, it won't take you very long."

"This is a total waste of time. It's so boring! The teacher must think we have nothing better to do. How is this going to help me in real life?"

"Jared, sometimes you just have to do what you have to do. That's life. I don't love everything I have to do on my job, but I do it anyway."

"Well, at least you get paid for it!"

"Your homework is your responsibility."

"Why should I have to spend my time coloring? That's just stupid. I'm not in kindergarten!"

"Jared, with all the time you spent arguing about this, you could have finished the whole thing! Just get it done!"

Everything that Jared's mother says is very sensible, but it doesn't seem to get through to Jared. That's because they're talking past each other. His criticism of the assignment is an expression of how he's feeling: bored, frustrated, condescended to, and controlled. Her comments are about the task: it's easy; it's required.

A general principle in dealing with kids is that when they don't feel heard, they tend to get *louder*. Because Jared feels as though his mother is ignoring or dismissing how he feels, his complaints escalate in intensity. The conversation deteriorates into a "Just do it!"—"I don't want to!" deadlock.

Jared's mother's comments are an effort to prod him into action. She is absolutely right that the assignment won't take him long once he gets to it, but her remarks seem to make him dig in his heels rather than get moving. Unfortunately, by responding to his frustration with commands, she unintentionally gives him a target for his frustration—someone he can push against. She allows him to turn the struggle into a "him versus her" battle and avoid having to cope with the real, internal struggle between the part of him that wants to comply and the part of him that doesn't.

Extrinsic Motivation: Gotta Get It Done

Being able to do what needs doing when it needs doing, whether or not we feel like it, is a sign of maturity. Apparently, Jared hasn't yet developed this maturity. Learning isn't always enjoyable; sometimes it's just plain work. This means that children need more than intrinsic motivation to keep them going with their studies. They also need extrinsic motivation, which is the desire to do something, not because it's fun, but because it's a means to a desired end. Extrinsic motivation enables children to see work in context, so they can persist despite difficulties or frustration.

Edward Deci and Richard Ryan at the University of Rochester and their colleagues have conducted some of the most compelling and useful research on motivation. They find that there are three main kinds of extrinsic motivation. We'll call these situation-based, approval-based, and value-based.

1. *Situation-based motivation* is determined by circumstances in the environment. Kids with situation-based motivation follow the rules. They might work hard in school in order to win money for good grades or to avoid being grounded for bad grades. This is the weakest kind of extrinsic motivation, because children can refuse to play the game, by declaring, "I don't care about those rules, rewards, or punishments." Children with situation-based motivation are also apt to decide, "I'm just going to do the minimum necessary to get the reward." Some bright children will even spend a lot of effort trying to figure out ways to get around the rules, or to make it appear as if they are complying when they really aren't.

2. *Approval-based motivation* involves "swallowing whole" other people's standards. Children with this kind of motivation live with a sense of constantly being judged. Their self-esteem depends on repeatedly proving their worth through visible accomplishments. They do things because they are afraid of others' disappointment or criticism or because they crave applause and public recognition. These children often work very hard, but they tend to give up when they believe the risk of a negative evaluation is too high or when the pressure to perform becomes too painful.

3. *Value-based motivation* is the most robust form of extrinsic motivation. It stems from children's consciously chosen and per-

sonally meaningful ideals. It enables them to persist with difficult or unpleasant tasks because they perceive that doing these tasks is somehow worthwhile. Value-based motivation comes initially from a sense of connection with a respected person or group. Ultimately, it can become part of a child's personal identity. When we say we want children to "care about learning" or "want to do their best," we're talking about value-based motivation. Value-based motivation can effectively fill the breach when intrinsic motivation lags (that is, when the task doesn't seem fun).

The table describes and compares the three types of extrinsic motivation. It also offers examples of statements illustrating each type.

Comparing Three Types of Extrinsic Motivation

More outwardly controlled ⟷ More self-determined

	Situation-based	*Approval-based*	*Value-based*
Focus	Rules, rewards, and punishments	Evaluations, approval, and disapproval	Personally chosen goals and values
Typical comments	"I'm supposed to . . ." "I'll get in trouble if I don't." "I do it so I can win points."	"I want the teacher to like me." "I'll feel bad about myself if I don't." "I want people to think I'm smart."	"I want to understand . . ." "I think it's important to . . ." "I'm the kind of person who . . ."
Response to failure	Excuses, blaming others	Anxiety, withdrawal, harsh self-criticism	Determined persistence

Source: Adapted from Ryan & Connell, 1989, and Ryan & Deci, 2000.

Motivation and Feelings

What difference does it make *why* kids do their work? Isn't the most important thing just that they get it done? Intriguing results from a study by Richard Ryan and James Connell at the University of Rochester suggest that different kinds of extrinsic motivation are linked to different feelings and outcomes. This study classified children in third through sixth grades according to their self-reported motivation for doing schoolwork. Students with situation-based motivation were the least interested in school, didn't see school as valuable, and reported the least effort toward achievement. They were also more likely to blame others for failure. Children with approval-based motivation reported more effort, but they also reported feeling very anxious and coping poorly with failure. When they didn't perform well, they worried and put themselves down or denied the importance of the setback. The most healthy responses were from children who said they had value-based motivation for doing schoolwork. These children showed the most interest, enjoyment, and effort. They also reported active, positive coping strategies in response to failure.

So how can we encourage children to have value-based motivation? On the basis of their extensive research, Deci and Ryan claim that value-based motivation is most likely to occur when three fundamental psychological needs are met: *competence*, *autonomy*, and *connection*. In the next sections, we consider each of these needs and describe practical strategies for addressing them.

STRATEGIES TO SUPPORT YOUR CHILD'S COMPETENCE

The first ingredient necessary for values-based motivation is *competence*. Children like to do things that they think they're good at because a sense of mastery is satisfying. A child who successfully makes a base hit will be eager to bat again. In contrast, children actively try to avoid activities in which they believe they can't be successful, because they don't want to feel embarrassed or inadequate. Here are some ideas about how you can help your child develop competence.

Address Possible Learning Issues

Some children who appear unmotivated are actually struggling with learning disabilities or attentional problems that compromise their performance. With bright children, these difficulties can be hard to detect because the children are able to compensate up to a point, especially in the younger grades. Also, parents and teachers may find it hard to fathom that, for example, a child who is extremely articulate might truly struggle to organize thoughts on paper, or that a child who grasped multiplication at an early age genuinely finds it difficult to avoid careless errors. When learning or attentional difficulties go undetected, it can lead to years of unnecessary misery, frustration, and self-doubt. If your child shows an ongoing pattern of underperformance, we strongly recommend that you speak with school personnel, an educational consultant, or a psychologist to help you determine whether testing is needed to identify or rule out learning difficulties.

Sometimes the issue is not a learning disability but a relative weakness or a learning gap. For example, if your daughter breezes through math but struggles with writing, she may decide, "I can't do writing" and just stop trying. Or, if your son went through a period of tuning out in math, he may have missed some foundational concepts, making it harder for him to grasp later material. Appropriate evaluation and tutoring can help increase academic competence and confidence.

Let Your Child Try

It's very easy for us parents to fall into the trap of doing too much for our children. We rush to the rescue because we hate to see them struggle, or because it's just easier and faster to do it ourselves. But when we leap in to solve a problem our children could solve themselves, we steal their opportunity to learn. Well-intentioned comments such as "Here, let me do it," "I'll talk to the teacher for you," or "I'll take care of it" tell children, "You can't handle this." By unnecessarily taking over, we prevent children from gaining the authentic self-confidence that comes from developing new skills and overcoming difficulties. Whether it's pouring milk from the big container or finishing a report on a famous inventor, when we let our children try, we express confidence in their ability to cope.

Explain the Criteria

Some bright children regularly ignore or misconstrue directions, which means they have only a vague idea of what the teacher wants. They often leave out key pieces of a project, or they misunderstand the teacher's questions, so they end up doing something that misses the point of the assignment. When their misdirected efforts are unsuccessful, they are apt to conclude that effort doesn't make a difference.

If your child has this tendency, you may want to make it a habit to go over directions *before* your child begins work. Having your child read instructions aloud and then restate them in his or her own words sometimes helps. Underlining or circling key words in directions can also be a useful strategy.

If the teacher provides a grading rubric for a major project, it may be helpful to review it carefully with your child. Ask questions to make sure that your child understands the criteria. "The teacher says the information is worth twenty points. What do you think your project needs to include to get all twenty information points?" "Artwork is worth five points, and the speech is worth thirty points. What does that tell you about where the teacher wants you to put your effort?" There's nothing more discouraging than spending a lot of effort and having it count for naught.

For large projects, you may want to suggest going over the rubric again, when the project is almost finished, to decide if adjustments are necessary. You may need to bite your tongue to refrain from mentioning all the ways you can think of to make the project even better. Be careful: if you take over, you will undermine your child's sense of competence. Think of your role as just making sure that your child is launched in the right direction, but let your child be the captain, steering the project.

Be Your Child's Biased Biographer

One of the most powerful ways that we as parents influence our children is through the stories that we construct about them and tell to them. Saying to a child, "You're so irresponsible! This is just like what you did last year! I keep telling you to put your homework in your folder, and you never listen!" suggests that the next chapter in the narrative will involve further mess-ups. This is discouraging rather than motivating. By being our children's positively biased biographers, we can help them see themselves as competent, which makes it easier for them to try.

Build a stockpile of your child's success stories, focusing on ones that involve struggle, followed by effort and resourcefulness, leading ultimately to a positive outcome. Tales of great effort or coping with adversity are more useful and inspiring than tales of instant, effortless success. Your child probably won't be interested in hearing these stories in the middle of an emotional motivation crisis, but bringing up these gems at other times can help shape your child's self-view as someone who is capable of handling challenges.

Start the inspiring success stories with a statement about some motivation-related ability or skill that you see in your child. For instance, you could say, "You know how to figure out good learning strategies for yourself," "You can choose to do the right thing, even when it's difficult," "You can come up with creative ways to solve problems," or "You're able to keep trying, even when it's hard." Then back up this statement with an anecdote. "I remember when you were learning to ride a two-wheeler. You were afraid of falling, and part of you wanted to just give up, but you kept trying until finally you did it!"

The stories don't have to involve major public triumphs. Small acts can have great meaning. "Last week, when it was so cold and rainy out, you didn't want to take Barney for a walk, but you know how much he needs exercise, so you took him anyway. I'm sure Barney appreciated that you cared enough about him to take him for a walk even though you didn't feel like doing it."

Maybe there are a lot more stories you could tell about times when your child *didn't* demonstrate responsibility, effort, or perseverance, but it's not helpful to bring those up. The times when your child got it right are the stories that need to be treasured and told.

You may also want to strategically tell stories about your child to adult family members within your child's hearing. Kids' ears perk up when they hear themselves being discussed. Try working a success story into a phone call to Grandma or an evening conversation with your spouse. Remember to emphasize the process rather than the outcome.

STRATEGIES TO SUPPORT YOUR CHILD'S AUTONOMY

The second ingredient for value-based motivation is *autonomy*. Autonomy means having a sense of personal control. It's human nature to want to steer our own course. Even two-year-olds insist, "I do it!" Motivation is most likely to persist when children feel that they have chosen to act in a certain way, rather than being forced to do it. Here are some strategies you can use to support appropriate autonomy for your child.

Be Cautious About Using Rewards

Research shows that external rewards can undermine value-based motivation. When children are rewarded for doing an activity that they enjoy or find satisfying, they often become less motivated to do that activity. Rewards that are given in a heavy-handed way can make kids think, "I'm only doing this to get the prize."

Despite this, rewards can sometimes be helpful on a temporary basis to get kids over a hump. For example, there is nothing fun about practicing math facts, but that practice is necessary so that children can compute effortlessly and move on to the more interesting task of solving problems. Rewarding kids with a fun activity after they finish practicing can make an unpleasant task more palatable.

Rewards are least likely to undermine value-based motivation if they are unexpected and intangible. Don't reward your child for every little thing. Let the reward be a delightful surprise when your child shows particularly good effort or reaches a competence milestone. Also, stick mainly with warm words or a special activity, rather than material rewards, because these enhance a sense of closeness.

You may also want to talk to your child about self-rewards. These can be very effective for inspiring and maintaining motivation without compromising autonomy. Kids can make a deal with themselves, along the lines of "If I do this, then I get to do that." Unlike any reward system you set up, knowing how to self-reward is something your child can carry throughout life.

Allow Choices

Giving your child choices about when and how schoolwork is done can increase your child's sense of autonomy: Living room or bedroom? Regular pencil or mechanical pencil? Spelling or math first? Don't overwhelm your child with too many choices, but try to allow enough wiggle room so that your child can feel some sense of self-direction.

Allowing choices includes allowing the choice of messing up. Some kids need to learn from experience what *doesn't* work with homework. They need to find out what happens if they don't study or don't bother to turn in a paper. While your child is in elementary school is a low-cost time for this kind of experimentation.

If your child messes up, don't rush to the rescue. Don't make excuses or offer to call the teacher. Just empathize with your child's disappointment and then calmly ask what your child thinks might help next time.

Provide a Rationale

Kids find it easier to do a task if they know why that task is important. If your child complains about an assignment, you may be able to explain why the teacher assigned it or how it relates to real-life skills or interesting topics.

If your child doesn't buy this explanation or you can't think of one, you may want to offer a rationale that focuses on process rather than content. Explain to your child that there are two things kids need to learn in school. One is the "what"—the specific information or skills that educated people know, such as punctuation rules or how to subtract big numbers. The other is the "how"—the more subtle, usually unspoken lessons about how to figure out what the teacher wants, how to learn new material effectively, how to break down large assignments into manageable steps, how to work on a group project, how to learn from mistakes, how to manage boredom, frustration, or anxiety . . . Even when your child can't see any relevance in the "what," the "how" is critically important, because these are the skills that your child will need in high school, college, and the working world. See if your child can figure out what the "how" lesson is in a particular assignment.

Have "Meaning of Life" Conversations

Once they're capable of thinking abstractly, most smart kids love to philosophize. Encouraging your child to articulate answers to the big questions about life in a warm and accepting environment can help your child begin to define personal values. These values, in turn, can instill motivation. Sometime when you're out for a walk or going on a long drive or hanging out together at night, try in a low-key way to engage your child in a conversation about philosophical issues. What does "a good life" mean? Are humans naturally good or evil? What makes people truly happy? What responsibility do we have to other people in the world? Listen attentively and respectfully to your child's responses, but recognize that your child's answers will evolve over time. Share your ideas, but don't try to convince your child that you're right and he or she is wrong. Ask questions to clarify and deepen your child's thinking. Choosing how we live our lives and what matters to us is the ultimate form of autonomy.

STRATEGIES TO SUPPORT YOUR CHILD'S CONNECTION

The third ingredient necessary for value-based motivation is *connection*, which refers to the quality of a child's relationship with a group or an adult. Children tend to identify with and imitate the people with whom they feel closest. Think of a toddler, delightedly clomping around the house in Mommy's shoes. Here are some motivation-enhancing ways to connect with your child.

Respond to the Feelings Behind the Complaints

The fastest way to diffuse complaints is just to listen and empathize. In the vignette involving Jared complaining that schoolwork is boring, things might have gone better if Jared's mother had been able to acknowledge his feelings from the start. This *doesn't* mean agreeing that the assignment is stupid (which would give his complaints too much weight). Nor does it mean giving him permission to avoid his work. It just means acknowledging how he's feeling at that moment, without trying to fix those feelings: "You're annoyed about having to color," "You wish you didn't have to do this," "You dislike artsy assignments." Jared's mom could keep reflecting until Jared winds down—until he sighs, "Yeah," and his body visibly relaxes. At that point, Jared would be more open to considering options and consequences or maybe even taking his mother's advice.

Reflecting feelings is not something that comes naturally to most parents. Logically, it seems as though jumping directly to solving the problem would be the most efficient approach. Practically, this rarely works with kids. When children are feeling emotional, they just can't listen to reason. Acknowledging feelings clears the air, making it possible for children to think. It also minimizes power struggles and builds a sense of connection between children and parents.

Provide Role Models

Having a role model can inspire children. Parents can be role models, but so can other adults. Silvia Rimm reports research which shows that there are three factors that predict whether a child will identify with an adult:

1. *Similarity*. Kids are more likely to identify with an adult when they believe that they are somehow like that adult.

2. *Warmth*. Kids are more likely to identify with an adult when they perceive that the adult cares about them and likes them.

3. *Power*. Kids are more likely to identify with an adult whom they perceive as effective in the world rather than helpless.

Think about how you and other adults in your child's life might fit this bill. You might try to arrange for your child to have contact with admirable adults. Invite a neighbor or colleague over for dinner and, in your child's hearing, ask about that person's career path. Speak admiringly about your child's teacher, sports coach, or scout leader. Making room for your child to have a mentor outside the family in no way diminishes your relationship with your child.

Enjoy Your Child's Company

When parents are worried about their children's school performance, it's easy for this concern to dominate all their interactions with their children. "How did you do on the test?" "Did you finish your homework?" "When are you going to get your poster done?" This well-intentioned and probably well-deserved nagging is very irritating to children. If you have to ask about schoolwork, make sure you talk about other, fun topics before and after. You may also want to decide that you won't mention schoolwork during certain times of the day.

If there's tension about schoolwork, it's especially important that you spend time with your child doing fun things together and just relaxing and enjoying each other's company. This helps your child feel loved and accepted, despite the difficulties.

DIANE: NOT APPLYING HERSELF IN SCHOOL

"Thank you for coming in to speak with me, Mrs. Granger," Diane's teacher began. "As I told you on the phone, I'm very concerned about Diane's school performance. She's clearly a bright girl, but she just isn't applying herself."

"Diane keeps telling me she's going to try harder. I thought she was doing better about handing in her assignments," Diane's mom said.

"She is, but her work is sloppy and careless. Look at this paper," the teacher said as she pulled out a page full of math problems. "I know Diane knows how to do long division, but many of these problems are wrong. She makes careless errors."

"Diane says math is too easy for her. She says it's boring."

"Well, how can I move her on to more advanced work, when she's making so many mistakes with the regular work? And it's not just math that's a problem.

"This is Diane's book report. The children were supposed to write a five-paragraph essay discussing how the main character changed over the course of the book, but Diane wrote only one paragraph. And what she did write is full of spelling errors and doesn't address the issue of character change. I know Diane's a strong reader, but she's just not showing effort with her schoolwork."

❧

The teacher feels frustrated by Diane's persistent lack of effort in school. Diane's mother feels helpless and worried. They both feel bewildered about why this smart girl doesn't seem to want to apply herself.

We suspect that Diane truly does want to do better in school. When she tells her mom that she's going to try harder, the desire to improve is genuinely there. Where she gets stuck is translating her goal into action. A goal without a plan is just wishful thinking. Unfortunately, no amount of wishful thinking can get her language arts paper written.

Fear of Effort

There are a lot of reasons why Diane might have trouble following through with her homework, but one possibility is that she's afraid of effort. Many smart kids somehow get the idea that "only stupid people have to try." Because learning has come easily to them in the past, they expect that success should be effortless. If they don't grasp a subject instantly, they tend to write it off completely, concluding, "I'm just not good at that."

With some bright children, lack of effort is a self-protective strategy. They tell themselves, "I could do it; I just don't want to." By never trying, they avoid putting that assumption to the test. Despite their bravado, these children harbor secret doubts about their abilities. We've noticed that the more adults tell them, "You're so smart! You could do so well if you'd just try!" the more these children resist trying. They protest that the subject is stupid or the teacher is mean, but inside these kids are scared. They worry that if they try, they might not do well. They fear that they don't even know how to try, because they've never done it.

Fixed Versus Growth Mindset

Research by psychologist Carol Dweck on mindset, which we discussed in Chapter One, is very relevant for these children. For instance, in a series of studies by Claudia Mueller and Carol Dweck, ten- to twelve-year-old children did problems from a nonverbal IQ test. The experimenter then told half the children, "Wow, you did very well on these problems. You must be smart at this," and the other half, "Wow, you did very well on these problems. You must have worked really hard." In other words, one group was praised for ability and the other for effort.

After giving this feedback, the experimenter offered the children a choice of doing either easy or more challenging problems. Most of the kids praised for ability chose the easy problems, presumably because they didn't want to jeopardize their "smartness" designation, but almost all of the kids praised for effort wanted to do the hard problems. The children were told they would get their choice at the end of the session "if there was extra time," but first they had to complete the prearranged tasks.

The experimenter then gave the children a second set of harder problems. Children praised for ability enjoyed the hard problems less than did kids praised for effort, and they were less likely to want to take them to work on at home. In contrast, many of the children praised for effort said the hard problems were the most fun. When offered a choice between reading (1) a folder containing information about "interesting new strategies" for solving the problems or (2) a folder containing information about "average scores" of unfamiliar children, 86 percent of children praised for ability wanted to know about how well other kids had performed, whereas 87 percent of those praised for effort chose to read about strategies. This suggests that being praised for ability led most kids to care more about their relative performance than about learning.

Next, the experimenter gave students a third set of problems that was easier, like the first set. The children praised for ability did substantially worse on the third set than they did on the initial set. Doing the difficult problems in between the first and third set apparently shook their confidence. In contrast, the children praised for effort did substantially better on the third set of problems, because they had learned strategies from doing the harder problems.

Finally, the experimenter told the children that they would be visiting other schools, and it would be very helpful if the children could describe their experience for students. The children received a paper with some space to write a paragraph about the experiment plus a small line where they could record their scores. Almost 40 percent of the students praised for ability *lied*, inflating their score. (Only 13 percent of those praised for effort exaggerated their performance.)

In her book *Mindset*, Dweck exclaims, "We took ordinary children and turned them into liars [and cowards], just by telling them they're smart!" Dweck has replicated her key concepts in many studies, with different samples, different ages, and different methodologies, including experimental and correlational studies, laboratory and naturalistic studies, and even brain scans.

Dweck's research points to the importance of cultivating a growth mindset rather than a fixed mindset in our children. Children with a fixed mindset believe that they are born with a certain amount of ability and that's it. Their performance is proof of their level of innate intelligence or talent. Failure means they're stupid, so these children are profoundly risk averse and prone to blaming others for difficulties. In contrast, children with a growth mindset believe that they can become smarter through effort. A poor performance to them means only that they need to work harder or learn better strategies. These children are resilient in the face of setbacks.

The implications of Dweck's research for parents of bright children are profound. We need to be very cautious about praising children's intelligence. We need to emphasize how they are growing rather than what they can do because of innate abilities. We need to help them embrace effort rather than feel frightened of or ashamed by it.

STRATEGIES TO ENCOURAGE YOUR CHILD'S EFFORT

Merely exhorting children to "Try harder!" rarely helps, because kids with motivation problems often don't know *how* to try hard. Learning to exert effort is a critical skill that enables children and adults to make the most of their abilities. Here are some ideas you can use to help your child embrace effort and let go of crippling assumptions about instant success.

Break Down Global Thinking

One of the key differences between children and adults is that children lack perspective. Kids just don't have enough life experience to place events in context. When adults make a mistake, they can usually say to themselves, "Well, I messed up on that, but I'm still a good person." Kids have a hard time doing this.

When they get a bad grade (which they might define as anything from an F to an A–), they're likely to see this as a global evaluation of their whole person. They tend to think, "I'm bad" or "I'm dumb." They feel ashamed, so they react by either wanting to hide the bad grade or by feeling furious at the grader. Their global thinking leaves them feeling helpless.

Most books on helping unmotivated children suggest starting out by having the child set goals that are specific, measurable, and achievable. This is fine for kids who are used to succeeding, but we don't recommend it for struggling performers. Spelling out explicit goals tends to make these children feel too exposed and vulnerable. If they voice their desire to do better and then don't, it's a crushing humiliation. So just assume that— underneath it all—your poorly performing child really wants to do better in school, then help your child overcome the helplessness that comes from immature global thinking.

One way to do this is to break the task of schoolwork down into a sequence of manageable steps and help your child identify sticking points. The figure on the following page illustrates an example of how you might do this, but you may need to adjust the sequence to make it relevant for your child. The sequence should include enough boxes that your child can honestly say that he or she is usually successful at completing most of the steps. Tell your child, "Great! You've got most of these steps down! Now we just need to come up with some ideas to make it easier for you to handle those couple of sticking points."

Brainstorm possibilities together for addressing the sticking points, and encourage your child to pick one or two options to try.

Do the Math to See the Impact of Not Turning in Work

Sometimes children don't realize how much they can hurt their academic performance by not turning in work. If your child

Where are the sticking points?

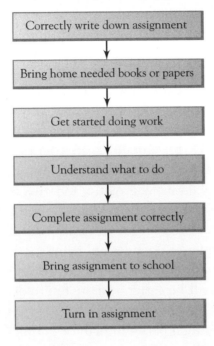

Correctly write down assignment

↓

Bring home needed books or papers

↓

Get started doing work

↓

Understand what to do

↓

Complete assignment correctly

↓

Bring assignment to school

↓

Turn in assignment

knows how to compute averages, you may want to use psychologist Michael Whitley's suggestion and have your child do the math to calculate how many 100 percent grades it takes to bring up a grade after a missed assignment. Not turning in an assignment results in a grade of zero. Not turning in an assignment and then getting 100 percent on the next assignment results in an average grade of 50 percent. A zero and three 100 percent grades yield an average of 75 percent. It takes nine grades of 100 percent following a zero to bring the average up to 90 percent. This exercise can help your child see that it's far better to turn in something than nothing for school assignments.

Help Your Child Construct If-Then Plans

Peter Gollwitzer at New York University explains that achieving goals requires that we solve problems related to getting started and persisting in the face of distractions, discomfort, or competing goals. His research looks at "if-then" plans that address when, where, and how goal-related activities will take place. These take the form of "If this situation occurs, then I will . . ." For example, "If my brother distracts me while I'm studying, then I will ignore him." "If it's 4:00, then I will start my homework." "If I get stuck with a math problem, then I will ask my teacher for help." These simple plans are surprisingly effective at enhancing performance. One study even shows that they affect the brain waves of children with ADHD while they are doing an attention-requiring task.

Gollwitzer maintains that if-then plans work because they make self-control more automatic and therefore less effortful. When children have an if-then plan, as soon as they encounter the specified situation, they know what to do. The situation itself serves as a reminder to do a desired behavior. Kids don't have to waste time wondering, "So what should I do? Do I really want to do this? Wouldn't it be easier or more fun to do something else?"

Explain the concept of if-then plans, but get your child to do the work of devising a personal plan or plans. You can ask questions, such as, "What if X happens?" "What do you think might get in the way of you doing that?" "What could you do to prevent or deal with that problem?" or "So, how could we say that as an if-then plan?" You may want to play the role of chief scribe, writing down the plan. For younger children, you may want to provide the "if" part of the equation and let them determine the "then."

Be careful not to overwhelm your child with plans. It's better to have a single plan that your child actually uses than a bunch of plans that your child falls short of and that only serve as a sign of failure. Once the first plan is a routine part of your child's life, you can add more if needed.

Discover Personal Learning Strategies

When adults say, "You need to try hard!" or "You need to show effort!" children tend to hear, "You need to suffer!" No wonder they often balk at these suggestions!

A healthier message for kids is, "You need to figure out which learning strategies work best for you." This is an example of *metacognition*, or thinking about thinking. Strong students are capable of effective metacognition: they know how to determine what they do or don't know and how to go about the process of learning.

Talk to your child about the difference between recognition and recall. Recognition means that sense of "Oh, yeah, I vaguely remember seeing this before." Recall means being able to retrieve information—to pull it out of our heads. Many bright children study only to the point of recognition. When the test comes, they get stuck ("I studied, but it didn't help!"), or they rely on their reasoning powers to fill in the gaps. Recognition only works with fairly simple topics and trivial tests, because it doesn't involve deeply understanding the material.

Unlike passive recognition, recall requires active involvement with the information. Repeated exposure and connecting to the information through multiple learning strategies make it easier for children to recall material. Here are some active learning strategies that your child might want to try:

- Anticipate teacher's questions and try to answer them.
- Fold a paper in half vertically. Write key words on one side and definitions on the other. Cover up the definitions and practice recalling them.
- Organize material by sorting it into piles or creating a list, outline, mind map, or chart.
- Invent a rhyme or saying to help you remember.
- Think through pros and cons, causes and effects, strengths and weaknesses.
- Discuss material with others.

Provide Opportunities for Refueling

Self-control is like a muscle that tires when it has been actively used for a while. Research shows that after doing tasks requiring effortful self-control, people are less able to persist on later tasks, and their blood glucose levels are lower. Self-control strength can be replenished through sleep, food, or experiencing positive emotions.

This has practical implications for parents. First, try not to make children do tasks that require effortful self-control when they are tired or hungry. Giving them a snack and some time to run around after school can make it easier for them to focus on homework. Second, help your child plan short breaks to clear the mind, stretch the muscles, or feed the body in order to sustain effort. Does your child prefer working for a certain amount of time (fifteen to thirty minutes) before taking a break, or taking a break after accomplishing certain tasks (for example, after finishing math homework but before starting spelling)? What does your child want to do during the break?

Parental contact offers another kind of refueling. We've emphasized that it's important for parents not to take over children's homework, but chatting with children or offering a hug during a study break can provide emotional refueling to enable them to return to work.

Help Your Child Catch Up and Keep Up with Schoolwork

If your child has a tendency to avoid doing schoolwork, consult with the teacher to find out what hasn't been completed. You and the teacher may need to figure out a reasonable plan for helping your child get back on track. On the one hand, you want to send a clear message to your child that schoolwork is not optional. On the other hand, the plan for moving forward has to be doable, not overwhelming. This may mean excusing your child from some past work or splitting it across several weekends. What is critical in situations like this is not that children realize how far behind they are (which is upsetting for kids), but rather the act of getting caught up and having a clean slate from which to try again.

Once your child is caught up, you may need to check in with the teacher once a week to help your child stay on top of things. Explain to your child, "You have a choice: you can do the work on the day that it's assigned, or you can complete it on the weekend, before you play with your friends (or get on the computer). Either way, it has to be done." State this confidently and calmly, in the same tone of voice that you would use to insist on teeth brushing.

If your child has to catch up on schoolwork on the weekends, aim for fifteen to forty-five minutes for a homework completion session, depending on the age of your child. Don't correct your child's work, because that would make finishing it unnecessarily painful. Just glance at it to see if it's complete (for example, there's the required half-page of writing, or all the problems have answers). Your goal is not to make your child suffer but to underscore the importance and inevitability of the work.

Recent research questions the educational usefulness of homework in early grades, but it's important that children learn respect and responsibility by meeting expectations. The tricky part is that *expectations should match children's individual capabilities and developmental stage*. It's never a good idea for young children to be up until ten o'clock at night doing homework. If that happens in your home, you need to talk with the teacher about adjusting the requirements. For some children, such as those who are very anxious or who have ADHD, it may make sense to negotiate with the teacher for a reduced homework load.

Consider Academic Acceleration or Enrichment

Because bright kids so often complain of being bored, parents frequently wonder whether academic acceleration (that is, moving a child up one or more grades in all or some subjects) would help their child become more engaged in school. Schools tend to resist acceleration because it can create logistical problems, and they don't want to set precedents that will be difficult to carry through ("What if lots of parents want . . . ?") Gifted associations tend to advocate for acceleration as a means of getting bright children into the instructional setting they need. The Iowa Acceleration Scale is a research-based measure that can help with this decision. Obviously, each case needs to be considered on an individual basis.

We're not educators, so we can't speak to the academic pros and cons of acceleration, but from a psychological perspective, we urge parents who are thinking about acceleration to consider their children's social and emotional maturity. Would your child do better, the same, or worse interacting with older kids?

Parents should also look closely at their children's motivation. If your child has a hunger to learn, frequently engages in independent projects outside of school, comes alive when you say, "Here's a hard problem," and willingly persists in the face of obstacles and setbacks, then acceleration could be the answer that offers the challenge your child craves, especially if your child wants to move up.

In contrast, if your child merely complains about being bored, generally seems passive and unmotivated outside school as well as in school, and shows effort only in areas where success comes easily, then acceleration probably would not be helpful, because your child hasn't yet learned to muster effort. Putting children like this in a more demanding academic situation would be a bit like throwing them into the deep end of a pool when they don't know how to swim. The extra challenge wouldn't be energizing for them; it would be scary and could lead them to feel inadequate, because they wouldn't know how to cope. For these children, enrichment activities outside school may be better than acceleration in school for helping them "get their feet wet" with the experience of exerting effort.

Develop Strategies for Mustering Motivation

Motivation is a state, not a trait. We all experience ups and downs in how motivated we are to do what we need to do. This is normal. But it also means we need to figure out effective ways to get ourselves moving. Ask what your child has found helpful for starting or persisting with schoolwork. Research with college students indicates that they deliberately try to increase their own motivation. How many of the self-motivation strategies listed in the table has your child tried?

Self-Motivation Strategies

Emphasize Learning	I tell myself to keep working so I can learn as much as possible.
	I think about wanting to become good at what I'm learning or doing.
	I convince myself to work hard just for the sake of learning.
Increase Relevance	I try to connect the material with something I like doing or find interesting.
	I imagine situations where it would be useful to know this stuff.
	I tell myself that I'll need to know this later in life.
Improve the Task	I make studying more fun by turning it into a game.
	I think of a way to make the work seem more enjoyable.
Manage the Situation	I try to study at a time when I can focus.
	I make sure I have as few distractions as possible.
	I eat or drink something so that I'm awake and ready to work.

(*continued*)

Self-Motivation Strategies

Plan Personal Rewards	I make a deal with myself that if I finish my work, I can do something fun afterward. I promise myself some kind of reward if I get my homework done.

Source: Adapted from Wolters, Pintrich, & Karabenick, 2005.

Self-motivation strategies are important because they put children in the driver's seat in terms of managing their effort and persistence. When—not if—their motivation starts to lag, they'll know what to do to help themselves continue.

Offer Encouragement

Having parents recognize their efforts helps children keep going. However, we need to be careful about how we do this. Abstract and overblown praise along the lines of "Fantastic! This is amazing! You're brilliant!" can actually inhibit children. They may feel that they *have* to be fantastic-amazing-brilliant to win your approval. This could make them ashamed of less-than-fantastic efforts and reluctant to try things where they might not be instantly successful. Moreover, if children disagree with the over-the-top praise, they might feel less trusting of the parent's truthfulness. They might think, "Mom says I'm fantastic. I don't feel fantastic. Mom must be lying."

One alternative is to comment, in a low-key manner, on your personal pleasure in your child's work. These comments must be sincere and not tied to future expectations. "I enjoyed reading your story." "Looking at your painting makes me smile." "I found those facts about penguins that you wrote on your poster very interesting."

Another option is simply to describe your child's efforts with warm approval in your voice. "You turned in every one of your homework assignments this week!" "I noticed you've been putting a lot of effort into your writing assignments lately." "Your drawing is full of detail." Because these remarks refer to observable facts, they can't be debated. Help your child own the victory by asking, "How are you managing to do this?" Listen attentively to whatever your child says in response. If your child replies, "I dunno," say, "Well, you might want to think about that, because whatever you're doing seems to be working for you." This emphasizes effort and strategy rather than innate ability. You can also reflect your child's feelings of satisfaction in a job well done by commenting, "It feels good to do your best."

SHOW THE WAY

Children's academic struggles tend to arouse strong feelings from parents: anger, frustration, worry . . . The instinctive response to these feelings is to clamp down harder on children: "No more soccer until you get those grades up!" "From now on, you have to show me every piece of homework, and I'm going to check them over for mistakes!" Unfortunately, these well-intentioned efforts to control the situation are likely to backfire. Motivation problems can't be solved by force or fear. In contrast, demonstrating your own positive attitude toward effort and growth can help bolster your child's motivation.

Share Your Enthusiasm for Your Work or Projects

How do you feel about your own work? Whether it's paid work, volunteer work, or running-a-household work, how you react sends a powerful message to your child. Too often, adults communicate to children, "I'm suffering, so you should too." Any healthy child will reject that message.

It's easy to fall into the habit of complaining about work. Certainly, any job has annoying and frustrating aspects, but most also have challenging, satisfying, and enjoyable parts. Think about how you talk about what you do. Make a point of sharing your enthusiasm.

Minimize Family Stress

Children's schoolwork often suffers when a family experiences significant stress. Even bright children are less available for learning when they're worried about the big argument that Mom and Dad had last night. Take an honest look at the level of stress in your home. Cut back, make changes, create routines, or get help if you need it. Do whatever you can to make your home a safe base from which your child can explore the world.

Attend Your High School Reunion

If you were a "good kid" who followed all the rules and did everything that was expected of you, it may be hard to imagine any alternative. Attending your high school reunion can shake up your belief in the straight-and-narrow path. Undoubtedly, you will encounter some former classmates whose academic performance was unexceptional in high school but who now have interesting and satisfying careers. You'll also find some former classmates who aced school but whose later accomplishments don't seem to match their early promise. Seeing the variety of life paths might help you worry less about your child, who is still learning to be a learner.

Postpone Worrying About College Admission

When parents come to see us in our practices, they almost always say something like, "I'm so worried about her future! If she keeps this up, she'll never be able to [manage on her own, be successful in life, get into a decent college]!" These worries are understandable, but projecting into the future this way is not helpful. Your child isn't going to college or even living alone anytime soon, so there's no reason to be alarmed by the fact that he or she doesn't seem close to being able to handle these responsibilities.

Children are not supposed to show adult-style discipline and drive. It's normal for them to prefer playing soccer to doing social studies homework. This doesn't mean that they lack motivation; it just means that they're kids. What grade your child got on the chapter three math test in second grade really has no bearing on future life accomplishments. Children grow and change tremendously, so we really can't predict what their future will be. Your best bet is to focus on the here and now and look for ways to nurture your child's sense of identity as a learner. Teach, strategize, or explain as needed, but keep in mind that one of the best gifts we can offer children is our faith that they'll figure things out and find a path that's right for them.

There are no quick fixes for motivation problems, so if your child is struggling in this area, you'll need to take a long-term view. In this chapter, we described ways to encourage your child's natural interests. We also looked at ways to cultivate a sense of competence, autonomy, and connection, so that your child can muster value-based motivation to persist with tasks that aren't intrinsically fun. Finally, we talked about ways to support your child in translating motivation into action, by focusing on learning strategies, plans, and growth.

The ability to work hard is important, but so is the ability to find happiness, which is the focus of the next chapter.

CHAPTER 7

FINDING JOY
What Makes Your Child Feel Happy?

 Does your child

○ Complain frequently?

○ Seem irritable and hard to please?

○ Tend to focus on the negative?

○ Find fault with even positive experiences?

· ○ Often put herself down?

○ Feel overwhelmed by ordinary demands?

○ Seem not to enjoy his accomplishments?

○ Seem to be "just going through the motions" rather than interested or enthusiastic?

○ Believe that being smart and being happy are mutually exclusive options?

"I just want my kid to be happy." Almost every parent has said or thought this. No matter how bright or accomplished our children might be, this is our most basic wish for them. At some level, everything we do for our children—insisting that they brush their teeth, driving them to soccer practice, asking whether they've finished their homework, reminding them to chew with their mouth closed, planning their birthday parties—is aimed at their present or future happiness.

But what do we really mean when we say we want our kids to be happy? If we could, we'd give them a trouble-free life, but we know that's impossible. There's nothing more delightful than hearing a child's joyful laughter, but we know that that kind of glee is fleeting. So when we wish for our children's happiness, we're hoping for something deeper than the absence of pain and more enduring than momentary enjoyment.

WHY HAPPINESS MATTERS

Our children's happiness is important not just because we love them and therefore want them to feel good but also because happiness predicts and precedes better life outcomes. Research with adults suggests that positive moods lead to an upward spiral toward psychological well-being. Feeling happy now is often linked, down the road, to better mental health, more supportive relationships, and even better physical health.

Negative moods narrow attention so we can focus on an immediate problem, but positive moods allow us to think broadly, creatively, and flexibly. Positive moods encourage us to try new things and seek out new experiences. They also make our interactions with others more enjoyable—it's just more fun to be around people who are in a good mood. Over time, positive moods fuel growth by prompting exploration, learning, and connection. Ultimately this can lead to greater knowledge and skills, as well as more supportive relationships. Because children are only beginning to develop coping skills and relationships outside the family, being able to cultivate positive moods could be especially important for supporting this growth.

Feeling Good *and* Being Good

In philosophy and psychology, there's often a distinction between pleasure and meaning as two separate, opposing paths toward well-being. The pleasure tradition emphasizes seeking enjoyment and comfort, whereas the meaning tradition emphasizes cultivating virtue and values-driven self-development. This distinction makes sense in theory, but in real life, pleasure and meaning are often intertwined. Meaningful activity often leads to happy feelings, and happy feelings can inspire meaningful activities, such as kindness and creativity. A particular activity, such as playing an instrument or spending time with friends, can be a source of both pleasure and meaning.

Research shows that the happiest people describe their lives as very enjoyable and also very meaningful. People who say they look for both pleasure and meaning report greater life satisfaction than those who emphasize one or the other or neither. Pleasure without meaning can lead to a sense of emptiness. Meaning without pleasure can yield feelings of drudgery and martyrdom. As parents, we want our children to feel good *and* to be good.

Positive Psychology

So how can we help our children be happy? Recently, there has been a tremendous amount of research about "positive psychology." This research focuses on the upside of human existence, such as positive emotions and personal strengths, and it has yielded a detailed and practical perspective on what makes adults happy. This literature conclusively shows that although happiness is strongly determined by genetic factors, there are things that adults can do to markedly increase their happiness.

Unfortunately, there is very little research about what makes kids happy. Asking children directly, "What makes you happy?" usually doesn't yield helpful information. They tend to answer, "Ice cream" or "If you buy me the new video game." Although these might bring momentary delight, as parents, we hope for deeper and more long-lasting answers for our children.

Interventions that work to increase happiness for adults don't necessarily translate to kids. For instance, a positive psychology exercise that is frequently recommended for adults is to write and deliver a gratitude letter. Adults tend to find this exercise very moving, as it fills them with a sense of love and appreciation for an important person in their lives. But in our own families, we've found that insisting that our children write thank-you notes to relatives has not particularly filled them with joy. And research bears out our at-home observations.

Jeffrey Froh at Hofstra University and his colleagues conducted a study in which students in third, eighth, and twelfth grades wrote a gratitude letter to an important person in their lives. The students worked on the letter for ten or fifteen minutes, on six days spread over two weeks. Although the content of the letters was emotionally vivid, participants in this program showed no increase in overall happiness compared to students who wrote about daily events. However, the investigators did find evidence that the gratitude letters were related to some increases in well-being among the most disengaged students.

Children are not simply short adults. Their way of thinking about and experiencing the world is qualitatively different from that of adults. This is true even for bright, articulate children who sound older than their years. Kids have limited life experience, and their sense of who they are is evolving. They have much less decision-making power than adults. Our clinical experience also suggests that, compared to adults, kids are more focused on the present (rather than the past or the future), have less ability to introspect, and tend to think more concretely and categorically (good or bad, black or white). Positive psychology interventions for children need to take all of this into account.

Although it's useful to talk about general ways to increase happiness, finding joy is a personal journey. Children need to know themselves—what delights them, what inspires them, what matters to them. One of our most important jobs as parents is to support our children in discovering these aspects of who they are.

MONICA: FINDING FAULT INSTEAD OF FUN

"Hi, sweetie. How was the birthday party?" Monica's mom asked.

"Okay, I guess. It was kind of boring."

"What do you mean 'boring'? Didn't you play miniature golf?"

"It wasn't *that* fun. It was really crowded, and we had to wait a lot between holes."

"Well, at least you got to spend time outside. Marisol had a beautiful day for the party. The weather couldn't have been nicer."

"It was too hot, and the sun kept getting in my eyes."

"What did you have to eat?"

"Pizza and cake, but the cake was yellow instead of chocolate, and we each only got a very tiny piece."

❧

Most kids enjoy birthday parties, but Monica is full of complaints. It's as though she has tunnel vision that only allows her to notice what's wrong. This behavior is undoubtedly annoying to people around her, but it also interferes with her own enjoyment. There's no law that says Monica has to love birthday parties or miniature golf, but her long list of complaints suggests that she has a habit of being negative that interferes with her ability to enjoy life.

Dampening Happiness with Critical Judgments

Monica's comments are all critical. By judging everything she encounters, she holds herself apart from experiences. She's mentally sitting on the sidelines rather than actively participating. With some bright children, we've had the sense that they feel as though it's their job to point out flaws, as if this makes them especially discerning. Unfortunately, focusing on what's wrong, what might go wrong, how things are not as good as they could be, how someone else is better off, and so forth dampens their ability to enjoy positive experiences.

To find joy, we need to be open to it. Few experiences are 100 percent positive, so believing that we can be happy only if everything is perfect is a sure path to misery. Joy involves engagement with life, and it's incompatible with an aloof, fault-finding stance.

Listening to children's negative judgments can be exasperating, but it's important to keep in mind that children like Monica aren't trying to be obnoxious or ungrateful. They suffer more than anyone else from their tendency to focus on the negative.

Arguing with children who are caught up in negativity never works—they just dig in their heels and offer more complaints. Instead of arguments, they need guidance so that they can recognize how negativity hurts them and develop ways to cultivate positive feelings.

Savoring

Fred Bryant at Loyola University has studied savoring for over two decades. He defines savoring as the "the capacity to attend to the joys, pleasures, and other positive feelings that we experience in our lives." Savoring involves the things we think and do to enhance and prolong positive feelings. It's about squeezing as much enjoyment as possible from our daily lives. People who regularly practice savoring tend to be happier and more optimistic. Positive circumstances naturally tend to lose their mood-enhancing luster as we get used to them. At first we're delighted, but after a while they just seem normal. Savoring is a way to keep our pleasure fresh. For adults, savoring can involve marveling at awe-inspiring phenomena or luxuriating in physical sensations.

Kids can certainly feel happy, and they know when they are happy, but are they mentally capable of true savoring in the sense of reflecting on positive feelings as they occur and deliberately enhancing their enjoyment of positive experiences? Probably not on their own. In the preadolescent years, savoring is mostly an emerging skill, but it's one that parents can help support and develop.

STRATEGIES TO HELP YOUR CHILD EXPERIENCE AND SAVOR PLEASURE

Supporting your child's ability to experience and savor pleasure requires a delicate touch. It also requires sensitive acceptance of your child's style of relating. Aim to nudge and invite rather than demand. Your goal is to help your child become more open to possibilities for genuine enjoyment, not to insist that your child act like a perky cheerleader at all times. Here are some strategies you may want to try to help your child become more engaged, aware, and reflective about positive experiences.

Discuss the Benefits of Seeing the Glass as Half Full

The classic description of optimism—seeing the glass as half full—seems trite to adults, but for many kids it's new information. Use a real glass of water or juice to make your explanation more vivid. Focus on choices and consequences rather than traits. In other words, rather than asking, "How do you generally see things?" or accusing your child of "always seeing the glass as half empty," emphasize that both perspectives are accurate, but they have very different impacts on how we feel. See if your child can predict the emotional consequences of the different perspectives.

Explain to your child that sometimes it takes real effort to see the "half full" side of things. "Half full" thinking doesn't mean denying unpleasantness. It does mean recognizing that a bad situation is salvageable in some way, to some degree, or that it won't last long. Work with your child to come up with some "half full" perspectives on the common childhood tragedies listed here. Using the prompt "At least . . ." may be helpful.

My best friend can't come over tomorrow after school.

> (At least I can invite a different friend; at least I can have my friend over for a longer play date on the weekend; at least I can do something I enjoy even though my friend won't be here.)

Dad said I can only have a small ice cream cone.

> (At least I'm having ice cream; at least the store has my favorite flavor.)

My favorite shirt is in the wash.

> (At least it will be clean for tomorrow; at least I can wear my second favorite shirt.)

I have a math test today.

> (At least it will be over soon; at least I know the material pretty well; at least it's only worth fifty points; at least we'll be done with fractions after this.)

My parents won't let me get a cell phone until I'm thirteen.

> (At least they're letting me have one when I'm thirteen.)

The next time your child is listing negatives, don't dispute these, because your child will dismiss your arguments and come up with even more complaints. Instead, just acknowledge the complaints in a general way by saying something like "A lot of things didn't turn out the way you hoped" or "You wish things were different." Then comment, "Remember how a glass can seem half full or half empty? Can you think of anything about the situation that *was* good?" If your child says no, don't push it. Just respond with mild sympathy by saying, "That's too bad" or "I'm sorry to hear that" and then change the subject. You've made the point that your child has another option, but your child is choosing not to use it at that time. If your child does manage to come up with something positive, respond with enthusiasm. You could say something like, "Good for you! Noticing the good stuff when there's lots of bad stuff is a hard thing to do!" then ask some interested questions about the positive observation.

Look for Little Joys

Little joys add up to a sense of well-being. In fact, our overall satisfaction with life depends more on how *often* we feel good than on how *intensely* we're delighted. We don't have to wait for extraordinarily wonderful events to feel happy.

To increase your child's awareness of little joys, read together the book *Happiness Is a Warm Puppy,* by Charles M. Schulz, the creator of Peanuts. Alternatively, print out the words from the song "My Favorite Things" from the musical *The Sound of Music* and sing them with your child.

Follow up by helping your child create a personalized book titled *Things That Make Me Smile.* Get a small photo album that holds 4-by-6 photos. Use 4-by-6 index cards to make the pages. Help your child draw, write, or cut out magazine pictures or photos for each page to illustrate a little joy. Encourage your child to focus on things and activities that are part of ordinary life.

Relive Happy Memories

Positive reminiscing is a common savoring strategy that allows people to extend their enjoyment of positive events. Most young children don't do this spontaneously in any elaborate way, but they can do it with adult guidance.

Shortly after a fun experience—maybe as you're traveling home or at the end of the day—talk with your child about the best aspects of the experience. Ask questions to draw out positive memories, such as "Which did you think was more fun?" "What was your favorite one?" "What did you like most about it?" to help your child draw out and reflect on pleasure. Also talk about your own positive feelings and reactions, and describe the relevant experiences in detail to model savoring.

You can also do this with older happy memories. Using physical prompts, such as photos or souvenirs, can help jog your child's memory. Focus on helping your child create a happy narrative about the memory by asking questions and making comments to highlight the sequence of events and sensory details. These details enable your child to relive and relish the experience. Ask your child, "Remember when . . . ?" "Remember how . . . ?" "Remember what happened next?"

Family stories can be a source of great delight for children, and they also create a sense of closeness and belonging. The stories don't have to be sophisticated, but they should be vivid. For instance, several years ago, one of us was out of town, and Grandpa was in charge of watching the kids. Unfortunately, he wasn't very experienced with domestic matters, and he accidentally put hand dishwashing detergent in the dishwasher. Frothy bubbles gushed out of the dishwasher, spewing all over the kitchen floor. The bubbles kept coming as Grandpa and the children worked frantically to scoop them up. After everything was mopped up, the kids asked, "Can we do it again?!" This simple story about a silly event is one of the children's favorite family stories, and it invariably elicits big grins and chuckles.

Relish Food

A common savoring exercise for adults is to spend five minutes eating a single raisin while noticing and enjoying the sensations. Few children would have the patience for this exercise, but, because it's concrete and familiar, food is useful for teaching kids about savoring.

The next time your family has a favorite meal or a special edible treat, invite your child to discuss what the best way is to eat it in order to most thoroughly enjoy it. Big bites? Little bites? Quickly? Slowly? Eating certain parts first or last or at the same time? Deciding to pick all the chocolate chips out of a muffin and save them for last may not meet any etiquette standards, but it's a sign that your child is learning to reflect on and enhance positive experiences.

Expand the Happiness Vocabulary

Words are powerful. The oft-quoted fact that Eskimos (Inuit) have many words for snow suggests that they make nuanced distinctions about snow. Words both influence and reflect our thought processes. When we have a word for something, we're able to see it more clearly and understand it more deeply.

If you ask most children to list emotion words, the list will be highly skewed toward negative feelings. Moreover, at least among American children, the positive feelings they list are likely to reflect an extroverted perspective on happiness and overlook more introverted forms. Helping children expand their happiness vocabulary can open their eyes to a range of possibilities.

Here are some of our favorite positive emotion words. Go over them with your child and explain any that are unfamiliar. See if your child can tell what sort of experience could arouse each feeling.

Excited	Content	Awed	Proud
Eager	Hopeful	Joyful	Relieved
Curious	Interested	Amused	Loving
Surprised	Inspired	Hopeful	Loved

You may want to help your child "collect" positive feeling words. Have your child write "I feel . . ." in the center of a poster paper, then write in as many positive feeling words as possible all over the paper in different colors. Keep adding to the poster over time. When you or anyone in the family feels happy, make a game of rushing to get the poster to help figure out exactly what kind of happiness is occurring. Naming positive feelings and reflecting on whether they are more like this or more like that is a form of savoring.

Get Moving

Sometimes adults live too much in their heads. We read, we talk, we have meetings, we surf the Internet, and we generally live our lives from the neck up. Unfortunately, this "heads only" bias is increasingly trickling down to young children, as schools shorten or even eliminate recess, assign more and more worksheets for homework, and emphasize preparation for high-stakes paper-and-pencil standardized tests. From a developmental perspective, this is misguided because children learn best when they are actively involved, moving and doing.

Physical activity is one of the strongest predictors of positive mood. There's even research suggesting that regular exercise is associated with increased self-esteem and reduced symptoms of anxiety and depression in children. When kids are physically active, they are directly participating in life rather than merely observing it.

Find a way for your child to be physically active. Sports are great, but kids don't have to be athletic to use and enjoy their bodies. Almost anyone can walk. Dance, yoga, tai chi, kayaking, and rock climbing are all possibilities that might appeal to kids who don't like popular team sports. Help your child discover what kind of physical activity he or she finds most enjoyable.

Get Outside

Personally, our best parenting answer to what ails ya is "Everybody outside!" Somehow just being outdoors seems to make everyone feel happier and more relaxed. Outside, there's space to breathe and run.

Exploring; climbing trees; creating a secret fort behind some bushes; playing catch, chase, or hide-and-seek . . . outdoor activities such as these are among the fondest childhood memories of many adults, but our busy, scheduled, goal-oriented modern lifestyle too often squeezes them out for our children.

There's research with adults showing that even five minutes of outdoor activity in the presence of nature (what scientists call "green" exercise) can enhance mood and self-esteem. We suspect that being outdoors is even more important for children.

"Cabin fever" seems to affect kids more than adults. If you live in an area that often has bad weather, don't let that stop you from getting your child outside. Kids love to stomp in puddles, and they seem to be impervious to cold when they're busy playing. Even a short burst of being outside can be restorative. If your child seems grumpy and the temperature is bitter, but you can't face the hassle of coats and hats and gloves and boots, suggest a "fresh air dash." Skip the outerwear and race with your child to the tree and back. Run as fast as you can, yelling about how cold it is. With a young child, you may want to hold hands as you do this. When you get back inside, you'll both be freezing and winded but also laughing and refreshed.

Encounters with nature can inspire many positive feelings, such as curiosity, exhilaration, peacefulness, and awe. Nature offers a glorious palette of sounds, sights, textures, and smells. Children often enjoy activities that help them learn about the natural world, but it's also great to get outside with no agenda whatsoever.

Sleep

We're convinced that sleep deprivation is the root of all evil. According to the National Sleep Foundation, children between five and twelve years of age need ten to eleven hours of sleep per night. Yet many children get far less than this on a regular basis. Research tells us that sleep-deprived children have trouble learning, and every parent knows that tired kids are more moody, more prone to whining, and less able to cope with ordinary frustrations. Modern lives are complicated, but making it a priority to get sufficient sleep could substantially enhance your child's ability to enjoy life.

Be Alert for Signs of Depression

Negativity is sometimes a sign of depression. Depressed children don't necessarily seem sad. They're often irritable; they may complain of vague physical symptoms or say they are always bored. If your child's irritability is persistent (lasting two weeks or more) and pervasive (affecting not just how she feels about one event but coloring how she views most activities, including ones she used to enjoy), and especially if it's accompanied by changes in sleep or appetite, talk to your pediatrician about whether your child could benefit from speaking with a mental health professional. A child who frequently feels miserable *needs help*. When kids consistently complain that they hate their lives or themselves, it's a serious problem. Unfortunately, depression in children is often overlooked. Their real symptoms are dismissed as whining, or they're accused of being spoiled. But these kids are hurting, and they need professional help. Depression is treatable, and early intervention can prevent a lot of suffering.

CONNER: SEARCHING FOR PERSONAL MEANING

"Congratulations!" Conner's father called from the bedroom doorway. "I hear you won the all-star academic award for your school. You must be really proud of yourself!"

"I guess," Conner muttered.

"Your teacher said it's quite an honor. They don't usually give that award to a sixth grader," his dad continued.

"Whatever. It doesn't matter." Conner picked up a book and pretended to read.

"Sure it does!" his dad enthused. "It means your hard work paid off."

"No, Dad! You just don't get it."

"What don't I get?" his dad asked, coming to sit on the bed next to Conner. "I thought you'd be happy about the award."

"I don't care about the stupid award. It's just a piece of paper. Besides, they may as well have announced, 'Congratulations, Conner, you are officially the biggest geek in the school.'"

"Now, Conner . . . ," his dad began.

"I'm sick of it!" Conner snapped. "Everyone keeps telling me how smart I am, but what good is that if no one really likes me? I'm sick of just being a brain."

"Conner, you're not just a brain. You're also a great piano player, and you have a brown belt in karate—"

"But I don't have a life! No one calls me up just to hang out. They only call if they want me to help with their homework. I want to be someone different. I wish I weren't even smart. Then maybe I'd have some real friends."

❧

Conner's accomplishments have garnered public praise and recognition from adults, but to him they feel pointless. Somehow Conner has come to believe that he can be smart or he can be happy, but he can't be both. This is tragic. It's also not true.

Connor is struggling to find a sense of personal meaning in his life. For him, being smart is not enough to be happy. Simply performing well doesn't feel satisfying unless it fits with our sense of who we are (or want to be) and what matters to us.

Meaning in Life

Thinkers as far back as Aristotle have tried to articulate what makes life meaningful, and modern positive psychology researchers are actively investigating this same question. Discussions of meaning in life refer directly or indirectly to values. The answers tend to involve developing our authentic selves and serving the greater good. They encompass having a sense of purpose, ongoing personal growth toward our best possible selves, and quality relationships with others. They incorporate ideals about what is worth living for—and maybe even dying for. Intuitively, it makes sense that a meaningful life is satisfying, and research consistently shows that when adults perceive their lives as meaningful, they also feel happier. (The reverse is also true: happy people tend to perceive their life as more meaningful.)

But how does this translate to children? Children's identities are in flux. What they do, think, and like can change drastically from year to year. In first grade, your daughter might insist on wearing only pink; in fourth grade, she might refuse to go anywhere near anything pink. When he's eight years old, your son might love Yu-Gi-Oh! cards, but when he's eleven, his passion might be major league baseball.

Elementary school children certainly don't have well-articulated personal philosophies, and they don't tend to wander around contemplating existential issues or paths to personal fulfillment. But children do have a sense that some things matter to them more than others. Kids can readily make value-laden judgments, classifying activities as "interesting" or "boring," actions as "kind" or "mean," and objects as "yucky," "nice," or "special to me." Children also have some sense that what they value is linked to their happiness.

Using both a structured interview and a collage activity, one study looked at kids' beliefs about what makes them happy. Third and fourth graders emphasized hobbies as well as people and pets as sources of happiness. Teenagers also valued people and pets, but they placed more emphasis on material possessions and achievement than did younger children. When asked what could be removed from their collages, children of all ages insisted that people and pets had to remain. In another study, investigators asked first graders what in their "whole life is most important" to them. The most popular response was social relationships (42 percent), followed by activities, such as sports and hobbies (21 percent). These results suggest that kids—like most adults—deeply value their relationships.

Two Themes Underlying Personal Meaning

The adult literature on meaning in life revolves around two main themes: authenticity and transcendence. Authenticity involves discovering and acting in accordance with the "true self." Transcendence involves awareness and connection to something greater than oneself, such as God, love, truth, community, or humanity in general. Discussion of these topics tends to be very abstract and adult-focused, but we believe that these two themes are quite relevant to children. In fact, we'd argue that the essential developmental tasks for children involve seeking authenticity, by discovering who they are; and cultivating transcendence, by becoming able to see and act beyond their self-interest.

Children's Authenticity and Parents' Wishes and Fears   The theme of authenticity suggests that the personal meanings that children find or create may not match what their parents value. This can be hard on parents.

Because most parents want their kids to "do well," we suspect that Conner's father felt a bit alarmed to hear Conner dismissing the importance of achievement and devaluing his intelligence. He might even have had a momentary image of Conner as an adult, unemployed and penniless because he rejected his abilities in sixth grade. This is understandable, but it's not helpful, because the future is impossible to predict. The issue isn't Conner's future occupational prospects but his present upset and struggles to figure out what matters to him. Fortunately, Conner's father doesn't resort to threats or dire predictions ("Well, you'd better care about academics, young man, or . . ."). Conner undoubtedly knows that his dad values achievement. What he needs help with is figuring out what achievement means to him.

The father's instinctive response was to argue—to try to convince Conner of the value of the award and his many talents. But Conner dismisses his father's reasonable comments. Arguments rarely persuade kids (or anybody else). Instead they tend to make children dig in their heels or move to a more extreme position. What works better is to acknowledge feelings and ask questions in order to understand what the world looks like through the child's eyes. Conner begins to open up when his father sits down and asks, "What don't I understand?" The father also might have asked, "What happened that got in the way of you enjoying receiving this award?" (We suspect a fellow student made a cutting remark.)

Laying out a values dilemma as an "and" rather than an "or" can be a useful way of expanding children's options and understanding. The father could say, "I know you care about school because I see you working hard, *and* you also want to feel like you have friends who care about you."

Conner's father should resist rushing to a solution ("Why don't you call Jason and invite him over?") or dismissing the problem ("That kid was probably jealous; just ignore him"). The struggle to figure out personal values is healthy and growth promoting. No immediate action or decision is required. The father's job is just to acknowledge this struggle and to support and have faith in Conner's efforts to figure things out. He could say, "That's a tough problem. I can see why you're upset. Do you have any ideas about what you might want to do about it?" An extra hug might also help.

Guiding and Supporting Children's Discovery of Personal Meaning   Adults frequently want to influence children's values. Nowadays, many schools have "character education" programs that involve a list of virtues, such as citizenship and cooperation, promulgated through posters and inspirational quotations. However, concentrating on abstract concepts doesn't fit how children think and learn.

In daily life, parents convey their values when they say things like "Share some with your sister" or when they do things like explaining a homework assignment or shoveling snow off an elderly neighbor's walkway. These can be powerful ways to convey values, because they pertain to specific situations and actions and because children generally want to please their parents. However, as any parent can attest, there can be a big gap between kids' knowing what they ought to do and actually doing it.

Early research on moral development focused on moral thinking. It involved describing and categorizing how children decide, "What's the right thing to do?" in imaginary situations involving moral dilemmas. But just because a child can offer a sophisticated analysis of the moral implications of stealing medicine to save a dying spouse doesn't necessarily mean that the same child will speak up for a classmate who is being bullied or refrain from raiding a sibling's candy stash.

What guides our responses to moral dilemmas is usually not careful, logical moral thinking but instead almost instantaneous "gut feelings" or emotional reactions that are later justified and elaborated on by moral reasoning. Moral emotions go beyond direct self-interest. They include contempt, guilt, compassion, and gratitude. They reflect our intuitive evaluations of ourselves or others. Moral emotions motivate us to act in certain ways, such as to comfort someone who is suffering or repay someone who has been kind to us.

The most powerful way for children to learn about values may be through having personal and emotionally compelling experiences and reflecting on these experiences. In the next section, we highlight some ways you can encourage this process.

STRATEGIES TO HELP YOUR CHILD HAVE MEANINGFUL EXPERIENCES

The activities that follow focus on child-size authenticity and transcendence. They are emotionally vivid ways to help children discover who they are and what matters to them, and to feel connected with something beyond themselves. But we urge you to tread lightly with them. Finding meaning is important, but gradual learning works better than cramming. Also, meaning needs to be balanced with pleasure so that life isn't endless toil.

Identify Personal Strengths

Psychologists Christopher Peterson and Martin Seligman argue that one path toward meaning involves using our signature strengths. The Web site www.authentichappiness.com contains an online test that your child can use to identify personal strengths, in rank order, out of a list of twenty-four possibilities. These include "Love of Learning," "Creativity," "Valor," "Perseverance," "Capacity to Love and Be Loved," "Humor and Playfulness," and "Zest."

Because the test is self-report, it's not clear whether results reflect strengths that respondents actually have or merely strengths they value. For our purposes, this doesn't matter. The benefit of completing the strengths questionnaire for children is that it can help them understand themselves in a more complex way. For instance, Conner, in the earlier vignette, saw himself as only smart. Completing the questionnaire could help him see himself in a more multifaceted way. If he chooses to act in ways consistent with those strengths, then he is cultivating them, whether or not he actually "has" them to begin with.

When you discuss your child's personal strengths, be careful to talk about them in terms of "strengths right now." Children grow and change dramatically, so their strengths are likely to change over time.

Explain to your child that there are two main paths to self-improvement: cultivating strengths or addressing weaknesses.

Most people do both. With this in mind, look over the full list of twenty-four strengths with your child. If your child could pick three strengths to have, which would they be? Why? Which ones would he or she like to develop more? Brainstorm with your child about ways to demonstrate or develop these strengths. You can find lists of over a hundred possible activities related to each of Seligman's signature strengths at http://people.virginia.edu/~jdh6n/Positivepsych.html or at http://www.viacharacter.org/Practice/Exercises/tabid/132/Default.aspx. These activities were designed for college students or adults, but most can be adapted to children.

Seek Flow

Have you ever seen your child completely absorbed in an activity? Maybe it was building with Lego, digging in a sandbox, reading, or drawing, but somehow the world melted away and time passed unnoticed, as your child became unself-consciously immersed in the activity. This is what psychologist Mihaly Csikszentmihalyi (pronounced *chick-SENT-me-high*) at the University of Chicago calls *flow*. He describes flow as a "state in which people are so involved in an activity that nothing else seems to matter; the experience itself is so enjoyable that people will do it even at great cost, for the sheer sake of doing it." He developed this concept while watching artists at work. He noticed that while the artists were painting, they were utterly absorbed in the process, but once the painting was finished, they lost interest. Flow involves an engrossing focus on a current activity that people experience as blissful and deeply satisfying.

Csikszentmihalyi went on to study flow in many other populations, including rock climbers, athletes, musicians, surgeons, file clerks, factory workers, and engineers. In beeper studies, in which he paged participants to ask them what they were doing and how they were feeling, he found that the more flow people have in their lives, the happier they are. He also found that people tend to be very bad at managing their leisure time. "I can't wait for the weekend" is a commonly expressed sentiment, but people are actually more likely to experience flow at work. This doesn't mean we should work all the time. It does mean we should think carefully about what we do during our leisure time and seek out experiences that give us this sense of active engagement.

We're most likely to experience flow when the challenge of the task matches our ability. If the task is too hard, we feel anxious; if it's too easy, we feel bored. That middle ground between boredom and anxiety offers the opportunity for the optimal experience and peak performance that's sometimes called "being in the zone."

Explain the concept of flow and help your child discover which activities are most likely to yield flow for him or her. The experience of flow is exhilarating and profoundly, personally meaningful.

Get a Pet

If allergies and living circumstances permit, getting a pet can be a wonderful source of meaning for children. They will gain the opportunity to love the pet (and, depending on the type of animal, be loved by the pet). Also, looking after the pet can enhance children's sense of responsibility and awareness of someone else's needs. Many adults still speak fondly of their childhood pets and would never live without one.

Cultivate Earned Self-Esteem

Many parents worry about their children's self-esteem. They may even try to bolster it by telling their children frequently and effusively how wonderful they are. It makes intuitive sense that if kids feel good about themselves, they ought to be more confident, generous, and successful, so making kids feel good about themselves should help them do well in life. Extensive research tells us that this idea is just plain wrong.

Roy Baumeister and his colleagues conducted an in-depth review of research on self-esteem and found that higher self-esteem does *not* lead to better school performance or better relationships, nor does it prevent kids from smoking, using alcohol or drugs, or engaging in early sex. Similarly, education research shows that academic programs that emphasize competence produce the greatest increase in self-esteem, whereas those that emphasize helping kids feel good about themselves had minimal or even negative impact on self-esteem and also produced the lowest academic achievement.

Self-esteem is also specific, rather than general. So, for example, children have beliefs about their adequacy in performing in math, baseball, video games, and being helpful to their parents. If we want our children to have better self-esteem in a particular area, we need to help them do better in that area. Anything else is just wishful thinking that won't stand up to the feedback of reality.

Do we want our children to have good opinions of themselves? Of course we do, because that's an aspect of happiness and well-being. But what research tells us is that there are no shortcuts to self-esteem. It can't be given; it has to be earned. Self-esteem is an outcome, not a cause, of meeting relevant standards of performance. Earned self-esteem is both meaningful and enjoyable for children.

Extracurricular activities can be one route toward earned self-esteem. When asked to tell about themselves, many elementary school children say things like "I play basketball," or "I take ballet." Activities can also provide a sense of meaningful belonging through shared interests.

Finding the right activities for your child sometimes takes creativity and resourcefulness. Look for activities that your child can (1) do with others and (2) work at to become increasingly skilled or responsible. Sports, music, or dance are common choices, but there are many other possibilities. The library has books on a wide range of hobbies that might interest your child, from drawing to juggling to performing magic tricks. It may take a few different attempts to discover an activity that resonates with your child, but that's part of discovering who he or she is.

Count Kindnesses

A recent study of college students found that simply counting their own acts of kindness for one week increased their feelings of happiness. This is an easy strategy to use with children.

You may want to create a dinnertime ritual of going around the table and having all family members report a kindness they did that day. (We've done this for years with our own children.) This ritual shows that you place a high value on kindness, creates the expectation that children should be engaging in kind behavior on a daily basis, encourages children to be alert to others' needs, and helps children see themselves as kind people.

If your child has no kindness to report, show little interest. Just comment mildly, "That's too bad," and move on. If your child does have a kindness to report, remark on how the act must have made the other person feel, to emphasize your child's ability to have a positive impact. You could say, "I bet he really appreciated that!" "That was a big help for her," or "I'm sure they liked that." If you want to, you can collect marbles in a jar to represent each act of kindness and celebrate when, collectively, you reach fifty or one hundred.

There are many standards in the world that your child may or may not meet. Your child may or may not get selected for the travel soccer team or the advanced band or the school play or the highest reading group. But kindness is always within everyone's reach, and there are numerous opportunities every day to demonstrate it.

Volunteer

Albert Schweitzer once told a graduating class of medical students, "I don't know what your destiny will be, but one thing I do know: the only ones among you who will be really happy are those who have sought and found how to serve." Volunteering is one way of putting our convictions into action, and it's also a source of what's popularly called "the helper's high."

Volunteering can have long-term effects on children. Adults who began volunteering as children are twice as likely to volunteer than those who didn't. For some people who continue to volunteer over time, volunteering can become an important part of who they are. It can be a source of meaning, positive moods, and social connection.

You may want to talk with your child about what kinds of volunteer activities he or she would find most meaningful: Working with animals? Teaching younger children? Cleaning up the environment? Then seek out opportunities to do these. If you're not sure what volunteer work is available in your area, the Web site www.volunteermatch.org has an advanced search function that can help you find kid-friendly volunteer opportunities of various types near your home.

Share Your Spiritual or Religious Beliefs

For many people, religion is a source of great meaning. It offers values, rituals to mark important milestones, a sense of community and connection to something greater than oneself, and comforting answers to difficult questions about life, death, good, evil, fate, and free will. For many parents, being able to convey their spiritual or religious beliefs to their children is critically important.

There's been a fair bit of research but no easy answers about children's spiritual development. It's clear that children's understanding of God evolves. For example, research that asks children of various religions open-ended questions such as "What makes you Jewish [or Protestant, or Catholic]?" and "What is a prayer?" finds a progression in the complexity of children's religious thinking.

Seven- to nine-year-old children see religion as determined by one's family. If a Catholic family has a cat, young children believe that the cat is Catholic. They also think concretely about prayer as something to do at certain times or in certain places, in order to make personal requests. Young children's views of God are vividly expressed in Stuart Hample and Eric Marshall's book, *Children's Letters to God*. Our favorite quotation is "Dear God, Thank you for the baby brother but what I prayed for was a puppy."

Nine- to twelve-year-olds start to see prayer in more abstract and emotional terms, involving a shared conversation and altruistic feelings. In the ten-to-fourteen age range, children have a more complex view of religion, seeing it as coming from within the person rather than imposed externally. Around age thirteen and fourteen is also when doubts about religion tend to emerge.

Children learn about their parents' spiritual beliefs through what parents do and say. When parents participate in religious activities, kids are more likely to do so, even when they grow up. When parents talk more about their beliefs, children understand them more accurately. The most intriguing research about children's spiritual development focuses on parallels between child-parent and child-God relationships. Young adults are most likely to adopt their parents' religious beliefs when they have a warm relationship with their parents. College students who feel they came from a home that was emotionally cold or unspiritual say they avoid intimacy with God. Those who believe they came from overprotective, rigid, and authoritarian homes also say they avoid intimacy with God, and they feel anxious about whether God loves them. So your best bet for ensuring that your child adopts your religious beliefs in the future may be to foster a close and caring relationship with your child now.

If your family is not religious, you may want to read *Parenting Beyond Belief*, edited by Dale McGowan, for ideas about sharing your values.

Read or Watch Inspiring Stories

Throughout history, people have used hero stories to describe what we human beings are like at our best, in order to inspire others. These stories are meaningful because they embody our most important values.

Hero stories can evoke *elevation*, which is a feeling that we experience when we're deeply moved or uplifted by acts of goodness, such as kindness, courage, loyalty, or compassion. It's often accompanied by a warm, tingling, heart-swelling feeling in the chest. Just seeing or hearing about a stranger's kindness to another stranger can be profoundly affecting and even inspire us to want to become better people ourselves.

In one study, college students watched video clips of either a touching documentary about Mother Teresa, an amusing excerpt from *America's Funniest Home Videos*, or an interesting but emotionally neutral film. The students who watched the Mother Teresa film felt more loving and inspired afterwards, and they more strongly wanted to be with and help others. They also were more likely to volunteer to work at a charitable organization following the study. Elevation connects people with what is good in the world, and fills them with feelings of hope, love, and inspiration.

What this suggests is that a powerful way to provide children with a sense of meaning might be to go for the heartstrings. In contrast to bland lectures about how they ought to behave, emotionally moving stories of people who acted out their highest ideals can connect children with those ideals in a personal and compelling way. Instead of being admonished, they can be inspired.

Stories that can elicit elevation are everywhere: in a newspaper account of a heroic firefighter or a gentle animal rescue worker, in a movie about a cancer survivor, in a biography about a leader who rose from adversity, in a novel about a child who stands up to a bully, or maybe even in your own family history.

Obviously, a steady deluge of elevation stories would diminish their impact, so use them sparingly. Also, it's probably best if the shining examples aren't too close to home, so that your child doesn't feel criticized by comparison. Keep your eyes open for stories that you find particularly moving and share them with your child to make your ideals come alive.

Praise Your Child in a Way That Embraces Growth and Communicates Acceptance

Parenting advice often swings from one extreme to another. Not so long ago, experts told parents that it was very important to praise children as much as possible for every little thing they did (so they'd have high self-esteem). This advice is misguided, because it renders praise cheap and meaningless, and it makes it hard for kids to learn what the standards really are. Love should be unconditional, but praise should not.

Lately, we've been reading advice that cautions parents *not* to praise children, because praise involves judging, and that will supposedly make children dependent on external judgments for their self-worth. We think this is too withholding, and it also doesn't fit developmentally with how children view the world. Children *want* to please their parents and other important adults. This is a good thing. Civilization depends on it. So does family harmony. If we avoid praise, we also avoid clearly communicating our values. Adults (by and large) understand what the relevant standards of behavior are. Kids are still learning these standards. We are "the boss of them" for good reason.

We recommend praising in a way that encourages growth. This means

- *Be specific.* Describe what you observed your child do.
- *Be sincere.* Only comment on behaviors that matter, either because they meet some objective standard or because they have a significant and positive impact on other people's feelings (including yours).

○ *Focus on effort or strategies rather than innate ability.* Children can control and adjust the first two of these, but innate ability is fixed.

○ *Notice improvement.* Offer encouragement along the way to acknowledge progress and enhance persistence.

Encouraging growth is important, but so is communicating acceptance. Some of the most unhappy people we've met in our practices are those who feel as though they were never good enough to win their parents' approval. No matter how well they performed, the message they received from their parents was always, "You could do better." But often they really couldn't do better, or the cost of doing better was too high. Some people in these circumstances spend their whole lives trying to please impossible-to-please parents. Others just give up and accept the judgment that they are somehow not good enough.

So how do we avoid this? How can we express our values, encourage growth, and at the same time communicate acceptance? The key to finding that middle ground between empty flattery and constant criticism is to truly see our children as precious, unique, and evolving individuals. This means that our standards for praise shouldn't be based only on abstract ideals or disembodied expectations about what children "should" do. Our standards need to be anchored by the past behavior of a particular child, and they need to encompass more than objective performance. A child who does "better" than he or she did in the past craves and deserves recognition for this progress. This recognition should be offered without exaggeration but with generosity—a simple "You did it!" unspoiled by comments that "It's about time!" or "If you try harder you could do even better!"

Children aren't born with their own standards, so they do seek the approval of important adults in their lives. They want to know that we think they're "a good kid." But the greatest praise an adult can give a child has nothing to do with objective performance, and it's more precious to a child than any grade or certificate. It's this: telling a child, "I really enjoyed your company."

SHOW THE WAY

Mental health is more than just the absence of mental illness. It's also the presence of positive feelings and functioning. As an adult, you're probably loaded down with responsibilities. Kids, home, paid or volunteer work . . . the to-do list is endless. Often this can lead to a grim, driven approach to life. We have to do what we have to do, and we certainly want to set an example of responsible living for our children, but for our own and our children's well-being, we also need to make happiness a priority.

Make a Conscious Effort to Connect

With our hurried lifestyles, too often a task-oriented focus intrudes on interactions with loved ones, and too many of our conversations end up sounding like checklists: "Did you . . . ? Could you . . . ? When will you . . . ?" To some extent, this type of conversation is necessary, just to keep things running smoothly, but sometimes it's important to set aside the to-do list.

When you see your child (or spouse) at the end of the school or work day, make a conscious effort to connect. You may want to make yourself a cup of hot tea, and for the length of time it takes you to drink that tea, just sit and try to be fully present. Ask. Listen. Share. Or, if you prefer a more physical way of connecting, you may want to make an activity like walking the dog, watering the plants, or playing catch part of your reconnection routine. Whatever you decide to do, try to think about how much your child (or spouse) matters to you as you are doing it.

You may also want to create a plan to get together regularly with adult friends. People routinely report that their relationships are the most important things in their lives, but relationships need tending or they wither. Set aside a certain time to reach out to friends by phone, e-mail, or Facebook. Better yet, get together in person. Consider setting up a regular date, once a month, for you and a bunch of friends to meet at a local restaurant, so no one has to cook or clean. Joining a book club, bowling league, choir, or school committee are other options for connecting with adults.

Avoid Multitasking

Adults frequently complain, "I have so much to do!" Often, they try to cope with too many demands by multitasking—doing two or more activities at the same time in an attempt to increase productivity and efficiency. Some people even brag about their ability to multitask. They're kidding themselves. Although it may be possible to do two trivial tasks at the same time (for example, folding laundry while listening to music), this strategy won't work for tasks that require attention.

Multitasking is a myth. Physically, it's impossible to concentrate on two things at once, so what multitaskers actually do is shift their attention back and forth between tasks. Each shift costs time, which cuts down on efficiency and raises the possibility of missing something important. Edward Hallowell, author of *CrazyBusy*, likens multitasking to playing tennis with two balls. "There is no way your game with two balls could be as good as your game with one," he insists. John Medina, author of *Brain Rules*, reports that multitasking makes people take 50 percent longer to accomplish a task and causes 50 percent more errors.

Part of the problem is the "Now, where was I?" effect. One study found that Microsoft workers took an average of fifteen minutes to return to demanding mental tasks after being interrupted by an e-mail or instant message. The interruptions threw them off track, and they ended up checking other e-mails or Web sites. Another study found that workers took an average of twenty-five minutes to resume interrupted work. Multitasking can sometimes be a form of procrastination, as people shift their attention away from demanding tasks.

There's also an emotional cost to multitasking. Gloria Mark at the University of California, Irvine, and her colleagues did a study that found that interruptions make people feel more stressed, frustrated, and time pressured. They lead people to work faster but produce less.

The alternative to multitasking is what psychologists call *mindfulness*, which involves being fully present to whatever we are doing in the moment, and deliberately immersing ourselves in the experience without judging it. The idea of mindfulness has been around since Buddha counseled his followers, "When you are walking, walk. When you are sitting, sit." Although Buddha-like serenity is beyond most people, concentrating on one thing at a time may help you be more productive and feel more peaceful.

Make Time for Activities That Feed Your Soul

The ability to delay gratification—to do a hard thing now in order to get a better outcome later—is a sign of maturity. But sometimes adults become too good at it. If you find yourself frequently thinking, "I'd love too, but I'm just too busy. Maybe someday . . . ," think again. If you are constantly postponing doing something that matters deeply to you until the stars are aligned and your life is perfect, someday will never come. If the press of everyday busyness routinely squeezes out the activities that you find most fulfilling, eventually you could feel bitter and resentful.

Maybe you wish you could get together with adult friends, read for pleasure, learn a skill, start a project, play music, or exercise regularly. Maybe the physical reality of your life is that you can't do as much as you'd like, but with some creative thinking and determined commitment, you can probably do something to incorporate these activities into your life. And something is much better than nothing. By making time to do things that matter to you, you're not only taking care of your own mental health but also showing your child that you think it's important to do things that make you happy.

Be Open to the Possibility of Happiness

Some adults deliberately muffle their own happiness. Instead of delighting in whatever pleasure or meaning they encounter, they do what psychologist Fred Bryant calls "kill-joy thinking." They immediately start imagining what could go wrong, how things could be better, how these circumstances are not as good as someone else's, or what they could or should be doing instead. It's as if they mistrust happy moods and choose to dampen them by trying to calm down or feel less excited. Or perhaps they believe that they can't be happy if circumstances are less than ideal.

If kill-joy thinking is something you tend to do, you may want to try to catch yourself in the act. The strategies we described earlier related to savoring, flow, and mindfulness might be useful. If these don't help, you may want to consult a mental health professional.

Share Positive Feelings

Expressing joy intensifies that joy. Also, shared feelings tend to be contagious, so when you express positive feelings, the people around you tend to pick up on and react to them. If you want your home or job to be a happier place, do your part to fan the flames of happiness. Make a point of smiling more. Greet people cheerfully. Express appreciation for something kind someone has done for you. Tell someone, "I love you." Share a funny story and laugh out loud. Although these actions may feel unnatural at first, they can make a difference. You'll feel happier and closer to the people around you, and they're likely to respond in kind.

Our children's happiness matters not only for their momentary enjoyment but also for their long-term well-being. Positive feelings enable them to broaden their thinking and build personal and social resources. Both meaning and pleasure contribute to happiness. Although children generally have less elaborate understandings of meaning than adults, they can move toward authenticity and transcendence by coming to know themselves better and learning to care about more than themselves.

CONCLUSION

The Pressure to Perform
Versus the Power to Grow

Of those to whom much is given, much is required.
—Luke 12:48, quoted by John F. Kennedy, Jan. 9, 1961

There are two ways to interpret this quotation. When John F. Kennedy said these words, he was referring to our responsibility to serve the greater community. But in our current anxiety-ridden and highly competitive culture, the meaning of the quotation has become distorted. It now seems like a demand for individual accomplishment, with an emphasis on surpassing everyone else. Kennedy was talking about giving, but today the emphasis seems to be on winning.

Winning is fun, and it's often satisfying, especially when we work hard for our victories, but it's not the whole story. Winning is fleeting. Even Olympic records rarely last for long. Of course we all want our children to "do well" in life, but if we overemphasize achievement, we risk placing our children on a treadmill of constantly having to prove their worth. They may mistakenly get the message that looking impressive is more important than being good.

BEYOND PERFORMANCE
TOWARD GROWTH

No performance can fully capture who your child is. Performance is a snapshot, a temporary presentation, a public display. Machines can be measured by their output, but people are far more complex. Yes, performance is important, but with people, and especially with children, what matters most is what's behind the performance: the engagement in real relationships, real learning, and real growth.

Your child's *true* potential is not an end point; it's the capacity to grow and learn. This is much bigger than performance. The seven challenges we describe in this book are all about developing inner strength and outward compassion. Mastering these challenges won't impress the neighbors and probably won't change whether or not your child gets into Harvard. But we believe that these challenges matter deeply for your child's ability to create a meaningful and satisfying life.

THE LANGUAGE OF BECOMING

Bright children tend to receive a lot of praise for their achievements. Unfortunately, the noise of the applause and the pressure to perform can make it hard for them to figure out who they are and who they want to be.

Author and family therapist Ellen Wachtel has written about the impact of different types of praise on children. She notes that abstract comments like "You're terrific! You're amazing!" are too vague to be meaningful to most children. Some kids may hear these comments as implied expectations: "You *must* be terrific! We *expect* you to be amazing!" For children who don't believe that they're terrific or amazing, this type of comment rings false, which can make them question the adult's sincerity ("You're just saying that").

Praising a specific behavior—"You did a fantastic job playing at the recital!"—is better, because at least children know what you're talking about. But again, if kids are feeling insecure, they're likely to dismiss these comments, thinking or saying, "It's no big deal. Anybody could have done that." They may also feel anxious about whether they can maintain the high level of performance that earned the praise.

Wachtel offers a third option, "the language of becoming," which she describes as "a way of speaking to children that enables them to see themselves as continually evolving and changing." It consists of a simple description of the child's behavior paired with a statement about how that child is growing or becoming. Here are some possibilities:

> "You played blocks with your little brother and cheered him up.
> "YOU ARE BECOMING **good at** noticing and responding to other people's feelings."

> "You managed to stay calm, even though you lost the game.
> "YOU ARE BECOMING **better able to** handle frustration."

> "You worked out a fair compromise with Miriam about what movie to see.
> "YOU ARE BECOMING **the kind of person who** knows how to resolve a disagreement."

The reason the language of becoming is so powerful is that it says to kids, "Never mind if you've messed up in the past. And never mind if you mess up tomorrow. Right here, right now, I see evidence of how you are growing." The language of becoming sends a message of hope, faith, and acceptance that is profoundly meaningful to children.

A TRUE REFLECTION

We've all heard the saying, "Life is a journey, not a destination," and this is especially true for children. We really can't predict where our kids are going to end up. It's their job and their privilege to figure this out. We can try to equip them for their journey by offering loving guidance and support, but we also need to get out of their way so that they can become competent and discover their own path.

As parents, we are our children's first mirrors. Our comments and reactions shape how they see themselves. The world will tell our kids that they're smart. They need our help to see that they are far more than that. What matters is not only what our children can do but also how they touch the lives of those around them. We need to show our kids that we treasure their kindness, humor, curiosity, determination, and compassion. We need to hold up a mirror to them that reflects, not just their performance, but a caring view of their true and evolving selves. By loving them for more than their abilities, we show our children that they are much more than the sum of their accomplishments.

SELECTED REFERENCES AND RECOMMENDED READING

Note: Asterisk (*) indicates publications written for a lay audience.

CHAPTER ONE: TEMPERING PERFECTIONISM

*Boice, R. (1994). *How writers journey to comfort and fluency: A psychological adventure.* Westport, CT: Praeger.

*Burka, J. B., & Yuen, L. M. (2008). *Procrastination: Why you do it, what to do about it now.* Cambridge, MA: Da Capo Lifelong.

*Dweck, C. S. (2007, December). The secret to raising smart kids. *Scientific American: Mind,* 36–43.

Ericsson, K. A., Krampe, R. T., & Tesch-Romer, C. (1993). The role of deliberate practice in the acquisition of expert performance. *Psychological Review, 100,* 363–406.

Flett, G. L., & Hewitt, P. L. (2002). Perfectionism and maladjustment: An overview of theoretical, definitional, and treatment issues. In G. L. Flett & P. L. Hewitt (Eds.), *Perfectionism: Theory, research, and treatment* (pp. 5–31). Washington, DC: American Psychological Association.

Flett, G. L., Hewitt, P. L., Oliver, J. M., & MacDonald, S. (2002). Perfectionism in children and their parents: A developmental analysis. In G. L. Flett & P. L. Hewitt (Eds.), *Perfectionism: Theory, research, and treatment* (pp. 89–132). Washington, DC: American Psychological Association.

*Green, J. (2007). *Famous failures: Hundreds of hot shots who got rejected, flunked out, worked lousy jobs, goofed up, or did time in jail before achieving phenomenal success.* West Hills, CA: Lunatic Press.

*Greenspon, T. S. (2001). *Freeing our families from perfectionism.* Minneapolis, MN: Free Spirit.

*Klutz Press. (1992). *Kids shenanigans: Great things to do that mom and dad will just barely approve of.* Palo Alto, CA: Author.

Luthar, S. S., Shoum, K. A., & Brown, P. J. (2006). Extracurricular involvement among affluent youth: A scapegoat for "ubiquitous achievement pressures"? *Developmental Psychology, 42,* 583–597.

*Quindlen, A. (1999, May 23). Commencement speech, Mount Holyoke College. Retrieved June 22, 2010, from http://www.mtholyoke.edu/offices/comm/oped/Quindlen.shtml.

Rice, K. C., Leever, B. A., Christopher, J., & Porter, J. D. (2006). Perfectionism, stress, and social (dis)connection: A short-term study of hopelessness, depression, and academic adjustment among honors students. *Journal of Counseling Psychology, 53,* 524–534.

*Romain, T., & Verdick, E. (1997). *How to do homework without throwing up.* Minneapolis, MN: Free Spirit.

*Rozakis, L. (2002). *Super study skills.* New York: Scholastic.

*Sachs, B. E. (2001). *The good enough child: How to have an imperfect family and be perfectly satisfied.* New York: Quill.

*Schacter, D. L (2001). *The seven sins of memory: How the mind forgets and remembers.* Boston: Houghton Mifflin.

*Scott, S. (2007, August 30). Do grades really matter? Retrieved June 22, 2010, from http://www.macleans.ca/education/postsecondary/article.jsp?content=20070910_109139_109139&page=2.

Sternberg, R. J., Grigorenko, E. L., & Bundy, D. (2001). The predictive value of IQ. *Merrill-Palmer Quarterly, 47,* 1–41.

*Stone, M. (2002). [Interview]. In M. Moore (Producer and Director), *Bowling for Columbine* [Motion picture]. United States: United Artists.

*Young, S. (2002). *Great failures of the extremely successful: Mistakes, adversity, failure and other stepping stones to success.* Beverly Hills, CA: Tallfellow Press.

CHAPTER TWO:
BUILDING CONNECTION

Asher, S. R., & McDonald, K. L. (2009). The behavioral basis of acceptance, rejection, and perceived popularity. In K. H. Rubin, W. M. Bukowski, & B. Laursen (Eds.), *Handbook of peer interactions, relationships, and groups: Social, emotional, and personality development in context* (pp. 232–249). New York: Guilford Press.

Asher, S. R., Rose, A. J., & Gabriel, S. W. (2001). Peer rejection in everyday life. In M. R. Leary (Ed.), *Interpersonal rejection* (pp. 105–142). New York: Oxford University Press.

Bowker, J.C.W., Rubin, K. H., & Burgess, K. B. (2006). Behavioral characteristics associated with stable and fluid best friendship patterns in middle childhood. *Merrill-Palmer Quarterly, 52*, 671–693.

Coie, J. D., & Kupersmidt, J. B. (1983). A behavioral analysis of emerging social status in boys' groups. *Child Development, 54*, 1400–1416.

Degnan, K. A., & Fox, N. A. (2007). Behavioral inhibition and anxiety disorders: Multiple levels of a resilience process. *Development and Psychopathology, 19*, 729–746.

Dodge, K. A. (1983). Behavioral antecedents of peer social status. *Child Development, 54*, 1386–1399.

*Elman, N. M., & Kennedy-Moore, E. (2003). *The unwritten rules of friendship: Simple strategies to help your child make friends.* New York: Little, Brown.

Finkelhor, D., Turner, H., Ormrod, R., & Hamby, S. L. (2010). Trends in childhood violence and abuse exposure. *Archives of Pediatric and Adolescent Medicine, 164*, 238–242.

Gazelle, H., & Ladd, G. W. (2002). Interventions for children victimized by peers. In P. A. Schewe (Ed.), *Preventing violence in relationships: Interventions across the life span* (pp. 55–78). Washington, DC: American Psychological Association.

Gottman, J. M. (1983). How children become friends. *Monographs of the Society for Research in Child Development, 48*.

Gottman, J. M., & Parker, J. G. (Eds.). (1986). *Conversations of friends: Speculations on affective development.* New York: Cambridge University Press.

Hartup, W. W., & Laursen, B. (1993). Conflict and context in peer relations. In C. H. Hart (Ed.), *Children on playgrounds: Research perspectives and applications* (pp. 44–84). Albany: State University of New York Press.

Hubbard, J. A., & Dearing, K. F. (2004). Children's understanding and regulation of emotion in the context of their peer relations. In J. B. Kupersmidt & K. A. Dodge (Eds.), *Children's peer relations: From development to intervention* (pp. 81–99). Washington, DC: American Psychological Association.

Kagan, J. (1992). Temperamental contributions to emotion and social behavior. In M. S. Clark (Ed.), *Review of personality and social behavior: Vol. 14. Emotion and social behavior* (pp. 99–118). Newbury Park, CA: Sage.

Kupersmidt, J. B., & Dodge, K. A. (2004). *Children's peer relations: From development to intervention.* Washington, DC: American Psychological Association.

Ladd, G. W., Herald, S. L., Andrews, R. K. (2006). Young children's peer relations and social competence. In B. Spodek & O. N. Saracho (Eds.), *Handbook of research on the education of young children* (2nd ed.) (pp. 23–54). Mahwah, NJ: Erlbaum.

*Laney, M. O. (2002). *The introvert advantage: How to thrive in an extrovert world.* New York: Workman.

Lansford, J. E., Putallaz, M., Grimes, C. L., Schiro-Osman, K. A., Kupersmidt J. B., & Coie, J. D. (2006). Perceptions of friendship quality and observed behaviors with friends: How do sociometrically rejected, average, and popular girls differ? *Merrill-Palmer Quarterly, 52,* 694–720.

Newcomb, A. F., Bukowski, W. M., & Pattee, L. (1993). Children's peer relations: A meta-analytic review of popular, rejected, neglected, controversial, and average sociometric status. *Psychological Bulletin, 113,* 99–128.

Olweus, D. (1993). *Bullying at school: What we know and what we can do.* Cambridge, MA: Blackwell.

Putallaz, M., & Wasserman, A. (1989). Children's entry behavior. In S. R. Asher & J. D. Coie (Eds.), *Peer rejection in childhood* (pp. 60–89). New York: Cambridge University Press.

Rimm-Kaufman, S. E., Fan, X., Chiu, Y. I., & You, W. (2007). The contribution of the Responsive Classroom approach on children's academic achievement: Results from a three-year longitudinal study. *Journal of School Psychology, 45,* 401–421.

Rubin, K. H., Coplan, R. J., & Bowker, J. C. (2009). Social withdrawal in childhood. *Annual Review of Psychology, 60,* 141–171.

Rubin, K. H., Coplan, R., Chen, X., Buskirk, A. A., & Wojslawowicz, J. C. (2005). Peer relationships in childhood. In M. H. Bornstein & M. E. Lamb (Eds.), *Developmental science: An advanced textbook* (5th ed.) (pp. 469–511). Mahwah, NJ: Erlbaum.

*Rubin, K. H., & Thompson, A. (2002). *The friendship factor: Helping our children navigate their social world—and why it matters for their success and happiness.* New York: Penguin Books.

*Thompson, M. G., Cohen, L. J., & Grace, C. O. (2004). *Mom, they're teasing me: Helping your child solve social problems.* New York: Ballantine Books.

*Thompson, M. G., Grace, C. O., & Cohen, L. J. (2001). *Best friends, worst enemies: Understanding the social lives of children.* New York: Ballantine Books.

Tickle-Degnen, L., & Rosenthal, R. (1990). The nature of rapport and its nonverbal correlates. *Psychological Inquiry, 1,* 285–293.

Twenge, J. M., Zhang, L., Catanese, K. R., Dolan-Pascoe, B., Lyche, L. R., & Baumeister, R. F. (2007). Replenishing connectedness: Reminders of social activity reduce aggression after social exclusion. *British Journal of Social Psychology, 46,* 205–224.

CHAPTER THREE:
MANAGING SENSITIVITY

*Aron, E. (2002). *The highly sensitive child: Helping our children thrive when the world overwhelms them.* New York: Broadway Books.

*Baker, J. (2008). *No more meltdowns.* Arlington, TX: Future Horizons.

*Chansky, T. E. (2008). *Freeing your child from negative thinking.* Cambridge, MA: Da Capo Press.

Crick, N. R., & Dodge, K. A. (1994). A review and reformulation of social information-processing mechanisms in children's social adjustment. *Psychological Bulletin, 115,* 74–101.

*Gottman, J. M., & DeClaire, J. (1998). *Raising an emotionally intelligent child.* New York: Fireside.

Gottman, J. M., Katz, L. F., & Hooven, C. (1996). Parental meta-emotion philosophy and the emotional life of families: Theoretical models and preliminary data. *Journal of Family Psychology, 10,* 243–268.

*Huebner, D. (2006). *What to do when you grumble too much: A kid's guide to overcoming negativity.* Washington, DC: Magination Press.

Kennedy-Moore, E., & Watson, J. C. (1999). *Expressing emotion: Myths, realities, and therapeutic strategies.* New York: Guilford Press.

*Kranowitz, C. S. (2006). *The out-of-sync child has fun.* New York: Penguin.

Mendaglio, S., & Tillier, W. (2006). Dabrowski's theory of positive disintegration and giftedness: Overexcitability research findings. *Journal for the Education of the Gifted, 30,* 68–87.

*Niebuhr, R. (1937). Serenity prayer. Retrieved June 22, 2010, from http://en.wikipedia.org/wiki/Serenity_Prayer.

Schachter, S., & Singer, J. (1962). Cognitive, social, and physiological determinants of emotional states. *Psychological Review, 69,* 379–399.

*Watterson, B. (1992). *Calvin and Hobbes tenth anniversary book.* Kansas City, MO: Andrews McMeel.

CHAPTER FOUR: HANDLING COOPERATION AND COMPETITION

Brewer, M. B. (2003). Optimal distinctiveness, social identity, and the self. In M. Leary & J. Tangney (Eds.), *Handbook of self and identity* (pp. 480–491). New York: Guilford Press.

*Carnegie, D. (1936). *How to win friends and influence people.* New York: Simon & Schuster, p. 123.

*Chansky, T. E. (2004). *Freeing your child from anxiety: Powerful, practical solutions to overcome your child's fears, worries, and phobias.* New York: Broadway Books.

Cizek, J. (1999). *Cheating on tests: How to do it, detect it, and prevent it.* Mahwah, NJ: Erlbaum.

Cressey, D. R. (1973). *Other people's money: A study in the social psychology of embezzlement.* Montclair, NJ: Patterson Smith. (Original work published in 1953). Cited in Wells, J. T. (2008). *Principles of fraud examination.* Hoboken, NJ: Wiley.

Educational Testing Service/The Ad Council. Academic cheating background. Retrieved June 22, 2010, from http://www.glass-castle.com/clients/www-nocheating-org/adcouncil/research/cheatingbackgrounder.html.

Felder, R. M. (2007). Random thoughts . . . Sermons for grumpy campers. *Chemical Engineering Education, 41*, 183–184.

Felps, W., Mitchell, T. R., & Byington, E. (2006). How, when, and why bad apples spoil the barrel: Negative group members and dysfunctional groups. *Research in Organizational Behavior, 27*, 181–230. Featured on Glass, I. (2008, December 19). 370: Ruining it for the rest of us. *This American Life.* [Radio broadcast]. Retrieved June 22, 2010, from http://www.thisamericanlife.org/radio-archives/episode/370/Ruining-It-for-the-Rest-of-Us.

*Huebner, D. (2005). *What to do when you worry too much: A kid's guide to overcoming anxiety.* Washington, DC: Magination Press.

Kennedy, D. E., & Kramer, L. (2008). Improving emotion regulation and sibling relationship quality: The More Fun with Sisters and Brothers Program. *Family Relations: An Interdisciplinary Journal of Applied Family Studies, 57*, 567–578.

Matthews, G., Davies, D. R., Westerman, S. J., & Stammers, R. B. (2000). *Human performance: Cognition, stress and individual differences.* Philadelphia: Psychology Press/Taylor & Francis.

*Rimm, S. B., & Rimm-Kaufman, S. (2001). *How Jane won: 55 successful women share how they grew from ordinary girls to extraordinary women.* New York: Three Rivers Press.

Vasey, M. W., Crnic, K. A., & Carter, W. G. (1994). Worry in childhood: A developmental perspective. *Cognitive Therapy and Research, 18*, 529–549.

*Weissbourd, R. (2009). *The parents we mean to be: How well-intentioned adults undermine children's moral and emotional development.* Boston: Houghton Mifflin Harcourt, p. 76.

*Wood, C. (2007). *Yardsticks: Children in the classroom ages 4–14* (3rd ed.). Greenfield, MA: Northeast Foundation for Children.

CHAPTER FIVE:
DEALING WITH AUTHORITY

Brehm, S. S. (1981). Oppositional behavior in children. In S. S. Brehm, S. M. Kassin, & J. X. Gibbons (Eds.), *Developmental and social psychology: Theory and research* (pp. 96–121). New York: Oxford University Press.

Burgoon, M., Alvaro, E., Grandpre, J., & Voulodakis, M. (2002). Revisiting the theory of psychological reactance. In J. P. Dillard & M. Pfau (Eds.), *The persuasion handbook: Developments in theory and practice* (pp. 213–232). Thousand Oaks, CA: Sage.

Cupach, W. R., & Metts, S. (1994). *Facework*. Thousand Oaks, CA: Sage.

*Faber, A., & Mazlish, E. (1999). *How to talk so children will listen and listen so children will talk* (20th anniv. ed.). New York: Harper Paperbacks.

Goffman, E. (1959). *The presentation of self in everyday life*. New York: Overlook.

Joussemet, M., Landry, R., & Koestner, R. (2008). A self-determination theory perspective on parenting. *Canadian Psychology, 49*, 194–200.

*Kurcinka, M. S. (2000). *Kids, parents, and power struggles*. New York: HarperCollins.

*Marchese, J. (2009, September 1). Is this the best school in Philadelphia? *Philadelphia Magazine*. Retrieved June 22, 2010, from http://www.kipp.org/news/philadelphia-magazine-is-this-the-best-school-in-philadelphia-.

Patterson, G. R. (1982). *Coercive family process*. Eugene, OR: Castalie.

*Siegel, D. J., & Hartzell, M. (2003). *Parenting from the inside out*. New York: Penguin, p. 204.

*Swift, M. (1999). *Discipline for life: Getting it right with children*. Southlake, TX: Childright.

CHAPTER SIX:
DEVELOPING MOTIVATION

Assouline, S., Colangelo, N., Lupkowski-Shoplik, A., Lipscomb, J., & Forstadt, L. (2009). *Iowa acceleration scale manual* (3rd ed.). Scottsdale, AZ: Great Potential Press.

Baumeister, R. F., Vohs, K. D., & Tice, D. M. (2007). The strength model of self-control. *Current Directions in Psychological Science, 16,* 351–355.

Cooper, H., Robinson, J. C., & Patall, E. A. (2006). Does homework improve academic achievement? A synthesis of research, 1987–2003. *Review of Educational Research, 76,* 1–62.

*Deci, E. L., & Flaste, R. (1996). *Why we do what we do: Understanding self-motivation.* New York: Penguin Books.

Deci, E. L., Koestner, R., & Ryan, R. M. (1999). A meta-analytic review of experiments examining the effects of extrinsic rewards on intrinsic motivation. *Psychological Bulletin, 125,* 627–668.

Duckworth, A. L., Peterson, C., Matthews, M. D., & Kelly, D. R. (2007). Grit: Perseverance and passion for long-term goals. *Journal of Personality and Social Psychology, 92,* 1087–1101.

Duckworth, A. L., & Seligman, M.E.P. (2005). Self-discipline outdoes IQ in predicting academic performance of adolescents. *Psychological Science, 16,* 939–944.

*Dweck, C. S. (2006). *Mindset: The new psychology of success.* New York: Random House.

Gollwitzer, P. M. (1999). Implementation intentions: Strong effects of simple plans. *American Psychologist, 54,* 493–503.

Henderlong, J., & Lepper, M. R. (2002). The effects of praise on children's intrinsic motivation: A review and synthesis. *Psychological Bulletin, 128,* 774–795.

*Kashdan, T. (2009). *Curious? Discover the missing ingredient to a fulfilling life.* New York: Morrow.

Lepper, M. R., Corpus, J. H., & Iyengar, S. S. (2005). Intrinsic and extrinsic motivational orientations in the classroom: Age differences and academic correlates. *Journal of Educational Psychology, 97,* 184–196.

Lepper, M. R., & Henderlong, J. (2000). Turning "play" into "work" and "work" into "play": 25 years of research on intrinsic versus extrinsic motivation. In C. Sansone & J. M. Harackiewicz (Eds.), *Intrinsic and extrinsic motivation: The search for optimal motivation and performance* (pp. 257–307). San Diego, CA: Academic Press.

Livingston, J. (1997). Metacognition: An overview. Retrieved June 22, 2010, from http://gse.buffalo.edu/fas/shuell/CEP564/Metacog.htm.

Mueller, C. M., & Dweck, C. S. (1998). Praise for intelligence can undermine children's motivation and performance. *Journal of Personality and Social Psychology, 75*, 33–52.

*Rathvon, N. (1996). *The unmotivated child: Helping your underachiever become a successful student.* New York: Fireside.

*Rimm, S. B. (1995). *Why bright kids get poor grades: And what you can do about it.* New York: Three Rivers Press.

Ryan, R. M., & Connell, J. P. (1989). Perceived locus of causality and internalization. *Journal of Personality and Social Psychology, 57*, 749–761.

Ryan, R. M., & Deci, E. L. (2000). Self-determination theory and the facilitation of intrinsic motivation, social development, and well-being. *American Psychologist, 55*, 68–78.

Tangney, J. P., Baumeister, R. F., & Boone, A. L. (2004). High self-control predicts good adjustment, less pathology, better grades, and interpersonal success. *Journal of Personality, 72*, 271–322.

*Whitley, M. D. (2001). *Bright minds, poor grades.* New York: Perigee.

Wolters, C. A., Pintrich, P. R., & Karabenick, S. A. (2005). Assessing academic self-regulated learning. In K. A. Moore & L. H. Lippman (Eds.), *What do children need to flourish? Conceptualizing and measuring indicators of positive development* (pp. 251–270). New York: Springer Science+Business Media.

CHAPTER SEVEN: FINDING JOY

Barton, J., & Petty, J. (2010). What is the best dose of nature and green exercise for improving mental health? A multi-study analysis. *Environmental Science and Technology, 44*, 3947–3955.

Baumeister, R. F., Campbell, J. D., Krueger, J. I., & Vohs, K. D. (2003). Does high self-esteem cause better performance, interpersonal success, happiness, or healthier lifestyles? *Psychological Science in the Public Interest, 4*, 1–44.

Brawley, L. R., & Culos-Reed, N. (1999, August). The physical activity of children and youth: Outcomes of participation, scientific summary of psychosocial outcomes. *Canadian Society for Exercise Physiology.* Retrieved June 22, 2010, from http://www.csep.ca/english/view.asp?x=720.

*Bryant, F. B., & Veroff, J. (2006). *Savoring: A new model of positive experience.* Mahwah, NJ: Erlbaum.

Chaplin, L. N. (2009). Please may I have a bike? Better yet, may I have a hug? An examination of children's and adolescent's happiness. *Journal of Happiness Studies, 10,* 541–562.

*Cornell, J. B. (1998). *Sharing nature with children: 20th anniversary edition.* Nevada City, CA: Dawn.

*Csikszentmihalyi, M. (2008). *Flow: The psychology of optimal experience.* New York: Harper Perennial Modern Classics.

*Diener, E., & Biswas-Diener, R. (2008). *Happiness: Unlocking the mysteries of psychological wealth.* Malden, MA: Blackwell.

Fredrickson, B. L. (2001). The role of positive emotions in positive psychology: The broaden-and-build theory of positive emotions. *American Psychologist, 56,* 218–226.

*Fredrickson, B. L. (2009). *Positivity: Groundbreaking research reveals how to embrace the strength of positive emotions, overcome negativity, and thrive.* New York: Crown.

Froh, J. J., Kashdan, T. B., Ozimkowski, K. M., & Miller, N. (2009). Who benefits the most from a gratitude intervention in children and adolescents? Examining positive affect as a moderator. *Journal of Positive Psychology, 4,* 408–422.

Haidt, J. (2003). Elevation and the positive psychology of morality. In C.L.M. Keyes & J. Haidt (Eds.), *Flourishing: Positive psychology and the life well-lived* (pp. 275–289). Washington, DC: American Psychological Association.

Haidt, J. (2009). The moral emotions. In R. J. Davidson, K. R. Scherer, & H. H. Goldsmith (Eds.), *Handbook of affective sciences* (pp. 852–870). New York: Oxford University Press.

*Hallowell, E. M. (2002). *The childhood roots of adult happiness.* New York: Ballantine Books.

*Hallowell, E. M. (2007). *CrazyBusy: Overstretched, overbooked, and about to snap! Strategies for handling your fast-paced life.* New York: Ballantine Books, p. 19.

*Hample, S., & Marshall, E. (1991). *Children's letters to God.* New York: Workman.

Holder, M. D., & Coleman, B. (2009). The contribution of social relationships to children's happiness. *Journal of Happiness Studies, 10,* 329–349.

Holder, M. D., & Coleman, B., & Sehn, Z. L. (2009). The contribution of active and passive leisure to children's well-being. *Journal of Health Psychology, 14*, 378–386.

Hood, R. W., Jr., Hill, P. C., & Spilka, B. (2009). *The psychology of religion: An empirical approach* (4th ed.). New York: Guilford Press.

Huta, V., & Ryan, R. M. (2009). Pursuing pleasure or virtue: The differential and overlapping well-being benefits of hedonic and eudaimonic motives. *Journal of Happiness Studies*, DOI 10.1007/s10902-00909171-4.

Iqbal, S. T., & Horvitz, E. (2007). Disruption and recovery of computing tasks: Field study, analysis and directions. In *CHI '07: Proceedings of the ACM conference on human factors in computing systems* (pp. 677–686). New York: ACM.

*Kabat-Zinn, J. (2005). *Wherever you go, there you are: Mindfulness meditation in everyday life* (10th anniv. ed.). New York: Hyperion.

King, L. A., Hicks, J. A., Krull, J. L., & Del Gaiso, A. K. (2006). Positive affect and the experience of meaning in life. *Journal of Personality and Social Psychology, 90*, 179–196.

*Langer, E. (1989). *Mindfulness*. Cambridge, MA: Perseus Books.

*Likona, T. (1994). *Raising good kids: From birth through the teenage years*. New York: Bantam.

*Lyubomirsky, S. (2008). *The how of happiness: A new approach to getting the life you want*. New York: Penguin.

Mark, G., Gudith, D., & Klocke, U. (2008). The cost of interrupted work: More speed and stress. In *CHI '08: Proceedings of the twenty-sixth annual SIGCHI conference on human factors in computing systems* (pp. 107–110). New York: ACM.

McDonald, A., Beck, R., Allison, S., & Norsworthy, L. (2005). Attachment to God and parents: Testing the correspondence vs. compensation hypothesis. *Journal of Psychology and Christianity, 24*, 21–28.

*McGowan, D. (Ed). (2007). *Parenting beyond belief: On raising ethical, caring kids without religion*. New York: AMACOM.

*Medina, J. (2009). *Brain rules: 12 principles for surviving and thriving at work, home, and school*. Seattle, WA: Pear Press.

*National Sleep Foundation. How much sleep do we really need? Retrieved June 22, 2010, from http://www.sleepfoundation.org/article/how-sleep-works/how-much-sleep-do-we-really-need.

Otake, K., Shimai, S., Tanaka-Matsumi, J., Otsui, K., & Fredrickson, B. L. (2006). Happy people become happier through kindness: A counting kindnesses intervention. *Journal of Happiness Studies, 7*, 361–375.

Peterson, C., Park, M., & Seligman, M.E.P. (2005). Orientations to happiness and life satisfaction: The full life versus the empty life. *Journal of Happiness Studies, 6*, 25–41.

Peterson, C., & Seligman, M.E.P. (2004). *Character strengths and virtues: A handbook and classification.* New York: Oxford University Press.

Piliavin, J. A. (2010). Volunteering across the life span: Doing well by doing good. In S. Stürmer & M. Snyder (Eds.), *The psychology of prosocial behavior: Group processes, intergroup relations, and helping* (pp. 157–172). Malden, MA: Wiley-Blackwell.

Taylor, S. J., & Ebersole, P. (1993). Young children's meaning in life. *Psychological Reports, 73*, 1099–1104.

Watson, D. (1988). Intraindividual and interindividual analyses of positive and negative affect: Their relation to health complaints, perceived stress, and daily activities. *Journal of Personality and Social Psychology, 54*, 1020–1030.

CONCLUSION

*Kennedy, J. F. (1961, January 9). Address of President-Elect John F. Kennedy delivered to a joint convention of the General Court of the Commonwealth of Massachusetts, the State House, Boston. Retrieved June 22, 2010, from http://www.jfklibrary.org/Historical+Resources/Archives/Reference+Desk/Speeches/JFK/.

Wachtel, E. F. (2001). The language of becoming: Helping children change how they think about themselves. *Family Process, 40*, 369–384.

ABOUT THE AUTHORS

Eileen Kennedy-Moore, PhD, is a clinical psychologist with a private practice in Princeton, New Jersey, where she works with children, adults, and families. She is coauthor of a book for parents, *The Unwritten Rules of Friendship: Simple Strategies to Help Your Child Make Friends* (Little, Brown), and a book for mental health professionals, *Expressing Emotion* (Guilford Press). She is also the author of an award-winning children's book, *What About Me? 12 Ways to Get Your Parents' Attention Without Hitting Your Sister* (Parenting Press). Dr. Kennedy-Moore frequently speaks at schools, conferences, and community group events about children's feelings and friendships. She and her husband have four lively school-age children. You can reach her at www.eileenkennedymoore.com.

Mark S. Lowenthal, PsyD, has helped many children and their families during his twenty-two years as a clinical psychologist. He has a full-time private practice in Maplewood, New Jersey, working with children, adolescents, and adults. Previously, he served as the director of the Child and Adolescent Outpatient Psychiatric Program at Trinitas Hospital, in Elizabeth, New Jersey. Dr. Lowenthal has been a longtime advocate on behalf of children with mental health issues, helping to shape policy on a state and local level. He and his wife, a pediatrician, have two children. His Web site is www.marklowenthal.com.

INDEX

A

Academic acceleration/enrichment,
231–232
Academic cheating, 136–138
Academic performance: addressing
possible learning issues impacting,
213; anxiety and, 140–142; cheating
to improve, 135–138; if-then plans
and enhanced, 227–228; impact of
not turning in schoolwork on, 226–
227; self-discipline as predictor of,
201; show the way for high, 235–
237; social and emotional costs of
excessive focus on, 119–120. *See also*
Expectations; Grades; Schoolwork
Acceptance: praising your child that
communicates, 265–267; relationship
repair through, 87
Accepting "good enough" strategies:
diminishing returns concept, 39–40;
focus on "reasonable effort," 35–36;
sharing a fable: The Last Handful of
Grain, 37–39; teaching anti-
procrastination tips, 36–37. *See also*
Feeling inadequate
Achievement: child's authenticity versus
parents wishes for, 254–255; family
context of, 147; language of
becoming versus praise for, 273–274;
pressures on your child for, 1–2.
See also Performance
Adults' anger: developing healthy
perspective on, 194–197; feeling

helplessness in face of, 194; scenario
on fretting about, 192–193; trying to
ward off, 193–194
Afghani children, 109, 110
After-school activities: benefits of
outdoor, 249–250; cooperation and
competition interwoven in, 118–119;
finding joy in physical, 249; fitting
your child's style with appropriate,
63; when your child avoids
challenging, 30–33. *See also* Play
dates; Team sports
America's Funniest Home Videos (TV
show), 264
Anger: acknowledge your child's, 195;
developing healthy perspective on,
194–197; don't deny your own, 195;
feeling helplessness in face of, 194;
find ways to taking action on adults',
195–196; relationship repairs to
recover from, 87–89, 197; teaching
child to focus on evidence of
consequences, 196; trying to ward off
adults', 193–194. *See also* Conflict;
Emotional outbursts; Feelings
Anti-procrastination tips, 36–37
Anxiety-performance curve, 141–142
Apology, 88–89
Approval-based motivation, 210, 211
Arguing: addressing child's habit of,
189–190; with authority figures, 177–
179; bright children's relishing of
verbal, 126–127, 178–179;
emphasizing values to stem child's,